LEARN
Adobe Premiere Pro CC
for Video Communication

Adobe Certified Associate Exam Preparation

Joe Dockery
and Conrad Chavez
with Rob Schwartz

ADOBE
PRESS

Adobe

LEARN ADOBE PREMIERE PRO CC FOR VIDEO COMMUNICATION
ADOBE CERTIFIED ASSOCIATE EXAM PREPARATION
Joe Dockery (video)
Conrad Chavez (book)
with **Rob Schwartz**

Copyright © 2016 by Peachpit Press

Adobe Press books are published by Peachpit, a division of Pearson Education.
For the latest on Adobe Press books and videos, go to www.adobepress.com.
To report errors, please send a note to errata@peachpit.com

Learn Adobe Premiere Pro CC for Video Communication is published in association with Adobe Press.
For the latest on Adobe Press books and videos go to www.adobepress.com.

Adobe Press Editor: Victor Gavenda
Senior Editor, Video: Karyn Johnson
Development Editor (book and video): Stephen Nathans-Kelly
Senior Production Editor: Becky Winter
Copyeditor: Liz Welch
Compositor: Kim Scott, Bumpy Design
Proofreader: Kim Wimpsett
Cover & Interior Design: Mimi Heft
Cover Illustration: Yury Velikanov, Fotolia.com

ISBN-13: 978-0-13-439641-5
ISBN–10: 0-13-439641-3

9 8 7 6 5 4 3 2 1

Printed and bound in the United States of America

Acknowledgments

I wish to personally thank the following people for their contributions to creating this book:

My loving and understanding wife, Laura, who puts up with all the crazy projects I get myself into. Thank you for your patience and support. My daughter Jewell and my brothers John and Brian for helping me create all the assets for the book. My good friend and founder of Brain Buffet, Rob Schwartz, who has been the driving force behind this book series. Thank you for your guidance and encouragement throughout the authoring process. My editor, Steve Nathans-Kelly, thanks for patiently catching all my errors. Your input made the book stronger. Lisa Deakes and the entire Adobe Education Leader crew for all your support. The Snoqualmie Valley School District and all my amazing students over the years. You have shaped the teacher and author that I am today.

—Joe Dockery

I'd like to thank Victor Gavenda at Peachpit for his support and encouragement, and Steve Nathans-Kelly for the editorial guidance that made this project go smoothly.

—Conrad Chavez

About the Authors

Joe Dockery (video author) has taught for 25 years in the Snoqualmie Valley School District and currently leads the Digital Media Academy at Mount Si High School. He engages his students in real-world design projects from their school and community to ensure they receive authentic learning experiences. As an Adobe Education Leader, Joe Dockery consults and trains nationwide on the use and integration of Adobe software. His awards include the The Washington State Golden Apple Award, The Radio Shack National Technology Teacher of the Year Award, Educator of the Year Award from the Snoqualmie Valley Schools Foundation, ISTE's "Best of the Best" and "Making IT Happen," Adobe Education Leader "Impact" Award, and The Give Good Awards: Educational Excellence 2015. Joe is an Adobe Certified Associate in Premiere Pro CC.

Conrad Chavez (primary book author) is an author and photographer with over two decades of experience with Adobe digital media workflows. During his time at Adobe Systems Inc., Conrad helped write the user guide for Adobe Premiere (the precursor to Adobe Premiere Pro). He is the author of several titles in the Real World Adobe Photoshop and Adobe Classroom in a Book series, and he writes articles for websites such as CreativePro.com and Peachpit.com. Visit his web site at conradchavez.com.

Rob Schwartz (author of book chapters 8 & 9) is an award-winning teacher (currently at Sheridan Technical College in Hollywood, FL) with over 15 years experience in technical education. Rob holds several Adobe Certified Associate certifications, and is also an Adobe Certified Instructor. As an Adobe Education Leader Rob won the prestigious Impact Award from Adobe, and in 2010 Rob was the first Worldwide winner of the Certiport Adobe Certified Associate Championship. Find out more about Rob at his online curriculum website at brainbuffet.com.

Contents

Getting Started   viii

1   Introduction to Adobe Premiere Pro CC   3

About Adobe Learn Books   4

Managing Files for Video Production   5

Unpacking and Organizing   10

Starting Premiere Pro   11

Setting Up the New Project Dialog Box   13

Setting Premiere Pro Preferences   17

Exploring the User Interface   18

Using Workspaces   27

Challenge   30

Conclusion   31

2   Editing Basics   33

Identifying Job Requirements   33

Setting Up Project Media   35

Editing a Video Sequence   39

Working with Titles   55

Exporting a Sequence to a Video File   61

Challenge   66

Conclusion   67

3   Editing an Interview   69

Preproduction   69

Setting Up a Project   70

Filling a Stereo Clip with a Mono Recording   70

Editing the Rough Cut   71

Applying Audio Transitions   75

Adding B-Roll Clips   76

Changing the Playback Speed of a Clip   78

Varying Clip Playback Speed Over Time   79

Nesting a Sequence and Freezing a Frame   81

Creating a Lower-Third Title   83

Designing Sound   86

Creating Rolling Credits   87

Stabilizing Shaky Clips   88

Exporting Final Video   89

Challenge: Mini-Documentary   91

Conclusion   91

4   Editing a Dialogue Scene   93

Preproduction   93

Setting Up a Project   94

Creating a Rough Cut   95

Fixing Audio in Adobe Audition   98

Applying Video Adjustments   99

Add a Still Image to the Sequence   103

Reviewing with Your Clients and Exporting the Final Video   107

Challenge: Create Your Own Dialogue Scene   109

Conclusion   109

5   Compositing with Green Screen Effects   111

Preproduction   111

Setting Up a Project   112

Compositing a Green Screen Clip with a New Background   115

Adding and Animating More Graphics   120

Exporting Final Video   126

Challenge: Create Your Own Composited Video   128

Conclusion   129

6 Creating a Video Slide Show   131
Preproduction   131
Setting Up a Slide Show Project   132
Creating a Sequence from Multiple Files Quickly   133
Exporting Multiple Versions with Adobe Media Encoder   140
Challenge: Your Own Slide Show   144
Conclusion   144

7 Reviewing Tools and Shortcuts   147
Setting Up a Project   147
Working in the Timeline Panel   148
Navigating in the Timeline Panel   150
Selecting and Moving Clips in the Timeline Panel   152
Trimming Clips   153
Changing Clip Speed and Duration   155
Splitting a Clip   155
Editing Keyframes with the Pen Tool   156
Finding Shortcuts That Make You More Efficient   157
Conclusion   159

8 Leveling Up with Design   161
Creativity Is a Skill   162
The Design Hierarchy   164
The Elements of Art   167
The Principles of Design   194
Wrapping Up the Design Concepts   203

9 Working with Outsiders   205
Who You're Talking For and Who You're Talking To   206
Copyrights and Wrongs   210
Think Like a Boss   216
Conclusion   225

10 Wrapping It Up!   227
Extending Premiere Pro CC with Adobe Creative Cloud   227
Where to Go Next   233

ACA Objectives Covered   235
Index   239

Getting Started

Welcome to *Learn Adobe Premiere Pro CC for Video Communication!* We use a combination of text and video to help you learn the basics of video editing with Adobe Premiere Pro CC along with other skills that you will need to get your first job as a video editor. Adobe Premiere Pro CC is a powerful program for capturing footage from a variety of devices and assembling it into professional-quality video with sophisticated transitions, special effects, and text. You can also use Premiere Pro to export your video to many popular formats that your viewers can watch on a wide range of screens, including desktop computers and mobile devices like phones and tablets.

About this product

Learn Adobe Premiere Pro CC for Video Communication was created by a team of expert instructors, writers, and editors with years of experience in helping beginning learners get their start with the cool creative tools from Adobe Systems. Our aim is not only to teach you the basics of the art of video editing with Premiere Pro, but to give you an introduction to the associated skills (like design principles and project management) that you'll need for your first job.

We've built the training around the objectives for the Video Communication Using Adobe Premiere Pro CC (2015) Adobe Certified Associate Exam. If you master the topics covered in this book and video you'll be in good shape to take the exam. But even if certification isn't your goal, you'll still find this training will give you an excellent foundation for your future work in video. To that end, we've structured the material in the order that makes most sense for beginning learners (as determined by experienced classroom teachers), rather than following the more arbitrary grouping of topics in the ACA Objectives.

To aid you in your quest, we've created a unique learning system that uses video and text in partnership. You'll experience this partnership in action in the Web Edition, which lives on your Account page at peachpit.com. The Web Edition contains 8 hours of video—the heart of the training—embedded in an online eBook that supports the video training and provides background material. The eBook material is also available seperately for offline reading as a printed book or an eBook in a variety of formats. The Web Edition also includes hundreds of interactive review questions you can use to evaluate your progress. Purchase of the book in *any* format entitles you to free access to the Web Edition (instructions for accessing it follow later in this section).

Most chapters provide step-by-step instructions for creating a specific project or learning a specific technique. Other chapters acquaint you with other skills and concepts that you'll come to depend on as you use the software in your everyday work. Many chapters include several optional tasks that let you further explore the features you've already learned.

Each chapter opens with two lists of objectives. One list lays out the learning objectives: the specific tasks you'll learn in the chapter. The second list shows the ACA exam objectives that are covered in the chapter. A table at the end of the book guides you to coverage of all of the exam objectives in the book or video.

Most chapters provide step-by-step instructions for creating a specific project or learning a specific technique. Many chapters include several optional tasks that let you further explore the features you've already learned. Chapters 8 and 9 acquaint you with other skills and concepts that you'll come to depend on as you use the software in your everyday work. Here is where you'll find coverage of Domains 1 and 2 of the ACA Objectives, which don't specifically relate to features of Premiere Pro but are important components of the complete skill set which the ACA exam seeks to evaluate.

Conventions used in this book

This book uses several elements styled in ways to help you as you work through the exercises.

Text that you should enter appears in bold, such as:

In the Link field in the Property inspector, type **https://helpx.adobe.com/premiere-pro.html**.

▶ **Video 5.1** *Working in the timeline*

Links to videos that cover the topics in depth appear in the margins.

The ACA objectives covered in the chapters are called out in the margins beside the sections that address them.

★ *ACA Objective 2.1*

Notes give additional information about a topic. The information they contain is not essential to accomplishing a task but provides a more in-depth understanding of the topic.

> **NOTE** *In time notation, the numbers after the last colon are frames. For video you read time as hours, minutes, seconds, and frames.*

Operating system differences

In most cases, Premiere Pro CC works the same in both Windows and Mac OS X. Minor differences exist between the two versions, mostly due to platform-specific issues. Most of these are simply differences in keyboard shortcuts, how dialogs are displayed, and how buttons are named. In most cases, screen shots were made in the Mac OS version of Premiere Pro and may appear somewhat differently from your own screen.

Where specific commands differ, they are noted within the text. Windows commands are listed first, followed by the Mac OS equivalent, such as Ctrl+C/Cmd+C. In general, the Windows Ctrl key is equivalent to the Command (or "Cmd") key in Mac OS and the Windows Alt key is equivalent to the Option (or "Opt") key in Mac OS.

As lessons proceed, instructions may be truncated or shortened to save space, with the assumption that you picked up the essential concepts earlier in the lesson. For example, at the beginning of a lesson you may be instructed to "press Ctrl+C/Cmd+C." Later, you may be told to "copy" text or a code element. These should be considered identical instructions.

If you find you have difficulties in any particular task, review earlier steps or exercises in that lesson. In some cases if an exercise is based on concepts covered earlier, you will be referred back to the specific lesson.

Installing the software

Before you begin using *Learn Adobe Premiere Pro CC for Video Communication*, make sure that your system is set up correctly and that you've installed the proper software and hardware. This material is based on the original 2015 release of Adobe Premiere Pro CC (version 9.0) and is designed to cover the objectives of the Adobe Certified Associate Exam for that version of the software.

The Adobe Premiere Pro CC software is not included with this book; it is available only with an Adobe Creative Cloud membership which you must purchase or it must be supplied by your school or other organization. In addition to Adobe Premiere Pro CC, some lessons in this book have steps that can be performed with Adobe Media Encoder and other Adobe applications. You must install these applications from Adobe Creative Cloud onto your computer. Follow the instructions provided at helpx.adobe.com/creative-cloud/help/download-install-app.html.

ADOBE CREATIVE CLOUD DESKTOP APP

In addition to Adobe Premiere Pro CC, this training also requires the Adobe Creative Cloud desktop application, which provides a central location for managing the dozens of apps and services that are included in a Creative Cloud membership. You can use the Creative Cloud desktop application to sync and share files, manage fonts, access libraries of stock photography and design assets, and showcase and discover creative work in the design community.

The Creative Cloud desktop application is installed automatically when you download your first Creative Cloud product. If you have Adobe Application Manager installed, it auto-updates to the Creative Cloud desktop application.

If the Creative Cloud desktop application is not installed on your computer, you can download it from the Download Creative Cloud page on the Adobe website (creative.adobe.com/products/creative-cloud) or the Adobe Creative Cloud desktop apps page (www.adobe.com/creativecloud/catalog/desktop.html). If you are using software on classroom machines, be sure to check with your instructor before making any changes to the installed software or system configuration.

CHECKING FOR UPDATES

Adobe periodically provides updates to software. You can easily obtain these updates through the Creative Cloud. If these updates include new features that affect the content of this training or the objectives of the ACA exam in any way, we will post updated material to peachpit.com.

Accessing the free Web Edition and lesson files

Your purchase of this product in any format includes access to the corresponding Web Edition hosted on peachpit.com. The Web Edition contains the complete text of the book augmented with hours of video and interactive quizzes.

To work through the projects in this product, you will first need to download the lesson files from peachpit.com. You can download the files for individual lessons or download them all in a single file.

If you purchased an eBook from peachpit.com or adobepress.com, the Web Edition will automatically appear on the Digital Purchases tab on your Account page. Continue reading to learn how to register your product to get access to the lesson files.

If you purchased an eBook from a different vendor or you bought a print book, you must register your purchase on peachpit.com:

1 Go to www.peachpit.com/register.

2 Sign in or create a new account.

3 Enter ISBN: 978-0-13-439641-5.

4 Answer the questions as proof of purchase.

5 The **Web Edition** will appear under the Digital Purchases tab on your Account page. Click the Launch link to access the product.

The **Lesson Files** can be accessed through the Registered Products tab on your Account page. Click the Access Bonus Content link below the title of your product to proceed to the download page. Click the lesson file links to download them to your computer.

Project fonts

All fonts used in these projects are either part of standard system installs or can be downloaded from Typekit, an Adobe service which is included with your Creative Cloud membership.

Additional resources

Learn Adobe Premiere Pro CC for Video Communication is not meant to replace documentation that comes with the program or to be a comprehensive reference for every feature. For comprehensive information about program features and tutorials, refer to these resources:

- **Adobe Premiere Pro Learn & Support:** helpx.adobe.com/premiere-pro is where you can find and browse Help and Support content on Adobe.com. Adobe Premiere Pro Help and Adobe Premiere Pro Support Center are accessible from the Help menu in Premiere Pro. Help is also available as a printable PDF document. Download the document at helpx.adobe.com/pdf/premiere_pro_reference.pdf.

- **Adobe Forums:** forums.adobe.com/community/premiere lets you tap into peer-to-peer discussions, questions, and answers on Adobe products.

- **Adobe Premiere Pro CC product home page:** adobe.com/products/premiere provides information about new features and intuitive ways to create professional-quality videos that play back on a wide range of devices.

- **Adobe Add-ons:** creative.adobe.com/addons is a central resource for finding tools, services, extensions, code samples, and more to supplement and extend your Adobe products.
- **Resources for educators:** adobe.com/education and edex.adobe.com offer a treasure trove of information for instructors who teach classes on Adobe software at all levels.

Adobe certification

The Adobe training and certification programs are designed to help video editors, designers, and other creative professionals improve and promote their product-proficiency skills. The Adobe Certified Associate (ACA) is an industry-recognized credential that demonstrates proficiency in Adobe digital skills. Whether you're just starting out in your career, looking to switch jobs, or interested in preparing students for success in the job market, the Adobe Certified Associate program is for you! For more information visit edex.adobe.com/aca.

Resetting preferences to their default settings

Premiere Pro lets you determine how the program looks and behaves (like tool settings and the default unit of measurement) using the extensive options in Edit > Preferences (Windows) or Premiere Pro CC > Preferences (Mac OS). To ensure that the preferences and default settings of your Adobe Premiere Pro program match those used in this book, you can reset your preference settings to their defaults. If you are using software installed on computers in a classroom, don't make any changes to the system configuration without first checking with your instructor.

To reset your preferences to their default settings, follow these steps:

1 Quit Adobe Premiere Pro.

2 Hold down the Alt key (Windows) or Option key (Mac OS).

3 Continue to hold the key and start Adobe Premiere Pro CC.

4 When the program's splash screen appears, release the key.

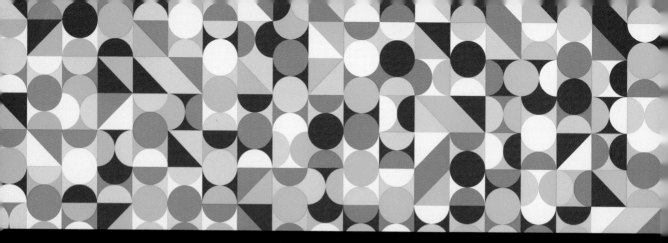

CHAPTER OBJECTIVES

Chapter Learning Objectives

- Explore file management overview.
- Set up project files.
- Open and save Premiere Pro projects.
- Learn scratch disk options.
- Configure your preferences.
- Explore the Premiere Pro user interface.
- Learn basic panel functions.
- Customize your workspace.

Chapter ACA Objectives

For more information on ACA Objectives, see pages 235–238.

DOMAIN 3.0
UNDERSTANDING ADOBE PREMIERE PRO CC

3.1 Identify elements of the Premiere Pro user interface, and demonstrate knowledge of their functions.

3.3 Navigate, organize, and customize the workspace.

DOMAIN 4.0
EDITING DIGITAL VIDEO USING ADOBE PREMIERE PRO

4.1 Create a new project.

CHAPTER 1

Introduction to Adobe Premiere Pro CC

On the surface, video editing might seem to be about mastering a video editing application. But successful video editing—even with an application as powerful and versatile as Adobe Premiere Pro CC—is often about much more than just pushing the right buttons on the computer. Video production typically involves a high degree of both integration and collaboration.

Integration means creating a seamless video program by pulling together media from potentially several different sources, such as conventional video cameras, smartphones, drones, action cameras, microphones, stock footage, music, graphics, and still images.

Collaboration is often required because the many elements that go into a project are typically created by a wide range of specialists—such as camera operators and audio recording engineers—and are coordinated by a producer. You will work with them as a team, so working successfully includes coordinating and cooperating with everyone on the team. That requires clear communication about standards and procedures.

Video 1.1 Welcome to the team

In the next chapter, you'll complete a project in which you'll act as a member of the Brain Buffet production team, working with them to create a 15-second promotional video for a client's online newsletter (**Figure 1.1**). In this chapter, you'll organize the media assets you'll use in the newsletter project. In the process, you'll get an introduction to the Premiere Pro user interface and some of the things you can accomplish with it.

Figure 1.1 Working on
the promo project

About Adobe Learn Books

Let's take just a second to explain what I'm trying to accomplish so we can be sure
we're on the same page (pun intended!). Here's what I (and the other authors) hope
to accomplish in this series.

Have fun

This is seriously a goal for me, as I hope it is for you! When you're having fun, you
learn more, and you're more likely to remember what you're learning. Having fun
also makes it easier to focus and stick with the task at hand.

Even if the projects you create as you complete the exercises in this book aren't the
kinds of things you'd create on your own, I'll make them as entertaining and fun as
possible. Just roll with it, and it will make the time you spend with this book more
enjoyable. Have fun, make jokes, and enjoy your new superpowers.

Learn Adobe Premiere Pro CC

This goes along with the previous item, but when you're working on the projects in this book, you have the freedom to explore and make your projects your own. Of course you're welcome to follow along with my examples, but please feel free to change text or styles to fit your own interests. When you're sure you grasp the concepts I'm talking about, I encourage you to apply them in your own way. In some projects, you may want to even take things beyond the scope of what appears in the book. Please do so.

Prepare for the ACA exam

This book covers every objective for the Adobe Certified Associate (ACA) exam, but I won't discuss them in order or make a big point of it. The authors of this series are teachers and trainers, and we've been doing this for a long time. We'll cover the concepts in the order that makes the most sense for *learning* and *retaining* the information best. You'll read everything you need to pass the exam and qualify for an entry-level job—but don't focus on that now. Instead, focus on having a blast learning Premiere Pro!

Develop your creative, communication, and cooperative skills

Aside from the actual hands-on work of learning Premiere Pro, this book explores the skills you need to become a more creative and cooperative person. These skills are critical for success—every employer, no matter what the industry, values creative people who can work and communicate well. This book describes the basics of creativity, how to design for (and work with) others, and project management.

Managing Files for Video Production

Let's talk about some fundamental practices that are common to essentially all professional video production. These procedures help a production team stay organized and make it easier for any member of the team to manage and locate all of the media that's involved in a project.

▶ **Video 1.2** *File management basics*

Linking to files instead of embedding them

In other applications you might have assembled a document by pasting or importing text and graphics into it. This is also known as *embedding* imported content. When you save that document, its file size grows because it contains all of the content you added. But embedding content is not practical for video projects, in part because video files themselves are very large. A single HD video clip can have a file size as large as thousands of text documents or photographs.

When you import content into a Premiere Pro project, the content is not copied into the Premiere Pro project file. Instead, Premiere Pro records the content's filename and folder path so it can retrieve the content from that location when it needs to display that content for you. The filename and folder path are the *link* to the content (**Figure 1.2**).

Figure 1.2 File path to linked content displayed in Premiere Pro

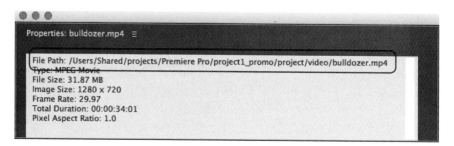

```
Properties: bulldozer.mp4  ≡

File Path: /Users/Shared/projects/Premiere Pro/project1_promo/project/video/bulldozer.mp4
Type: MPEG Movie
File Size: 31.87 MB
Image Size: 1280 x 720
Frame Rate: 29.97
Total Duration: 00:00:34:01
Pixel Aspect Ratio: 1.0
```

If you change the name of a file or move a file to a different folder, you break the link: Premiere Pro will lose track of the file and will be unable to load it. Fortunately, if that happens, Premiere Pro has tools that can help you quickly resolve links to lost files.

Because imported files are kept outside the project file, the project file size won't balloon as you add video. Another advantage is that if you need to swap in updated files for some that are already in the project, you have the option of simply replacing the old files with newer ones that have the same filename and location; Premiere Pro will simply pick up the newer ones.

But linking also means that you have the responsibility to make sure all of the assets imported into a project are always accessible to the project. If you delete a linked video file that's used in a video project, the project will have a blank segment where that video used to be. Linking also means that you have the responsibility to make sure that when you create a backup of your project, you back up not just the project file but every file you imported. Naturally, that's easier to do if you've stored your files in an organized way.

Deciding where to store your files

When you use your computer, it's constantly responding to requests for file access from the operating system and from the applications you're using. For most applications, such as web browsers and word processors, the files that are accessed are relatively small and there are long breaks between reads and writes, so your computer has no problem keeping up with them.

But video production is different. As you edit video, and especially as you scrub through video looking for specific frames or checking your work, your computer continuously reads frame after frame after frame from your video files. It's basically reading (and sometimes writing) thousands of different pictures all the time, and this constant activity places unusually high demands on your computer. And there are many ways in which video editing can strain your system even more. For example, editing 4K video is much more demanding on your computer than editing 2K (1080p) video. The burden on your system is even higher if you're layering multiple video clips or applying image corrections or special effects to your footage. The more ambitious the project, the more difficult it is for your computer to keep up.

The unusually high performance requirements of video editing affect where you store video project files on your computer. If you store everything on the same drive, such as your main system drive, it's more likely that your computer will be unnecessarily slow while video editing. That's because the system and your video application will constantly be competing for access time on the same drive. Whenever either has to wait, you have to wait.

WORKING WITH MULTIPLE DRIVES

To avoid the performance problems associated with competing demands on one storage drive, video professionals spread out project files across multiple drives. Typically, the system drive stores the operating system and the video application (in this case Premiere Pro). But the media files that you're assembling into a project (video, audio, still images, etc.) are usually stored on a completely separate drive. Temporary working files that are generated during video editing, such as preview files and cache files, might be stored on a third drive.

The great advantage of distributing files across drives is that when the operating system needs access to its files and, at the same time, Premiere Pro requests access to video files and cache files, they aren't going to compete for the same drive. Now that each drive has just one job, it can more easily concentrate on maintaining its own data stream without interruption. You experience this as better responsiveness and smoother performance while editing video.

Splitting project data across drives is necessary when you use hard disk drives (HDDs). They have a set of heads that move together to retrieve files from the disk, and these mechanical heads are limited in how fast they can move from place to place on disk. When your data is on more than one drive, your computer can retrieve data faster, because now you have multiple sets of drive heads working simultaneously on different data transfers at the same time.

You may have heard that solid-state drive (SSD) storage is much faster than hard drive storage. That's true, and it's because SSDs don't rely on mechanical heads—they are solid-state memory modules. With no moving parts, SSDs can access large amounts of stored data at once. Although SSDs are more expensive than HDDs, they are so much faster that they can reduce the need to split project files across drives for performance reasons. But because the newer formats such as 4K video are raising required data rates even more, distributing files across multiple SSDs is still a good way to help make sure your video editing system is as responsive as it can be.

What about network storage? Because of the high performance demands of video editing, it's not practical to store linked video on the most common types of network servers; the network transfer speed is too slow for real-time playback. There are network technologies that are fast enough, but they require such specialized and expensive equipment that you might only encounter them in a few high-end production studios.

COORDINATING ORGANIZATION WITH YOUR TEAM

How should you distribute the files across drives for your projects? If you work alone, you can decide for yourself based on your performance needs and your budget.

But in the project you're working on for this book, you're working as part of a team. And that means you need to coordinate file organization with the production manager. When the company you're working for has established its own standard practices for organizing files, you need to follow them. These practices are typically set up so that a set of project drives can be passed among team members who all understand the agreed-upon organization of those drives. That way, if anyone on the team needs to work on the project, they can connect the drives to their computer and begin working without delay.

Logging and naming clips

When you edit a project that uses many video clips and other content files, to work efficiently you'll want to quickly find the files you need. While Premiere Pro CC shows you thumbnail images of clips, you'll often rely on filenames to pick out the correct clips to insert into the right parts of your production. You also don't want to waste time playing back bad clips in case they might contain footage you need. For these reasons, before you begin editing, you should perform a pass through all captured clips to delete bad takes and give each file a meaningful name.

You might put all of the initially available files in a Pre-Production folder and use that folder as a starting point for organizing the content into the project folders you'll actually use.

Managing project folders

To help make it easier to find the right content, it's often a good idea to keep different media types in different folders within your project folder. For example, you might want to keep all video clips in a Video folder, all audio clips in an Audio folder, and all still images and graphics in an Images folder.

Consider adjusting the complexity of your folders to match the complexity of your project. For example, if you have many voiceover clips and background music clips, you may want to keep them in separate Voiceover and Music folders inside your Audio folder.

It's also a good idea to have an Exports folder that serves as a destination for exporting your project drafts and finished video (**Figure 1.3**).

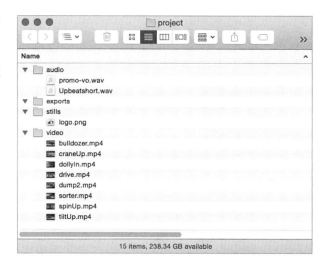

Figure 1.3 A sample folder arrangement for a project

Unpacking and Organizing

For the projects in this book, you've been provided with a ZIP file containing the content you'll use. A ZIP archive is a convenient way to combine multiple files into a single package that's easy to transfer online, so it's one way you're likely to receive project content.

Video 1.3
Organize your media files

The ZIP format is also popular for online transfers because it has built-in file compression; converting to ZIP can dramatically reduce the file size of some types of documents. However, many video and audio formats are already compressed, so adding those formats to a ZIP archive won't necessarily compress them any further.

UNPACKING A ZIP FILE

While extracting content from a ZIP file works the same way in Windows and Mac OS, the results are slightly different.

In both platforms, simply double-click the ZIP file:

- Windows opens the ZIP file as a window that displays its contents. If you close the window, you still have the ZIP file.

- Mac OS extracts the ZIP file into a new folder containing its contents. You now have both the original ZIP file and the new folder containing the contents of the ZIP file (**Figure 1.4**).

Figure 1.4 In Windows 10, even though the .zip filename extension is not visible, you can tell it's a compressed folder because of the description in the Type column and because the top of the window offers Compressed Folder Tools. (In Mac OS, the Kind column would say ZIP Archive.)

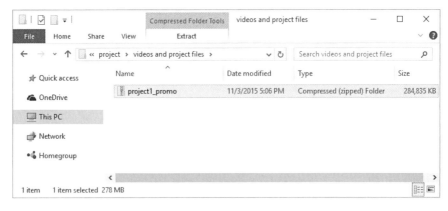

ORGANIZING FILES INTO FOLDERS

With the ZIP file opened, you're ready to organize its contents into folders before you start editing.

In the following steps, it's naturally more efficient to drag more than one file at a time whenever possible. Use the multiple selection techniques of your operating system to do this; for example, Shift-select a range of files to select multiple files for dragging.

1   Create a new folder, and name it **Video**.

2   In the window containing the expanded contents of the ZIP file, select the video files and then drag them to the Video folder.

3   Create a new folder, and name it **Audio**.

4   In the window containing the expanded contents of the ZIP file, select the audio files and then drag them to the Audio folder.

TIP

To see document types (video, audio, and so forth) more clearly, change a folder window to List view.

Starting Premiere Pro

You start Premiere Pro just as you start any other application you use, but what might be a little different is what Premiere Pro presents to you immediately after it starts up.

★ *ACA Objective 3.1*

1   To start Premiere Pro, do one of the following:

▶ *Video 1.4 Start Premiere Pro*

- In Windows, click the Adobe Premiere Pro CC application icon on the Start menu, Start screen, or Taskbar as available. If a shortcut icon for Premiere Pro exists on the desktop or in a folder window, you can double-click that.

- In Mac OS, click the Adobe Premiere Pro CC application icon in the Launchpad or Dock as available. If an alias icon for Premiere Pro exists on the desktop or in a folder window, you can double-click that.

TIP

You can also start Premiere Pro from the Adobe Creative Cloud desktop application, or by typing its name into Windows' desktop search or Mac OS's Spotlight search.

2 Choose an option from the Welcome screen (**Figure 1.5**).

Figure 1.5 The Welcome screen in Premiere Pro

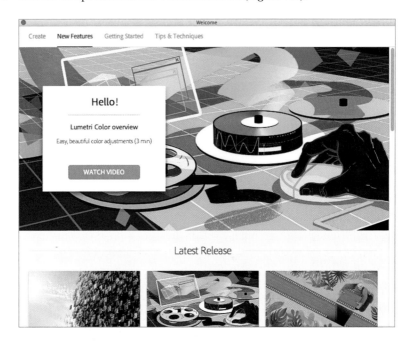

ABOUT THE WELCOME SCREEN

Instead of starting with a blank workspace, the Welcome screen is designed to help you start working or learning about Premiere Pro. As a beginner, you might take advantage of the Getting Started tab for tutorials. As an intermediate user, you might use the New Features and Tips & Techniques tabs to get caught up with the latest enhancements.

In day-to-day use, the first thing you'll often want to do after starting Premiere Pro is to work on your current projects right away. When the Welcome screen appears, click the Create tab, which contains the New and Open Recent lists. Those are shortcuts for the File > New command and the File > Open Recent commands.

If you prefer not to see the Welcome screen when Premiere Pro starts up, scroll to the bottom of the New Features, Getting Started, or Tips & Techniques tabs and select Don't Show Welcome Screen Again.

You can display the Welcome screen at any time by choosing Help > Welcome.

Setting Up the New Project Dialog Box

If you're the type of person who clicks OK as soon as a dialog box appears, you don't want to do that with the New Project dialog box. That's because it contains settings that define fundamental aspects of your video project, including where some working files are stored. Although it's possible to change New Project settings after you've started working on a project, it's much easier and better to set New Project settings mindfully and correctly the first time.

★ *ACA Objective 4.1*

▶ *Video 1.5 Set up preferences*

Configuring the General tab

A project can contain multiple named video sequences, and you can export final video from any of those sequences. The name of the project doesn't have to match any of those sequences, but it's a good idea for the project name to account for all the work inside the project.

With each new project, in the General tab of the New Project dialog box (**Figure 1.6**), double-check the Location as well as the Name. If you don't change the Location, Premiere Pro will save the project in the folder where the previously created project was saved, which may not always be what you want.

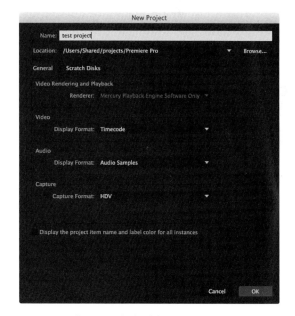

Figure 1.6 The General tab of the New Project dialog box

1   For Name, type **Promo**. You don't need to enter a filename extension; it will be added automatically.

2   Click Browse, and set the Location of the project to the folder you created for the promo video, where you unpacked and organized the promo project files.

3   For the Renderer option, choose the Mercury Playback Engine GPU Acceleration option when possible. This option uses all available and compatible opportunities to accelerate performance on your computer, particularly the graphics processing unit (GPU).

The Mercury Playback Engine Software Only option is provided in case incompatibilities or other issues exist with using full GPU acceleration. This option typically makes rendering much slower, so you should choose it only if a problem prevents you from completing your project with the GPU Acceleration option on.

ACCELERATING PERFORMANCE WITH THE MERCURY PLAYBACK ENGINE

The Mercury Playback Engine is a set of technologies that Adobe developed to make video editing faster and more responsive whenever possible. Whether you have the Mercury Playback Engine set to Software Only or GPU Acceleration, it accelerates your work by coordinating and making the best use of 64-bit CPU processing, multithreaded CPU processing, RAM, and scratch drives. Acceleration is more effective with larger amounts of installed RAM, more CPUs, more free space available on scratch drives, and faster drives (such as SSDs instead of HDDs).

Selecting the GPU Acceleration option usually results in much faster rendering. It can enhance performance even more using powerful graphics card technologies such as OpenCL and CUDA. The performance benefits of GPU Acceleration are so dramatic that video professionals specifically choose graphics cards that support it.

If the GPU Acceleration option is not available, it means your computer has a graphics card that doesn't meet the system requirements for the Mercury Playback Engine. You may need a graphics card that is newer or more powerful. Adobe maintains a list of compatible graphics cards on its website:

https://helpx.adobe.com/premiere-pro/system-requirements.html

4   When editing video from digital cameras, leave the Video and Audio Display Format options at their default settings: Timecode and Audio Samples, respectively.

5   Set the Capture Format to HDV for video projects captured using high-definition digital formats. The DV option is for older standard-definition digital video formats.

Configuring the Scratch Disks tab

You learned the benefits of spreading out your video project files across multiple drives in "Working with Multiple Drives" earlier in this chapter. You can use the following steps to set up a three-drive system for media file storage:

1 In the New Project dialog box, click the Scratch Disks tab (**Figure 1.7**).

Figure 1.7 The Scratch Disks tab of the New Project dialog box

2 To store the project's media assets on the second drive in the same location as the Premiere Pro project file, choose Same As Project from the Captured Video, Captured Audio, and Project Auto Save drop-down lists.

3 To store the project's preview files on the third drive, set the Path options for Captured Video and Captured Audio to the second drive. If the drive is not used for any other purpose, simply set the Path to the top (root) level of the drive.

Locating a project and editing its settings

There may be times when you're not sure of the folder or even the drive where a project is stored. Fortunately, the folder path to a Premiere Pro project file is always listed in the title bar for the application window (**Figure 1.8**).

Figure 1.8 Project path in the application window title bar

If you need to change the settings you entered in the New Project dialog box, choose File > Project Settings and then choose either the General or Scratch Disks command.

If you're trying to change settings such as Frame Rate and Frame Size, those are settings for a sequence, not a project. A project can contain multiple sequences. To change the settings for individual sequences within a project, choose Sequence > Sequence Settings when a sequence is selected or active.

Setting Premiere Pro Preferences ★ *ACA Objective 3.1*

It won't be too surprising if you feel overwhelmed when you open the Preferences dialog box in Premiere Pro, due to the sheer number of options. Rest assured that you don't necessarily have to change any preferences, and there's no need to review all of them. The reason so many preferences exist is that people work in different ways and within different workflows, so it isn't possible to design an application that fits perfectly into all workflows.

Preferences are options related to the daily use of the program, affecting actions you perform over and over. A good way to approach preferences is to look them over for options that might not work the way you'd like and then change those options. Examples of settings you might change at this point include the unit of measure for transitions, Default Scale to Frame Size, how items open in bins, and the Auto Save interval for the project.

Another approach is to leave these items alone until you realize there's something about Premiere Pro that you wish worked differently and then look through Preferences to change it.

A variation of that last approach is when you connect external devices that you want Premiere Pro to use. If the device isn't working as expected, it's often a good idea to look through Preferences to see if the device must be configured there. The video tutorial uses the example of going into the Audio Hardware preferences to make sure the USB microphone is selected. For connected devices, you want to look at the Audio Hardware, Control Surface, and Device Control preference panels.

To adjust Premiere Pro CC preferences:

- In Windows, choose Edit > Preferences and choose a command from the Preferences submenu.
- In Mac OS, choose Preferences from the Apple menu and choose a command from the Preferences submenu.

If you aren't sure where to start, choose General from the Preferences dialog box (**Figure** 1.9).

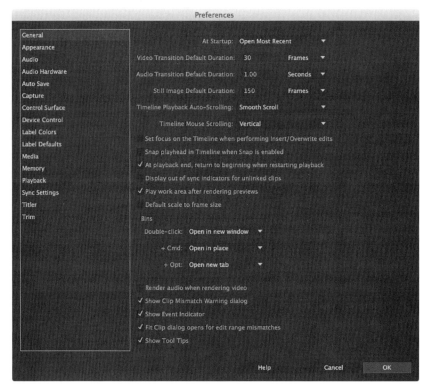

 TIP

If the list of preference panes is highlighted, you can move through the panes by pressing the up arrow and down arrow keys.

★ *ACA Objective 3.1*

Exploring the User Interface

The Premiere Pro CC user interface is designed to be powerful and flexible enough for professional workflows. Like other applications you may have used, it has menu commands with keyboard shortcuts as well as floating panels of options that you can arrange.

If you've used other Adobe Creative Cloud applications, you may already be familiar with how panels can be arranged, grouped (tabbed), and docked along each other's edges. Unlike the design-oriented Adobe applications such as Adobe Photoshop CC and Adobe Illustrator CC, the video- and audio-oriented Adobe applications also let you combine panels within the application window with shared dividers.

The tutorial video demonstrates some of these general guidelines for using the Premiere Pro user interface:

- In Premiere Pro, you'll spend most of your time using controls in panels. If you can't find the control you're looking for, the panel that contains it might be hidden. To see a list of panels available in the program, click the Window menu (**Figure 1.10**).

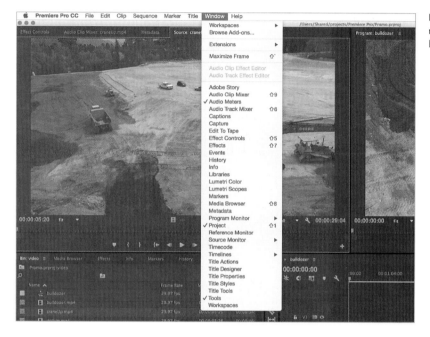

Figure 1.10 The Window menu in Premiere Pro CC lists all available panels.

- To learn more about a task you're trying to accomplish, click the Help menu (**Figure 1.11**) and choose Adobe Premiere Pro Help or Adobe Premiere Pro Support Center.

- To open a project you recently used, choose File > Open Recent.

Figure 1.11 The Help menu

Looking at the primary panels for video editing

If you haven't used a professional video editing application before, the panel arrangement in Premiere Pro may be unfamiliar. It's based on the traditional window layout for video editing. You'll also find this layout in other video editing applications because it's based on how dedicated video monitors were arranged in an edit bay in the days of tape-based video editing.

The three largest panels in the application window are the Source and Program panels across the top half and the Timeline panel across most of the bottom half (**Figure 1.12**). They are open only when a sequence is open in a project. The Timeline and Program panels are two views of a sequence: The Timeline panel shows how the video clips and other content are arranged in time within the sequence, and the Program panel shows the current state of the video at a specific time in the sequence. As you play back a sequence, the playhead (a vertical line in the timeline) moves along the Timeline and Program panel displays the video at the time indicated by the playhead.

At the bottom-left corner is the Project panel. This contains all the media that's been imported into the project, including media that you haven't yet used in a sequence.

Source Monitor   Program Monitor

Figure 1.12 The Source, Program, and Timeline panels in their default arrangement

Timeline

Video editing typically involves the following traditional video editing workflow. If you want your test project to have content for you to try out for the rest of this chapter, you can follow these steps:

1   View a video clip in the Source panel, usually by double-clicking it in the Project panel, and then trim that clip's beginning and end in the Source panel if needed.

2   Add the clip to the timeline, either by dragging and dropping or using a keyboard shortcut. Clips have to be added to a sequence, so if a sequence isn't already open in the timeline, dragging a clip to the timeline creates a sequence based on that clip.

3   See the results in the Program panel, and replay the clip if needed to review whether the resulting program plays back as expected.

This cycle of moving from the Project panel to the Source panel and then to the Timeline and Program panels is fundamental to assembling a video program. You'll use it to build your program from beginning to end by adding clip after clip to the timeline.

Exploring other important panels

A video sequence isn't just about video clips in a timeline. It will often include audio, effects applied to the video, and other content such as still images and titles. The Premiere Pro user interface includes panels that let you work with all of those.

- The Project panel (**Figure 1.13**, top) contains all media imported into the project, as you've seen before. Sometimes a project has a very long list of media, which can make it challenging to locate a specific file, so you can create named Bins inside the Project panel. Bins in the Project panel work much like folders on your desktop; you can nest bins inside bins just as you can nest folders inside folders.

- The Effects panel (**Figure 1.13**, bottom) includes lists of effects and transitions for video and audio along with color grading presets.

Figure 1.13 Project and Effects panels, which may be grouped together

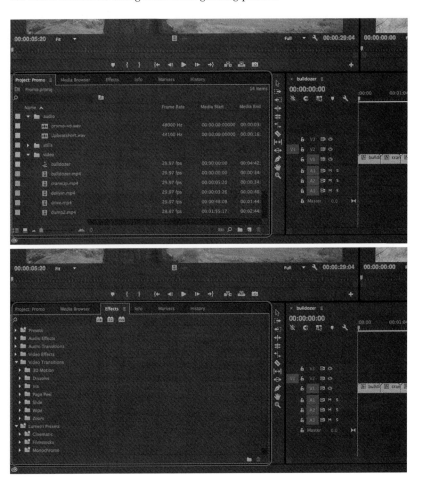

- The Audio Meters panel (**Figure 1.14**, right) shows you the audio level at the playhead. It includes clipping indicators so that you can instantly see if audio levels are too high.

- The Tools panel (**Figure 1.14**, left) contains tools that you can use to edit and view media interactively.

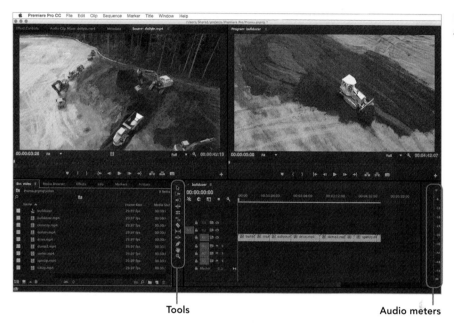

Figure 1.14 Tools panel and Audio Meters panels

Tools   Audio meters

Arranging panels

The first time you start Premiere Pro, you'll see all panels contained within a single application window. Panels share dividers with adjacent panels, so making one panel smaller makes another panel larger. You can separate any panel from the window by floating it, which creates a new window. In this exercise you'll work with panels in the user interface.

1 Position the pointer over the vertical divider between the Source and Program panels, drag horizontally until the divider is about two-thirds of the way across the width of the application window, and then release the mouse button (**Figure 1.15**). As you make one panel larger, the adjacent panel becomes smaller.

Figure 1.15 Dragging a divider

Figure 1.15 Dragging a divider

2 Click the panel menu in the Metadata panel tab, and choose Close Panel (**Figure 1.16**).

This is how you can close any panel. Some panels also have an X icon in the panel tab; if they do, you can click the X icon to close the panel.

Figure 1.16 Closing a panel from the panel menu

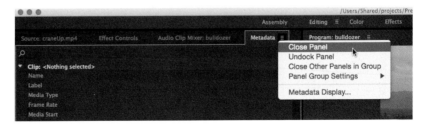

3 Choose Window > Metadata.

You're able to reopen the Metadata panel because all panels are listed under the Window menu.

4 Drag the Metadata panel tab and then, without releasing the mouse button, drag the panel over other panels. One or more of three things will happen:

- Notice the drop zone overlays that temporarily appear over a panel when you drag another panel over it and how the drop zone under the pointer is always the darkest.

- If you drop a panel over a center drop zone, the panel you drop will become grouped with the panel you drop it onto.

- If you drop a panel over an edge drop zone, the panel you drop will be inserted next to that edge of the panel you drop it onto.

5 Position the pointer over the left drop zone of the Program panel, and when it's highlighted, release the mouse button.

The Metadata panel is now inserted between the Source and Program panels (**Figure 1.17**).

Figure 1.17 Dropping the Metadata panel on the left edge drop zone of the Project panel (top) inserts the Metadata panel to the left of the Program panel (right).

■ Click the panel menu in the Project panel, and choose Undock Panel (**Figure 1.18**).

The panel is detached from the application window so you can reposition it independently. Other panels can be docked and grouped within this new window.

Figure 1.18 Undocking a panel

Premiere Pro CC remembers all of the changes you make to the panel arrangement across sessions, so after you exit, the next time you start the application it will restore the panel arrangement you were using in the previous session. But sometimes you want to revert to the panel arrangement as it was before you modified it. The panel arrangement is called a *workspace*, and you can reset the workspace to restore its original arrangement.

6 Choose Window > Workspaces > Reset to Saved Layout.

Using Workspaces

★ ACA Objective 3.3

You've learned how to customize the arrangement of the panels in Premiere Pro. But what if you want to create different arrangements of panels for different types of editing? When you used the Reset to Saved Layout command, you may have noticed that above that command was a list of named *workspaces*. Each workspace represents a different saved arrangement of panels. Those workspaces are built into Premiere Pro, but you can save your own.

1. Change the panel arrangement to your liking.

2. Choose Window > Workspaces > Save as New Workspace.

3. Give your new workspace a name, such as **Personal**, and click OK.

4. Choose Window > Workspaces, and notice that the name of the workspace you just created has been added to the Workspaces submenu (**Figure 1.19**).

Figure 1.19 The Workspaces submenu, now with the new Personal saved workspace

5 Choose Window > Workspaces > Assembly. You have now switched the panel arrangement to the Assembly workspace (**Figure 1.20**).

Figure 1.20 The Assembly workspace with the Workspaces panel across the top

Notice that there is now a new strip across the top of the application window that lists the workspaces. The strip is actually the Workspaces panel docked to the top of the window. Saved workspaces remember not only where panels are arranged, but which panels are displayed and hidden. The Workspaces panel is hidden in the default Editing workspace, but it is part of the Assembly workspace.

6 In the Workspaces panel, click the Color workspace.

The panels are now arranged for color grading, and that's also why the Lumetri Scopes panel is now displayed to the left of the Program panel and why the Lumetri Color panel now appears along the right side of the application window.

7 Return to the Editing workspace using the Workspaces panel or the Window > Workspaces submenu.

8 Choose Window > Workspaces > Edit Workspaces.

You can use the Edit Workspaces dialog box to hide, delete, and change the order of the workspaces in the list.

9 Drag the workspace you created to a different position in the list.

In **Figure 1.21**, the Personal workspace has been dragged to the second position from the top.

Figure 1.21 The Editing workspace order in the Edit Workspaces dialog box

10 Click OK to close the Edit Workspaces dialog box.

The workspace edits you made have changed both the Window > Workspaces submenu and the Workspaces panel when it's visible in the application window.

TIP

There are times when it's useful to maximize one of the panels. To do this without permanently modifying the workspace, position the pointer over a panel and press the tilde (~) key. Press the tilde key again to restore the panel to its usual place in the workspace.

Challenge

You've taken a look at getting media ready for production, and you've also gone on a grand tour of the general Adobe Premiere Pro CC user interface. Now it's time for you to take a closer look.

As a challenge, take some clips from one of your own personal projects and revisit how you got them organized for a project. If you had to prepare that media for editing today, do you think you might be able prepare them more effectively than in the past, given what you've learned in this chapter?

Another challenge you can try is going through each of the Preferences in Premiere Pro, looking out for settings that might have slowed you down when working in Premiere Pro before or in other video editing applications. Adjust them so that your future Premiere Pro sessions are more efficient and enjoyable.

Conclusion

Congratulations! You've reached the end of Chapter 1. You should now have a solid understanding of both file organization and the overall Premiere Pro user interface. You learned how to organize source media folders for a project, configure Premiere Pro to handle the project files it generates, and adjust application and workspace preferences.

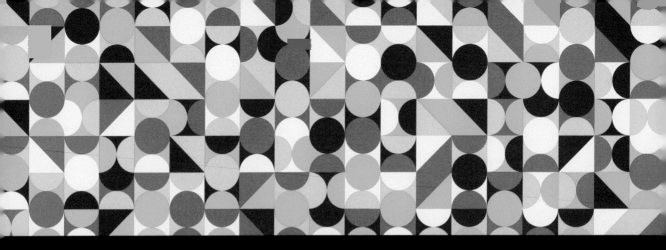

CHAPTER OBJECTIVES

Chapter Learning Objectives

- Import files into the Project panel.
- Use rough cut with the Source Monitor.
- Work with the timeline and sequences.
- Work with audio.
- Work with video transitions.
- Master title basics.
- Explore exporting basics.

Chapter ACA Objectives

For more information on ACA Objectives, see pages 235–238.

DOMAIN 1.0
SETTING PROJECT REQUIREMENTS
1.1, 1.2, 1.3, 1.4

DOMAIN 2.0
UNDERSTANDING DIGITAL VIDEO
2.1

DOMAIN 3.0
UNDERSTANDING ADOBE PREMIERE PRO CC
3.1, 3.2, 3.3, 3.4

DOMAIN 4.0
EDITING DIGITAL VIDEO USING ADOBE PREMIERE PRO
4.2, 4.3, 4.4, 4.5, 4.6, 4.7, 4.8

DOMAIN 5.0
EXPORTING VIDEO WITH ADOBE PREMIERE PRO
5.1, 5.1a, 5.1b, 5.1c, 5.1d, 5.1e, 5.1f

CHAPTER 2

Editing Basics

Your first project is a simple 15-second promotional video for one of our clients. It will be used as an introduction to their electronic newsletter. You'll assemble a series of aerial shots of the client's construction site. In this first project, you'll walk step by step through the video editing process and the Adobe Premiere Pro CC interface.

Identifying Job Requirements

During preproduction you should clearly describe the purpose, audience, deliverables, and other considerations for the promo video that need to be resolved before production begins:

- **Client:** Joe's Construction Cruisers. They use heavy equipment to prepare the land for large construction sites. Their tagline is "We Get the Dirty Jobs Done Right."

- **Target audience:** Joe's Construction Cruisers' clients are construction companies that build malls, schools, and large office buildings.

- **Purpose:** To lead off an e-newsletter in a way that's interesting enough to maintain client attention and motivate more clients to open the newsletter and read its contents.

- **Deliverable:** A 15-second video featuring high-quality video clips and music with a positive, upbeat feel and clearly delivering the client's tagline. Technically, the video should be in H.264 YouTube 720p HD format, and it should be compressed so that it loads quickly online while still retaining acceptable image quality.

★ *ACA Objective 1.1*

★ *ACA Objective 1.2*

★ *ACA Objective 1.3*

★ *ACA Objective 1.4*

▶ **Video 2.1** *Project planning*

Listing available media files

In this project, some media has already been acquired for the project. What do you have to work with?

- Aerial clips from a construction site
- Music from the Brain Buffet stock library
- Company logo from the client
- Voiceover audio files

That set of media is sufficient to complete the job, so you don't need to acquire any more media and editing can begin.

Addressing legal issues

You can shoot anything you see, but you can't necessarily use it. Reproducing a likeness of a person or personal property and using it to promote a business can interfere with the legal and privacy rights of people and property owners. To avoid unwanted legal consequences, be sure to obtain all necessary permissions and clearances through model and property releases.

For this promotional video:

- The aerial clips are covered by location releases from the property owners and model releases for any recognizable people.
- The music from the stock library is licensed for distribution in this type of production, and the music has been approved by the client.
- The client's logo is covered by an artist release.
- The voiceover is covered by a model release for the recognizable voice.

Be mindful of other media too. Watch out for things like music unintentionally recorded as part of the ambient audio of a location video clip, or a copyrighted poster on the wall of a room. If you're not sure, consult a lawyer familiar with video production. Another reason it's a good idea to work with a lawyer is that requirements can vary; for example, legal requirements for commercial productions may be stricter than for editorial uses.

Setting Up Project Media

If you've worked on projects in other media, such as print or websites, you already know that you need to bring media into a project. In video editing it's typically a two-step process where you first import video, and then you trim the video before adding it to a sequence.

Importing media into a project

Premiere Pro is similar to other professional media editing and management tools in that you don't copy and paste content into it; you import files into it. Importing makes it possible for Premiere Pro to record the folder path to the content's source file so that the file can be linked.

★ ACA Objective 4.2

You'll import media into the Project panel. The Project panel is the central repository for all media that you've either used in your project or set aside for potential use in your project.

▶ **Video 2.2** Import your video files

Bins are nested subsections of the Project panel that you can break off and float independently of the panel. In that way, bins are a lot like subfolders on your desktop. You can work with media in bins the same way that you can in the Project panel.

Importing in Premiere Pro is flexible enough to let you bring in media using the way that is most productive for you. You can drag and drop files directly into a project, or you can use menu commands or keyboard shortcuts.

1   Open the Promo project you created in Chapter 1.

2   Make sure the Project panel is visible, or just choose a workspace that makes the Project panel visible.

3   Import media using any of the following methods:

- Drag and drop individual files into the Project panel. This may be easier if you resize the Premiere Pro application window so that you can see the desktop window that you want to drag from.

- Drag and drop folders into the Project panel (**Figure 2.1**). Each folder becomes a bin in the Project panel.

- Choose File > Import, select an image, and click Import.

- Choose File > Import, select a folder, and click Import. The folder becomes a bin in the Project panel.

TIP

Want to import sequentially numbered still images as a single video clip, such as a time lapse? Choose File > Import, select the first image, and select the Image sequence option at the bottom of the Import dialog box. You'll learn more about this in Chapter 7.

- Press the keyboard shortcut for the Import command: Ctrl+I (Windows) or Command+I (Mac OS).
- Double-click inside Project panel or bin. This opens the Import dialog box.

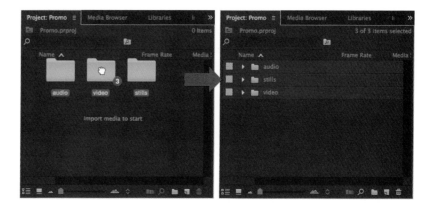

Figure 2.1 Importing media by dragging it into the Project panel

IMPORTING ALTERNATIVE: THE MEDIA BROWSER PANEL

Don't like going through the Import dialog box again and again? Without leaving Premiere Pro, you can use the Media Browser panel to browse your computer and all of the volumes connected to it, including network volumes and media cards. When you locate media using the Media Browser panel, you can import it in one step by simply dragging it into the Project bin, or you can select it in the Media Browser panel and choose File > Import from Media Browser. Whether or not you use the Media Browser, before you import media always make sure you first copy it to a drive that will be connected to your computer when you edit.

★ *ACA Objective 3.1*

★ *ACA Objective 4.3*

Using the Project panel

The Project panel isn't just for storage. You can use it to preview, arrange, and trim media.

▶ *Video 2.3* Explore the Project panel

The Thumbnail view of the Project panel is useful for previewing and arranging your content:

- Preview the contents of a video clip by hover-scrubbing: Move the pointer horizontally over a video thumbnail image (**Figure 2.2**).

- As you hover-scrub a clip you can trim it. To set an In point, press the I key, or to set an Out point press the O key.

- Drag to arrange clips in the order in which you'd like them to appear when you create a sequence.

Figure 2.2 Hover-scrubbing is a quick way to preview a video clip.

List view is useful when you want to inspect information details about your media (**Figure 2.3**):

- You can see bins as a hierarchy and expand them to see their contents.

- You can sort the list by clicking a column heading.

- You can change the column order by dragging column headings horizontally.

- You can customize which metadata columns are displayed by choosing Metadata Display from the Project panel menu.

TIP

Be sure to scroll List view all the way to the right to see all of the columns that are available, such as the column that lets you mark media as Good.

Figure 2.3 List view can provide you with detailed information about your clips.

WHAT ARE IN AND OUT POINTS?

It's good practice to record extra video around a scene by starting the camera before the beginning of a scene and stopping it sometime after the end of a scene. This provides *handles* that give you editing flexibility, such as allowing the ends of clips to overlap for transitions. But it also means that you need to tell Premiere Pro how far into a clip it should start playing in a sequence and how far from the end it should stop. The In point sets the starting frame of a scene, and the Out point sets its ending frame.

You don't need to worry about perfectly setting In and Out points before adding clips to a sequence because they are easy to adjust later. But many editors prefer to set approximate In and Out points before editing a sequence just so that the "rough cut" first draft of a sequence is a good starting point.

IMPORTING WITH THE CAPTURE WINDOW

If you're shooting with current digital video cameras, you might never need to use the Capture window because you can simply copy the digital video clip files from the camera media to your computer. But if you need to import footage that's only available on videotape, the footage will need to be *captured* to digital video files. To capture videotape, you need to play back the tape from a video camera or deck that can be connected to your computer. In Premiere Pro, you would choose File > Capture to open the Capture window, which you can use to control the camera or deck, mark clips for capture, and play back the tape while the Capture window transfers the footage to your computer.

The way you set up capture depends on whether the videotape is analog or digital. Capturing analog videotape, such as old VHS tapes, usually requires converter hardware that can be connected between the tape deck and your computer, or installed as an expansion card in a desktop computer. For digital videotape, whether you need extra hardware depends on whether the camera and computer have compatible ports that can be connected with a cable. There are so many potential variations that if you need to do this, research the specific capture workflow for the format you're trying to capture and how it needs to interface with the type of computer you use.

Editing a Video Sequence

What's a sequence? It's a timeline within a project. A sequence isn't the same as a project because a project can contain multiple sequences. This is a great advantage because it means you can create sequences with different specifications within a single project. For example, a project can contain multiple versions of the same video program, as different sequences. If you're editing a long movie, one sequence might be the full-length, full-resolution version edited and color-graded for a digital cinema projector in a movie theater, whereas another sequence might be a version of the same content edited and graded for viewing on a home television. You might also have sequences that are a two-minute theatrical trailer and a 30-second television commercial derived from the main sequence.

But sequences don't have to be multiple versions; they can also be nested to organize a video program. If you're editing a long three-act program, it might be easier to create a separate sequence for each act and then drag those three acts into a master sequence that organizes the entire program.

In a typical sequence workflow, you take clips from the Source Monitor or a bin, add them to a sequence to create a rough cut, and then use established editing techniques to tune the edits until the sequence has the pacing and flow you want. If the program has a specific duration requirement, such as a 30-second TV commercial, part of the goal of editing is telling the story properly while fitting all the required clips within that time limit.

Creating a sequence

★ *ACA Objective 4.3*

▶ **Video 2.4** *Create a sequence*

When creating a new sequence, you must ensure that the specifications of the sequence—such as frame rate, aspect ratio, and pixel aspect ratio—are appropriate. And that doesn't necessarily mean that the specs should match the final export specifications. For example, a project may need to be output in multiple formats for targets such as HDTV, smartphone, and web.

Premiere Pro is designed so that it's perfectly okay to mix media types in a single sequence, so don't be afraid to mix clips from a 4K cinema camera, a 1080p camcorder, a smartphone, and an action camera. You might want to set the sequence itself to the highest-quality format you expect to deliver.

But how do you do that? The Sequence Settings dialog box can be intimidating because it contains many options labeled with technical terminology. Fortunately, you may not need to set those options individually because Premiere Pro provides a simple shortcut: You can create a sequence based on the technical specifications of a clip you've imported into the project. For example, if you know you want to create a sequence that fully supports the 1080p footage from your camcorder, you can create a sequence based on one of its clips. There's more than one way to do that.

In the Project panel or a bin, do one of the following:

- Select a clip and choose File > New > Sequence from Clip.

- Drag a clip to the New Sequence button in the Project panel or bin.

- If the Timeline panel is empty, drag and drop a clip from the Project panel or bin into the Timeline panel (**Figure 2.4**).

- Right-click (Windows) or Control-click (Mac OS) a clip and choose New Sequence from Clip.

TIP

The clip you use to create a sequence will become the first clip in the new sequence, so it's best to use the clip that you actually want to appear first.

Figure 2.4 Drag a clip to an empty Timeline panel to create a new sequence based on the specifications of that clip.

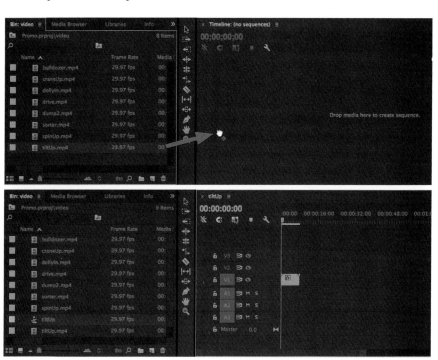

Creating a rough cut

A rough cut is like a first draft of a video program. You can use it to make sure that the basics of the program work well, such as the order of clips and the total running time. For a rough cut you don't have to obsess over the finest details of timing and editing.

★ ACA Objective 4.3

★ ACA Objective 4.4

Earlier you learned about In and Out points and how they can be set for clips in the Project panel or a bin. You can set In and Out points more precisely using the Source Monitor.

▶ **Video 2.7** *Create a rough cut*

1 Make sure the sequence you want to work on is open, so that it's visible in the Timeline panel.

2 In the Project panel, double-click a clip. It opens in the Source Monitor.

3 Use the Source Monitor controls to find the frame where that clip's action should start.

4 Click the Mark In icon, or press the I key.

5 Use the Source Monitor controls to find the frame where that clip's action should stop.

6 Click the Mark Out icon, or press the O key.

7 In the Timeline panel, make sure the playhead is at the time where you want to add the clip that's open in the Source Monitor.

8 Do one of the following:

   ▪ To add the clip at the playhead so that its duration moves all following clips later in time, click the Insert button.

   ▪ To add the clip at the playhead so that it replaces any clips that occupy its duration, click the Overwrite button.

The playhead automatically moves to the end of the clip you added (**Figure 2.5**).

NOTE *If the clip is added to a different track than the one you were expecting, check the blue rectangle in the first column in the Timeline panel. The track containing that rectangle is the one where clips are added by Insert or Overwrite.*

Figure 2.5 Adding a trimmed clip from the Source Monitor to the timeline

9 Go back to step 2 to add another clip at the playhead time, and repeat steps 3–8 until all the clips you need are added to the sequence.

As you build your sequence, you'll want to become familiar with the control layouts in the Source Monitor and Program Monitor (**Figure 2.6**).

Figure 2.6 Important controls in the Source Monitor and Program Monitor panels

A Playhead Position time display

B Buttons for adding markers and In/Out points

C Magnification

D Playhead transport controls

E Playback resolution

F Settings icon

Navigating time quickly is important for editing efficiently. Anywhere you see a Playhead Position time display in Premiere Pro, you can navigate time using these techniques:

- Drag the playhead.
- Use the transport control buttons or their keyboard shortcuts to move forward or backward along the timeline.
- Scrub the Playhead Position time display (drag the pointer horizontally over it).
- Click the Playhead Position time display, type the time to which you'd like the playhead to move, and press Enter or Return.

NOTE

In time notation, the numbers after the last colon are frames. For video, you read time as hours, minutes, seconds, and frames.

TIP

You can enter time quickly by entering only the numbers, and without the leading zeros. For example, to move the playhead to 00:01:29:03, enter **12903**.

If you've already arranged clip thumbnails in the order you want in the Project panel or a bin, you can create a sequence from those clips in one step. Select the clips and choose Clip > Automate to Sequence, or click the Automate to Sequence button in the Project panel or bin.

BUILDING A ROUGH CUT WITH KEYBOARD SHORTCUTS

Many experienced video editors prefer to work much faster by using only the keyboard. Premiere Pro is designed to accommodate this style of working so that you can use it when you feel that you're sufficiently familiar with the editing workflow. For example, you can perform the following functions using keyboard shortcuts:

- Switch to the Project panel or bin by pressing Shift+1.
- Select a clip in the Project panel or bin with the arrow keys.
- Open the selected clip in the Source Monitor by pressing Shift+O.
- Navigate the clip in the Source Monitor by pressing L or spacebar to play, K to stop playback, and J to play in reverse. Those keys are next to each other on the keyboard, so the "JKL" set of shortcuts was designed to form a reverse/stop/play set of shortcut keys that you can use to navigate video with three fingers.
- When you find your In point and Out point frames, press I or O respectively.
- Press the , (comma) key to insert the clip into the program at the playhead in the timeline, or press the . (period) key to overwrite. Those shortcuts are designed as an adjacent pair right under the JKL keys.

If you like to work this way, you can study a complete list of keyboard shortcuts here:

https://helpx.adobe.com/premiere-pro/using/default-keyboard-shortcuts-cc.html

The keyboard-driven editing workflow in Premiere Pro is based on shortcuts that have become standard over many years in professional video editing suites. That means you can generally use the same shortcuts, such as the JKL set, to edit quickly on other professional video editing systems you may encounter.

WHAT TO DO IF PLAYBACK ISN'T SMOOTH WHILE EDITING

Editing can be frustrating if playback isn't smooth. Simple one-track sequences might play back smoothly in the Source Monitor or Program Monitor, but playback may stutter or seem to be unresponsive if you use higher-resolution source footage (such as 4K media), add effects or overlay tracks, or edit on a less powerful computer. Premiere Pro provides tools for letting you know how well your computer is performing and to edit more smoothly.

The render bars above the timeline (**Figure 2.7**) have different colors depending on the ability of Premiere Pro to keep up with the performance demands of your sequence.

- No color is okay. It means Premiere Pro is confident it can play back that media at full quality in real time without having to render a preview file for it.

- Green is okay. Premiere Pro has rendered a preview file for that segment and the preview file is up to date, so playback will be at full quality in real time.

- Yellow is usually okay. Premiere Pro thinks it can play back at full quality, but you might see occasional stuttering.

- Red means that Premiere Pro thinks that segment is complex enough that you're probably going to see a lot of stuttering and delays. For real-time playback, you'll want to choose one of the Sequence > Render commands.

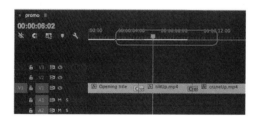

Figure 2.7 Colored render bars above the timeline

If Premiere Pro is having trouble playing back your sequence smoothly, there are two main approaches you can take to solve the problem:

- Adjust playback resolution in Premiere Pro. The Source Monitor and the Program Monitor both have a Select Playback Resolution menu. If you choose a lower resolution, you will lower the amount of work Premiere Pro has to do to render each frame, making it easier to achieve smooth playback.

- Upgrade your computer. The specific upgrades you need depend on where the bottleneck is. You may need to add more RAM, use faster storage, spread scratch files across more drives, or add a graphics card that's supported by the Mercury Playback Engine so that you can take advantage of GPU acceleration.

▶ *Video 2.8* Work in
the Timeline

Working with the Timeline panel

In Premiere Pro you'll probably spend the bulk of your time using the Timeline panel, so it's good to be familiar with the layout of its controls (**Figure 2.8**).

The main area of the Timeline panel is where you see audio and video tracks and the clips and other media sequenced. Here are some of the primary tasks you'll perform in the Timeline panel:

- Zoom the time magnification level using the scroll bar at the bottom, the Zoom tool, or the + (plus)/– (minus) keyboard shortcuts.

- Move the playhead in time by dragging it, entering the time into the Playhead Position time display, or using keyboard shortcuts such as spacebar to play/pause your video playback.

- Control which tracks are targeted, locked, hidden, muted, and so forth using the icons along the left side of the Timeline panel.

Figure 2.8 Important controls in the Timeline panel

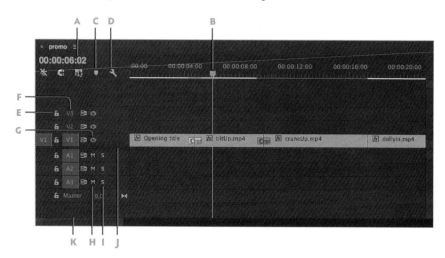

A **Playhead Position time display**

B **Playhead**

C **Add Marker (to sequence, not a clip)**

D **Timeline panel settings**

E **Lock track**

F **Track labels (Video 1, Video 2, Audio 1, Audio 2...)**

G **Show/hide track in Program Monitor**

H **Mute audio track**

I **Solo audio track**

J **Video/audio track separator**

K **Time magnification**

TIP *The \ (backslash) key is very useful in the Timeline panel, because it toggles between the current magnification and fitting the entire sequence within the visible width of the Timeline panel.*

TIP *When you use the JKL keyboard shortcuts for shuttling through a clip or sequence, pressing J or L more than once increases playback speed. For example, pressing LL or LLL results in higher speeds.*

Editing in the Timeline panel

★ ACA Objective 2.1

★ ACA Objective 3.2

★ ACA Objective 4.5

In the Timeline panel you fine-tune the trimming of each clip until the sequence has the right order, pacing, flow, and duration. Another way to look at trimming is that it's an adjustment to the In or Out point of clips in the timeline.

Keep in mind that trimming is nondestructive. In and Out points are merely markers that affect when playback of a clip starts and stops; they don't delete frames from the original clip. If you make a clip shorter by setting a later In point, you can subsequently restore the lost frames by setting an earlier In point for that clip.

▶ **Video 2.9** *Fine tune the edit*

You'll want to get to know the Tools panel (**Figure 2.9**), because most of the tools are there to help you handle different editing situations.

Figure 2.9 The Tools panel

A **Selection tool**

B **Track Select Forward tool**

C **Track Select Back tool**

D **Ripple Edit tool**

E **Rolling Edit tool**

F **Rate Stretch tool**

G **Razor tool**

H **Slip tool**

I **Slide tool**

J **Pen tool**

K **Hand tool**

L **Zoom tool**

Trimming clips in the Timeline panel is different from trimming in the Source Monitor. In the Source Monitor, you trim the clip by itself. In the Timeline panel, you trim while being aware of how a clip interacts with the clips that are before and after it in the program and how an edit affects the total duration of the entire sequence. These factors affect which technique you choose to make a specific edit.

1 To get ready to trim a clip in a sequence, move the playhead to the correct point in the Timeline panel and zoom into that time.

2 Choose an editing technique:

- To trim the end of one clip without altering the rest of the sequence in anyway, use the Selection tool ( ) to drag the end of a clip. This may leave a gap between clips.

Figure 2.10 Ripple Edit tool pointer indicating that you'll drag from the end of the first clip

- To trim the end of one clip without leaving a gap by automatically shifting all following clips in time, use the Ripple Edit tool (🔳) to drag the end of a clip (**Figure 2.10**).

- You can remove a clip from the timeline by pressing the Delete key, but you might prefer to perform a Ripple Delete by pressing Shift+Delete (Windows) or Shift+Forward Delete (Mac OS) so that the following clips shift to fill the gap.

- To adjust an edit so that one clip becomes shorter and the adjacent clip becomes longer, use the Rolling Edit tool (🔳).

- To change the frame rate (and therefore the speed) of a clip by dragging, use the Rate Stretch tool (🔳).

- To split one clip into two, click inside the clip with the Razor tool (🔳).

- To shift a clip in time without affecting adjacent clips, drag the clip with the Slip tool (🔳). This changes the In point and the Out point of the clip you drag. The duration of the clip and the adjacent clips don't change, but you shift the "window" of time seen in the clip you dragged.

- To shift a clip in time by automatically adjusting the Out point of the previous clip and the In point of the next clip, drag the clip with the Slide tool (🔳). The duration of the clip you dragged doesn't change, but the durations of the adjacent clips do change.

In addition to adjusting an edit on either side of a clip, you can move entire clips in time.

- To move one or more clips to a different time, select them with the Selection tool and drag them.

- To move one or more clips to a different time while automatically shifting clips that the moved clips would otherwise overwrite, select clips with the Selection tool and Ctrl-drag (Windows) or Command-drag (Mac OS) them. This performs a ripple move.

- To quickly select multiple clips on all tracks after a certain time, click the Track Select Forward tool (▶) in the timeline at the time where you want selection to start. The Track Select Backward tool does the same thing with tracks before the time at which you click the tool.

You can add audio to the Timeline panel the same way that you add video: Drag it in from the Project panel or a bin to an audio track, or add it with keyboard shortcuts.

If you add video that has audio, you'll see that both video and audio tracks are added to the Timeline panel, and they're linked to each other. If you want to edit a clip's video and audio separately, select the clip and choose Clip > Unlink.

Recording a voiceover

Voiceover audio is so common that Premiere Pro provides a way for you to record it directly into a project.

Voiceover recording starts in preproduction, where you should write, edit, and proof your voiceover scripts in advance. In the tutorial video, the voiceover is much simpler: just the client's slogan, "We get the dirty jobs done right."

Don't underestimate the value of audio; it can be as important as video in giving viewers the impression of quality in your production. If you'll be recording voiceovers frequently or for high-value clients, you'll want to research how to make better recordings in your studio. While it can start with buying a good-quality microphone for voice, how your studio is set up also makes a big difference. For example, speaking close to the microphone and installing acoustic treatments to reduce room reflections can make your recordings sound more professional. Here's the general workflow for recording a voiceover. You'll begin by preparing for recording.

1   Open the Audio Track Mixer panel (Window > Audio Track Mixer) (**Figure 2.11**).

★ *ACA Objective 4.6*

▶ **Video 2.10** *Record a voiceover*

NOTE

When you're setting up to record a voiceover, make sure you're working in the Audio Track Mixer panel, not the Audio Clip Mixer panel.

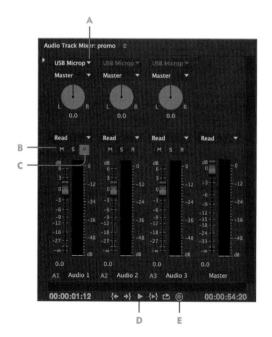

Figure 2.11 Audio Track Mixer panel prepared for a voiceover recording

A Track Input Channel (microphone should be selected here)

B Mute Track button

C Enable Track for Recording button

D Play/Stop toggle button

E Record button

2 If there are any tracks you don't want to hear while recording, click the M (Mute) button for those tracks.

3 In the Audio Track Mixer panel, click to enable the R button (Enable Track For Recording) for the audio track into which you want to record the new voiceover.

4 Make sure the correct microphone is selected at the top of the track you enabled. If the microphone isn't listed, open the Preferences dialog box, click the Audio Hardware panel, and make sure your microphone is set up there.

5 At the bottom of the Audio Track Mixer panel, click to enable the Record button for the mixer. Premiere Pro is now armed for recording, but not actually recording yet.

6 Right-click (Windows) or Control-click (Mac OS) the audio track just after the S (Solo) button, and choose Voice-Over Record Settings from the context menu (**Figure 2.12**). Verify that the settings are correct, test microphone levels, and then click Close.

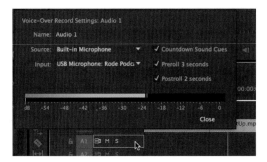

Figure 2.12 Opening Voice-Over Record Settings

Now you'll record your voiceover.

1 When you're ready to record, click the Play button in the Audio Track Mixer panel and begin speaking.

2 When you're finished recording, click the Stop button in the Audio Track Mixer panel. In the Timeline panel, the new voiceover should appear in the audio track you enabled for recording in the Audio Track Mixer panel.

3 If you aren't going to create any more recordings, make sure the R button is disabled for all tracks in the Audio Track Mixer panel.

Editing audio

★ ACA Objective 4.6

▶ **Video 2.11**
Sweeten the audio

Audio editing is an essential part of most video productions. Fortunately, you'll find that basic audio editing is somewhat similar to basic video editing: You can arrange audio clips in the Timeline panel, trim their ends, fade them in and out, and apply effects to clips or tracks.

As you work with audio, always be aware of whether you are working with an audio track or an audio clip. For example, it's possible to apply an effect to a clip or a track; if you apply it to a clip, the rest of the track won't have that effect.

To apply an audio effect to an entire track:

1 Open the Audio Track Mixer panel (Window > Audio Track Mixer > [track name]).

2 Click the Show/Hide Effects and Sends triangle near the top-left corner of that panel to reveal the list of effects and sends.

3 Click one of the pop-up triangles and choose the effect you want to add. For example, to process a voiceover, choose Special > Vocal Enhancer (**Figure 2.13**).

4 To make basic effect edits, use the controls that appear at the bottom of the effects/sends list. To make more detailed edits, double-click the effect in the list to open an editor window (**Figure 2.14**).

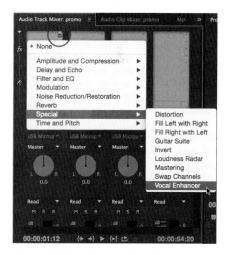

Figure 2.13 Applying the Vocal Enhancer audio effect to a track

Figure 2.14 Editing the Vocal Enhancer effect

There's one more thing you often have to do with audio and that's set the audio to an appropriate level throughout the timeline. This often involves making the levels of different clips consistent with each other.

There's a horizontal *rubber band* (line) across each audio clip that you can drag up and down to adjust volume for that clip (**Figure 2.15**).

Figure 2.15 Dragging vertically to adjust clip volume

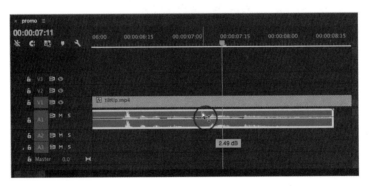

TIP

You can drag beyond the top and bottom of the clip. That way, you have finer control over the levels by dragging over a larger area.

You can also vary the audio level over time:

1 Select the Pen tool ( ) and click the audio level rubber band to add points where you want the level to change.

2 With the Selection tool ( ), drag the points you added up or down to shape the audio level over time (**Figure 2.16**).

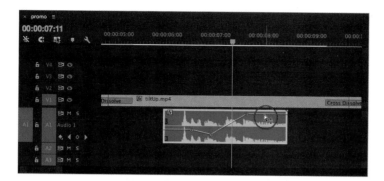

Figure 2.16 Dragging points added to the rubber band line to vary clip volume over time

TIP

You can add points while the Selection tool is active by Ctrl-clicking (Windows) or Command-clicking (Mac OS) the audio level rubber band.

Using video transitions and effects

★ *ACA Objective 4.8*

 **Video 2.12** *Add transitions*

After you've trimmed sequence clips to the point where you're probably done editing, you can start to enhance your sequence by applying video transitions and effects to clips. The main differences between the two is that you apply a transition only to the beginning or end of a clip, and a transition can affect the clips on both sides of an edit.

To add an effect to a clip:

1 Open the Effects panel (Window > Effects).

2 Expand the Video Effects category.

3 Drag the effect you want, and drop it onto a clip in the Timeline panel.

To add a transition to a sequence:

1 In the Effects panel, expand the Video Transitions category.

2 Drag the transition you want, and then in the Timeline panel, drop the transition at the edit point between two clips or onto the start or end of a clip (**Figure 2.17**).

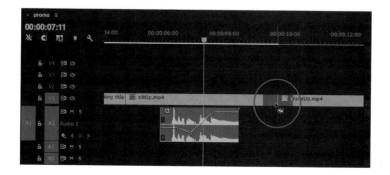

Figure 2.17 Dragging a transition between two clips

You can edit the duration of a transition directly in the Timeline panel by dragging either end with the Selection tool, just as you edit the In point or Out point of a video or audio clip. The transition will automatically maintain an equal amount of time before and after the edit, but if you want to adjust only one side of the transition, Shift-drag either end of the transition with the Selection tool.

> **TIP** Just before you drop an effect or transition, pay attention to which parts of clips are highlighted under the pointer. For example, you'll usually want to make sure the clips on both sides of an edit are highlighted before you drop a transition between those clips.

You can make fine adjustments to effects and transitions in the Effect Controls panel (**Figure 2.18**).

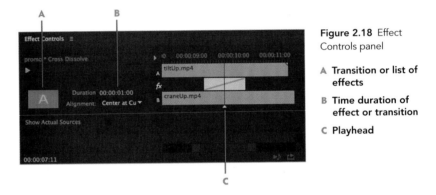

Figure 2.18 Effect Controls panel

A Transition or list of effects

B Time duration of effect or transition

C Playhead

1   Open the Effect Controls panel (Window > Effect Controls).

2   Select the clip containing the effect you want to edit, or select the transition you want to edit.

3   Use the options in the Effect Controls panel to edit the effect or transition.

   If multiple effects are applied to the clip, you'll see each effect listed with its settings in the Video Effects or Audio Effects sections of the Effect Controls panel.

HAVING ENOUGH EXTRA TIME FOR A TRANSITION

After you add a transition, is the transition not as long as you intended? This can happen when at least one of the clips involved in the transition doesn't have enough extra material to make it work. For example, if you want a one-second transition centered between clips, the first clip must have an extra half-second of footage after its Out point and the second clip must have an extra half-second before its In point. If that extra time wasn't captured in the original clip, you have to choose among these alternatives:

- Shorten or delete the transition
- Let the transition extend into the scene time
- Let Premiere Pro repeat end frames to create the extra time

In many cases those alternatives are not ideal. To avoid having insufficient time to create a transition, it's best to record more video than you need for a particular clip. Start recording a few seconds before the intended beginning, and stop recording a few seconds after the intended end. Many videographers don't stop the camera between takes, as long as there is enough free space on their media.

USING TRANSITIONS WISELY

Premiere Pro comes with a long list of video transitions, which are often overused by beginners. As with any video tool, you should choose transition effects that serve the way you want to tell the story. The next time you watch TV or a movie, note which transitions are used for the type of program. You'll probably find that professional editors use transition effects sparingly, sticking to basic cuts and fades most of the time.

Working with Titles

Whenever you see text superimposed over video, that's called a *title*, even though the text doesn't have to be just a title. You can create title text to introduce acts or scenes, as lower third graphics to identify locations or people, or for end credits.

Creating and adding a title

▶ *Video 2.13*
Add titles

You create and edit titles in the Title window (**Figure 2.19**), which contains its own set of panels and floats independently of the application window. Creating a title may seem familiar to you if you have experience using a drawing application like Adobe Illustrator, because the tools are similar.

Figure 2.19 The Title window

A **Hide/show background**

B **Title Tools panel**

C **Title Styles panel**

D **Title Properties panel**

E **Title Actions panel**

F **Preview area**

G **Type object**

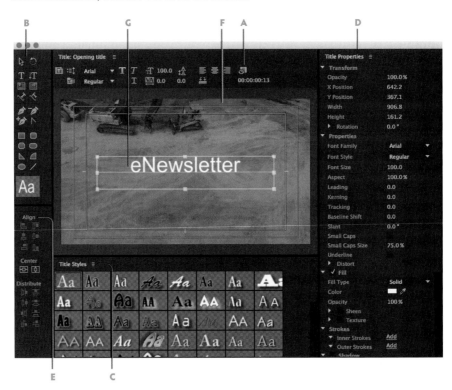

To create a new title:

1   If you want to preview the title over a specific time in the sequence, move the playhead to that time in the Program Monitor or Timeline panel.

2   Choose Title > New Title and then choose a title type from the submenu.

3   Change settings if needed, and click OK.

If you want to edit a title that already exists in the project, find the title in the Project panel or bin and double-click it.

To add text to a title:

1 In the Title window, select the Type tool and click or drag it in the title preview area.

2 Enter text.

3 Select all of the text, either by choosing Edit > Select All when there is a blinking insertion point in the text or by clicking the Selection tool so that the entire text object is selected.

4 Format all of the text.

It's often best to click a style in the Title Styles panel as a starting point and then adjust it using the options in the Title Properties panel. Title styles are saved presets of Title Properties.

5 If you want some of the text to be formatted differently, use the Type tool (T) to select part of the text, and then apply the formatting you want (**Figure 2.20**).

Figure 2.20 Formatting selected text in a title

6 If you want to animate the title with a roll or crawl, such as rolling end credits, choose Title > Roll/Crawl Options, specify options, and click OK.

To add a shape to a title, select one of the shape tools and drag it over the title preview area. Then customize the appearance of the shape using the Title Styles panel and the Title Properties panel; for example, use the Fill option in the Title Properties panel to change the fill color of the shape.

TIP

If the title text is already exists in another document, you can copy and paste it into a text object in the Title window. First use the Type tool to click an insertion point in the text object and then paste the text.

EDITING VALUES

While you have had the opportunity to enter values into settings in other areas of Premiere Pro, so far the Title window is probably the place where you'll want to make the most adjustments such as changing font size, leading (line spacing), or opacity. It's a good time to look at the various ways in which you can enter values in Premiere Pro so that you can use the methods you find most productive.

When you want to enter a value, do one of the following:

- Click the value so that it becomes selected, type a new value, and then press Enter or Return.

- Position the pointer over the blue value, and drag horizontally to interactively edit the value. While doing this, you can often see the effect of the change in the corresponding preview panel, such as the Title preview area or the Program Monitor.

- A shortcut for highlighting the next value in the same panel is to press Tab. To go to the previous value, press Shift-Tab.

To add an image to a title:

1 Choose Title > Graphic > Insert Graphic.

2 Use the Selection tool to reposition the image by dragging, or resize it by dragging its handles (**Figure 2.21**). To resize the image proportionally, Shift-drag a handle.

Figure 2.21 Positioning a graphic added to a title

3 Use the Title Properties options to style the image as needed. For example, you can use the Strokes option to add a border.

If you need to adjust the way that text, shapes, and graphics overlap, select an object and choose Title > Arrange and then choose a command to send the object forward or backward in the stacking order.

Adding a title to a sequence

★ *ACA Objective 4.7*

 **Video 2.14** *Create an overlay*

Once you've created a title, you can add it to a sequence the same way you add other media: Simply drag the title from the Project panel or a bin to a track in the timeline.

Be mindful of where you want to drop the title in the timeline. If you want the title to overlay other video, drop the title on a higher video track than that video (**Figure 2.22**). If you want the title to be added at the beginning of a sequence but there's already a clip at the beginning, Ctrl-drag (Windows) or Command-drag (Mac OS) the title at the beginning to perform a ripple insert, where all other video is automatically shifted down to make room for the duration of the title.

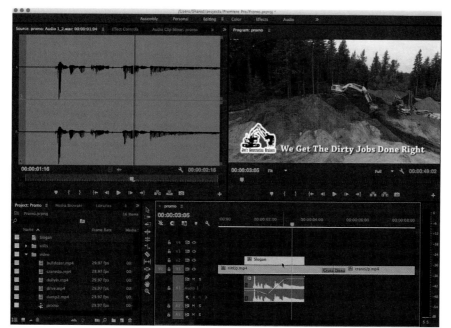

Figure 2.22 Superimposing a title over video by adding it to a higher track

You can always edit the duration of a title the same way you edit the duration of video and audio clips: by dragging its ends with the appropriate tool, such as the Selection tool or the Ripple Edit tool.

ABOUT SAFE MARGINS

You may see a double set of margin guides around the edges of the Title panel. These are called *safe margins* (**Figure 2.23**). The inner margin is called the safe title margin, and the outer margin is called the safe action margin. You can show or hide them by choosing them from the Title > View submenu.

Figure 2.23 Safe action margin (left) and safe title margin (right) in the Title panel

Safe margins were more commonly used back in the days when many televisions were set at the factory to enlarge the picture slightly, to better fill the smaller screens at the time. This effect was called *overscan* partly because enlarging would cut off the edges of the image. There was no standard for how much to overscan, so to make sure important content was not cut off on various televisions, the industry developed the concept of safe margins that were thought to be visible on most TVs. Videographers and video designers were instructed to keep all important activity inside the safe action margin and keep all text inside the safe title margin.

If you're creating a video program that may be distributed widely and viewed on a range of displays, including older televisions, it can be a good idea to respect the safe action and safe title margins. But the safe margins are much less necessary for video that will be shown on recent digital displays such as computer screens or high-definition televisions, because overscan is much less likely to be used on them.

Exporting a Sequence to a Video File

★ ACA Objective 5.1

▶ **Video 2.15** *Clean up the timeline and export your project*

When your sequences are complete and ready to be rendered out to final video files, you can export them. When you export, Premiere Pro not only has to assemble all of the components of a sequence into a single document, it might also have to convert all the media in the sequence to a different format and compress data to keep the file size down. Doing those tasks for every single frame will keep your computer very busy and can take a long time. Higher resolutions (such as 4K frames), heavy use of effects, and longer sequences can extend the exporting time further; that time can be cut down by using a computer with more RAM, faster drives, or a more powerful graphics card that's compatible with the Mercury Graphics Engine.

You set up an export using the Export Settings dialog box (**Figure 2.24**). It includes multiple panels containing a large number of settings. Don't panic—there's an easy way out. As long as your intended output is a standard destination, you can set up the entire dialog box in one step by simply choosing the preset for your destination.

For this exercise, you'll export a sequence with settings that are appropriate for YouTube.

Figure 2.24 The Export Settings dialog box.

A Format menu

B Preset menu

C Output Name

To export a sequence for YouTube:

1 Make sure the sequence you want to export is either active in the timeline or selected in the Project panel or bin.

2 Choose File > Export > Media.

3 Click the Format pull-down menu and choose H.264.

   This step is important because the format determines which presets are available in the Preset pull-down menu.

4 Click the Preset pull-down menu and choose YouTube 720p HD.

   That's the specification Brain Buffet is using for final output of the client video. This single step has now altered all export settings to match the selected preset.

5 Click the blue Output Name text to set the location and filename for the exported video.

6 Click Metadata. In the Metadata Export dialog box you can enter rights and licensing information, keywords that make it easier to find the video online, and so on. Enter any metadata that your project or client require, and click OK.

   TIP *If you expect to enter the same metadata for many projects, in the Metadata Export dialog box you can create Export Templates that contain that metadata. Then all you have to do is select a template to fill in the dialog box.*

   TIP *You may be accustomed to being able to add metadata to photos. For video, keep in mind that it's generally much easier to add metadata to a video during export than after it's been exported.*

7 Click the Queue button. This will send the sequence to the render queue in Adobe Media Encoder CC.

   You can also click the Export button to export directly, without using Media Encoder. If you aren't sure whether you should click Queue or Export, see the "Adobe Media Encoder CC or direct export?" sidebar.

8 If you have another sequence that you'd like to set up for export, such as another version of the project, do so by repeating steps 1 through 7 in Premiere Pro.

9 Switch to Media Encoder (**Figure 2.25**).

In the Queue panel you can see all of the sequences or other media that you've sent to Media Encoder. If you want, you can change the processing order of the items by dragging them up or down in the list.

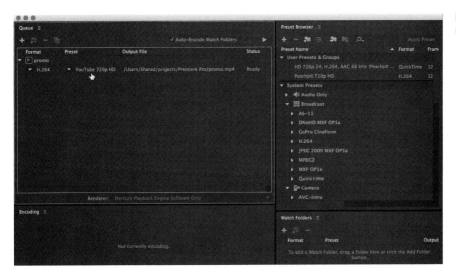

Figure 2.25 Adobe Media Encoder CC

WHAT'S WITH THE BLACK BARS?

When you preview your output in the Export Settings dialog box, you may see black bars along two sides of your sequence. This means that there is a mismatch between the aspect ratio (proportions) of the sequence and of the export settings. If you expected your exported video to have the same aspect ratio as your sequence, black bars can be a clue that the wrong preset or format is selected, so double-check them.

Sometimes you see black bars because the aspect ratios of the source material and the target output simply don't match, such as when you include clips from old VHS videotapes (4:3 aspect ratio) in a movie made for a widescreen HD format (16:9 aspect ratio). Black bars will appear along the sides because the 4:3 content cannot fill the width of a 16:9 aspect ratio frame if you want to preserve the original proportions. You can change the Width and Height values in the Premiere Pro Export Settings Video tab to match a 4:3 aspect ratio so that the video file itself maintains the original proportions with no black bars. But it will still play with black bars on a 16:9 display.

If the same black bars appear in Premiere Pro, that means the frame aspect ratio in Sequence Settings doesn't match that of the content.

TIP

If you realize you need to change the export settings, click the Preset arrow or text for the item in Media Encoder. To change the filename or export location, click the Output File name. You can change settings at any time before the item starts rendering.

10 Click the green Start Queue button. Media Encoder begins processing the items in the queue. The Start Queue button becomes a Pause Queue button while the queue is being processed.

Because Media Encoder processes in the background, you can switch to other programs while it's working. However, the Export queue will process faster if you run as few other programs as possible while it's processing, to avoid having programs compete for the processing power of your computer. Also, other programs may run slower while Media Encoder is processing.

If you realize there is a more important task to complete, you can click the Pause Queue button.

11 When the last export in the queue is complete, you can check your exports and exit Media Encoder.

ADOBE MEDIA ENCODER CC OR DIRECT EXPORT?

There are two ways to export a sequence to a video file. You can export it from Premiere Pro directly to a video file, or you can export to Adobe Media Encoder CC, a separate program that comes with Premiere Pro. Using Media Encoder has several benefits:

- Media Encoder can process exports in the background, so if you'd like to return to Premiere Pro to work on other sequences while your exports are processing, you can.

- Media Encoder can queue multiple exports. Instead of exporting a sequence from Premiere Pro and waiting until it's done to export the next one, you can send a number of sequences from Premiere Pro to Media Encoder where they will be queued up and automatically processed in turn.

- If you need multiple versions of a sequence and the only difference between the versions are the export settings, you can export that sequence once from Premiere Pro, duplicate it in Media Encoder, and change the export settings for each duplicate. This will be much faster than exporting a sequence multiple times from Premiere Pro to Media Encoder.

Because Media Encoder is a standalone video converter, you can even use it on its own to convert video files from their current format to another, a process called *transcoding*. For example, you can drag multiple video files into the Media Encoder queue and apply an export settings preset that converts them all for YouTube.

Now that you've taken a project from creation through editing and all the way to the final export, you probably have a good idea of how well the default Premiere Pro panel arrangements work for you. Remember that you can customize the workspace and save your own named workspace if that will help you adjust Premiere Pro for your own personal working style.

Video 2.16 *Panel review*

Challenge

Video 2.17
*E-newsletter
challenge*

Create a short promotional video for your school, your club, or a local business or nonprofit organization. Make it about 15–30 seconds long, like a TV commercial or public service announcement. Combine a collection of video clips that highlight your subject with titles, music, and a voiceover.

If you need background music, you can search the web for music licensed under Creative Commons. There are multiple types of Creative Commons licenses, so make sure you agree to the details of the license for the music you use. Some types of licenses may have requirements, such as attribution, for being able to use music for free. A good source of music recommended by Joe Dockery (author of the videos that accompany this book) is Incompetech:

www.incompetech.com/music/royalty-free/collections.php

After you complete the project, share it with your client and publish it online.

Remember Joe Dockery's Keys to Success from the video:

- Keep it short.
- Plan. Sit down with the client first so that you agree on the specifics of what the video should do.
- Shoot good-quality video. Keep the camera steady, and control the quality of light.
- Pay attention to file management.
- Use music licensed under Creative Commons if you're on a tight budget.
- Share your creation with the world!

Conclusion

Completing this chapter is a major step forward for you, because you've used Premiere Pro to create a new project; add media; edit the media in a sequence, including titles, transitions, and effects; and export it to specific output requirements. With these fundamental skills under your belt, you're ready to take on the next Brain Buffet project assignment!

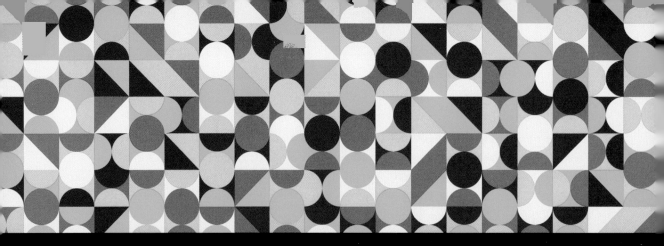

Chapter Learning Objectives

- Edit in the Timeline panel.
- Compare lift and extract edits.
- Export a JPEG format image.
- Create L and J cuts.
- Create a lower-third title.
- Insert a graphic into a title.
- Create rolling credits.
- Work with B-roll.
- Apply speed changes and time remapping.
- Adjust volume.
- Stabilize shaky clips.
- Export your video.

Chapter ACA Objectives

For more information on ACA Objectives, see pages 235–238.

DOMAIN 1.0
SETTING PROJECT REQUIREMENTS
1.1, 1.2

DOMAIN 2.0
UNDERSTANDING DIGITAL VIDEO
2.4, 2.5

DOMAIN 4.0
EDITING DIGITAL VIDEO USING ADOBE
PREMIERE PRO
4.2, 4.4, 4.5, 4.6, 4.7, 4.8

DOMAIN 5.0
EXPORTING VIDEO WITH ADOBE PREMIERE PRO
5.1

CHAPTER 3

Editing an Interview

Your second Adobe Premiere Pro CC project is a short, interview-based highlight video about a Brain Buffet employee. As in previous chapters, this is a hypothetical exercise created to help you explore some aspects of editing in Premiere Pro. You'll practice new video editing skills while building on the ones you learned in the previous project.

Preproduction

As you've learned, production can't start until the project requirements are clearly understood, so it's time to review those before you begin:

- **Client:** Brain Buffet Media Productions
- **Target audience:** Young professionals and students from 16 to 26 years old
- **Purpose:** The purpose for producing the employee highlight videos is to help customers connect with the people at Brain Buffet. Communicating what Brain Buffet employees are passionate about will help customers connect more strongly with the Brain Buffet brand.
- **Deliverable:** The client expects a 1-to-2-minute video featuring an interview with an employee that pairs high-quality video clips; music with a positive, upbeat feel; and a lower-third title featuring the company logo. The video should be in H.264 YouTube 720p HD format.

★ *ACA Objective 1.1*

★ *ACA Objective 1.2*

▶ *Video 3.1*
New project:
Snowboarding
highlight video

Listing available media files

In this project, some media has already been acquired for the project. What do you have to work with?

- Interview clip

- Snowboarding shots

- Background music—2 minutes of upbeat stock music

- Brain Buffet logo

That set of media is sufficient to complete the job, so you don't need to acquire any more media, and editing can begin.

★ *ACA Objective 4.2*

Setting Up a Project

▶ **Video 3.2** *Set up the project*

Start the editing stage of production by practicing the project setup techniques you learned earlier in the book:

- Unzip the project files using the same techniques you used for the previous project.

- Start a new project.

- Switch to a workspace that displays the Project panel, such as the Assembly workspace.

- Import media into the Project panel.

- Create a sequence based on a clip.

★ *ACA Objective 4.6*

Filling a Stereo Clip with a Mono Recording

▶ **Video 3.3** *Work with audio*

Many microphones provide just one channel of audio. That's considered *monophonic,* or mono, audio. But audio tracks in Premiere Pro often use multiple channels, from two-channel (*stereophonic,* or stereo) audio to surround sound audio such as 5.1 or 7.1 channels (the .1 is a subwoofer channel).

If mono audio is recorded as a multichannel clip, it probably won't sound right if it plays back in only one channel. For example, a mono microphone recording in a stereo channel might play back only in the left channel or only in the right channel. You can even out the sound across both channels by using a Fill audio effect.

1   In the Timeline panel, play back a stereo clip with signal in only one channel, such as the interview.mp4 video. As it plays back, notice how the Audio Meters panel shows audio playing in one channel; in the case of interview.mp4, all audio is in the left channel.

2   Expand the view of the audio track so you can see the audio waveform in only one of its channels (**Figure 3.1**).

    You can expand a track by vertically dragging the horizontal divider line between tracks or by using the scroll wheel on your mouse or the vertical scrolling gesture on your trackpad.

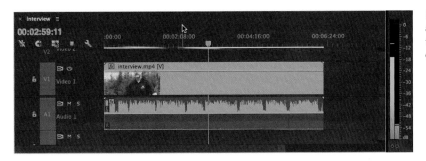

Figure 3.1 Audio meters and audio waveform when there is signal in only one of two channels

3   In the Effects panel, expand the Audio Effects folder.

4   In the Audio Effects folder, drag the Fill Right with Left effect and drop it on the clip in the timeline.

5   Play back the audio while watching the Audio Meters panel. If the correct effect was added, the audio signal should now be indicated in both the left and right channel level meters, and you should be hearing the audio through both channels as well.

Editing the Rough Cut

★ *ACA Objective 4.5*

You can refine the rough cut of the interview sequence by using tools and techniques you've been introduced to before. This time you can use and explore those techniques in more detail.

▶ **Video 3.4** *Trim your video in the timeline*

Performing ripple edits

The ripple edit is useful whenever you want to trim the beginning or ending of a clip without leaving a gap between it and an adjacent clip. You don't need to use a ripple edit to trim the last clip in a sequence because there aren't any clips after it, so you can simply drag the end of the last clip with the Selection tool ( ). But when you want to trim at any other edit within a sequence, including the beginning, you'll probably want to use a ripple edit.

One way to do a ripple edit is to drag the end of a clip using the Ripple Edit tool (**Figure 3.2**).

Figure 3.2 Before and after a ripple edit

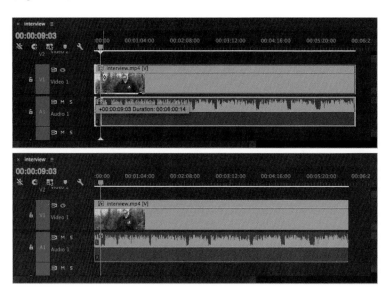

If the Selection tool is active, it can perform a ripple edit if you hold down the Ctrl (Windows) or Command (Mac OS) key while dragging the ends of clips with the Selection tool.

TIP

If your keyboard has Home and End keys, you can use them to navigate the sequence. To go to the first frame of a sequence, press Home. To go to the last frame, press End.

Deleting parts of a clip with or without leaving gaps

The interview clip contains several periods where the interviewee is saying nothing because the interviewer is asking a question. Those parts need to be removed from the interview.mp4 clip.

To mark part of a clip for deletion, do one of the following:

- Move the playhead to the time when the unwanted section starts, and click the Mark In button in the Program Monitor. Then move the playhead to the time when the unwanted section ends, and click the Mark Out button (**Figure 3.3**).

Figure 3.3 Sequence In and Out points right after clicking the Mark Out button

- Select the Razor tool ( ) and click inside the clip. If you want to delete a part from the middle of the clip while leaving the two ends, make two cuts: Click at the two frames where the unwanted section starts and ends.

As with trimming the ends of clips, you can remove part of a clip so that it either leaves a gap or automatically closes the gap that results from the edit.

- If you marked the start and end of the unwanted section using an In point and an Out point, click the Lift button to remove the section and leave a gap, or click the Extract button to remove the section and close the gap with a ripple delete (**Figure 3.4**).

Figure 3.4 Clicking the Lift button leaves a gap. For a ripple delete, click Extract instead.

- If you made cuts with the Razor tool, select the unwanted part of the clip and then press the Delete key to leave a gap, or press Alt+Del (Windows) or Option+Delete (Mac OS) to close the resulting gap by performing a ripple delete.

NOTE *You can also do a ripple delete of a selected clip by pressing Shift+Backspace (Windows) or Shift+Forward Delete (Mac OS); see the sidebar "Backspace/Delete and Forward Delete: Similar but Different Keys."*

TIP

Looking at the audio waveform can help you spot the quiet passages you want to remove, such as in the interviewer questions in the interview.mp4 clip.

BACKSPACE/DELETE AND FORWARD DELETE: SIMILAR BUT DIFFERENT KEYS

A PC (Windows) keyboard has a large Backspace key at the top-right corner of the keyboard, and an extended keyboard has a separate, smaller *forward delete* key (usually marked Del). In some applications, including Premiere Pro, these keys do different things. A Mac keyboard has a large Delete key at the top-right corner of the keyboard, and an extended keyboard has a smaller, separate forward delete key (confusingly marked Delete); those can also be programmed to do different things. When you study keyboard shortcuts, be sure you understand whether you should be pressing the Backspace/Delete key or the forward delete key.

Compact keyboards, such as on laptop computers, might only have the Backspace (PC) or Delete (Mac) key at the top-right corner of the keyboard. If you need the function of the forward delete key, you can usually get it by also pressing the Fn key. For example, on a compact Mac keyboard you can use the Delete key as a forward delete key by pressing Fn-Delete.

It's common to accidentally confuse the Backspace/Delete and forward delete keys, so if you're trying to use a shortcut that involves the Backspace/Delete key and it isn't working, see if the shortcut is supposed to use the forward delete key instead.

If you're not sure whether a Premiere Pro shortcut uses the Backspace/Delete or forward delete key, check the list of its keyboard shortcuts posted online by Adobe:

https://helpx.adobe.com/premiere-pro/using/default-keyboard-shortcuts-cc.html

Renaming clip instances in the Timeline panel

If you use the same clip multiple times in a sequence, it may be confusing as to what each instance of the clip represents. Fortunately, you can rename a clip instance in the timeline. When you do this, you change only the name of the selected clip instance in the timeline. The name of the clip in the Project panel or bin does not change, and neither does the original filename of the clip's source document.

To rename a clip instance in the Timeline panel, select the clip, choose Clip > Rename, type a new name, and click OK (**Figure 3.5**).

Figure 3.5 After renaming a clip instance to "approach" in the Timeline panel

Applying Audio Transitions

Where do you find audio transitions? Like video transitions and audio effects, audio transitions have their own group in the Effects panel (Window > Effects).

The three audio transitions are Constant Gain, Constant Power, and Exponential Fade. You'll usually use one of the first two, but you can easily listen to all three to see which one fits your project best.

As with video transitions, you can drop an audio transition between clips or to the beginning or end of a clip to fade audio in or out (**Figure 3.6**).

★ ACA Objective 4.6

★ ACA Objective 4.8

▶ **Video 3.5** Add transitions between audio clips

Figure 3.6 An audio transition selected between clips

With interview-based projects such as this one, cutting out parts of a clip can result in jarring jump cuts where there is an obvious break in the video. To smooth over this break you can apply the Morph Cut (Premiere Pro CC 2015 or later) video transition to be consistent with the audio crossfade. You'll find it in the Video Transitions > Dissolve group in the Effects panel.

PREVIEWING TRANSITIONS

You learned about some of the performance considerations involving playback in the sidebar "What to Do If Playback Isn't Smooth While Editing" in Chapter 2. You might notice that rendering bars indicating lower performance show up more often over transitions than over a single clip. Why is that?

It isn't hard to play back a single clip; your smartphone can probably do that. When you apply a transition, you're asking Premiere Pro to play back the two clips involved in the transition plus the transition itself. Because the transition combines the two clips, it doesn't look like either of the original clips, so Premiere Pro can't simply read it off your storage. The transition has to be calculated. If Premiere Pro believes the transition might be too complex to render in real time, you'll see a yellow or red render bar over the transition.

You usually don't need to be too concerned about a yellow render bar. But if the transition isn't playing back smoothly and you would like it to, select the transition and choose Sequence > Render Selection. This creates a new preview file that Premiere Pro can read directly from storage and quickly display, so the render bar becomes green.

★ *ACA Objective 4.4*

▶ **Video 3.6** *Add B-roll*

Adding B-Roll Clips

Video productions often consist of primary and secondary video footage. For example, in this interview project, the primary video consists of Joe talking, and the secondary video shows Joe snowboarding. Primary video is traditionally referred to as A-roll, and secondary footage is B-roll. The A and B terms came from tape-based video editing bays where you would load tapes into two source video tape decks marked A and B, and assemble them into your sequence on your program video monitor.

B-roll is used to help maintain the viewer's interest with engaging supplementary video or to provide informative visual background and context for the voiceover.

In this example, the snowboarding clips both enhance your understanding of Joe's personality and give you an opportunity to relate to him through his snowboarding hobby. The B-roll also adds visual interest beyond simply watching him talk to the camera.

You can add B-roll clips by dragging them into the timeline. You can drag them into gaps left by the removal of parts of clips on the main video track, or you can drag them to a higher track.

Clips on higher tracks completely cover clips on lower tracks. If you want lower tracks to show through, you have to modify the clip on the upper track by lowering its opacity or adding a mask to it.

It's common to use only the video of B-roll clips. For this reason, the Source Monitor makes it easy to bring just the video or just the audio part of a clip into a sequence. To control which parts of a clip you add, do one of the following in the Source Monitor:

- To add both audio and video, drag the preview image to the Timeline panel.
- To add just video, drag the Drag Video Only button ( ) to the Timeline panel (**Figure 3.7**).
- To add just audio, drag the Drag Audio Only button( ) to the Timeline panel.

TIP

To prevent audio on the main video track (usually V1) from being altered by edits on other tracks, in the Timeline panel you can click the lock icon ( ) for the main video track.

Figure 3.7 Adding a B-roll clip to the Video 2 track

Changing the Playback Speed of a Clip

★ *ACA Objective 4.8*

▶ **Video 3.7** *Adjust clip playback speed*

It's easy to change the playback speed of a clip, but be aware that playback speed and duration are tied together. For example, if you play a clip at 50% speed, it will take twice as long to play the entire clip. If you want to change the speed of a clip but maintain its duration, you'll need to show less of the clip's total length.

To change the speed of a clip, select it in the timeline and choose Clip > Speed/Duration. Specify the following options as needed, and click OK:

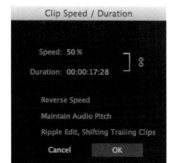

Figure 3.8 Clip Speed/Duration dialog box

- To change clip speed by a percentage of the original speed, enter a percentage value into the Speed option (**Figure 3.8**).

- To change clip speed to a specific length, enter a time value into the Duration option.

- To play the clip backwards, select Reverse Speed.

- To minimize audio pitch changes when the clip speed is changed, select Maintain Audio Pitch. Keep in mind that audio may still sound unusual after selecting this option because although pitch might be maintained, the speed of dialogue and other sounds will still change along with the new clip speed you've entered.

- To adjust clips that follow the selected clip, select the Ripple Edit, Shifting Trailing Clips option. This can save you the trouble of manually dragging clips to fill gaps created by a shortened duration or to create space to accommodate a lengthened duration.

If you want to adjust a clip's duration by dragging, use the Rate Stretch tool (⬚). This tool is useful when you don't know exactly how much you need to change a clip's duration to fill a space but you can see that gap in the timeline. Just use the Rate Stretch tool to drag the edges of a clip until it fills the gap, and the duration will be changed for you. Unlike trimming with the other tools, when you change clip duration with the Rate Stretch tool, the clip's In and Out points are maintained so no frames are hidden or revealed. The only change is that the clip will play faster or slower.

Varying Clip Playback
Speed Over Time

★ *ACA Objective 4.8*

You've probably seen action videos and TV commercials where clips are not only sped up or slowed down, but where the speed changes over time within a single clip. For example, you see a snowboarder start at a normal or faster playback speed, and then the speed changes to slow motion. You can do this in Premiere Pro using the Time Remapping feature.

▶ *Video 3.8* *Time remapping*

When you worked with audio levels, you learned how keyframes let you change values over time. To work with Time Remapping, you need to be able to see video keyframes and the clip rubber band:

1 In the Timeline panel, click the Timeline Display Settings icon (the wrench) and make sure Show Video Keyframes is selected.

2 Expand the video track containing the clip you want to adjust.

3 Right-click (Windows) or Control-click (Mac OS) the fx badge ( ) of the video clip you want to adjust, and choose Time Remapping > Speed (**Figure 3.9**). Now the rubber band over the clip controls clip speed.

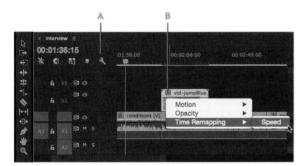

Figure 3.9 Timeline Display Settings icon (**A**) and fx badge (**B**)

Now you're ready to use Time Remapping.

1 Do one of the following to create a keyframe:

   ▪ With the Selection tool, Ctrl-click (Windows) or Command-click (Mac OS) the clip rubber band where you want to add a keyframe.

   ▪ Move the playhead to the time where you want to start changing clip speed, and in the Effect Controls window, click the Add Keyframe button ( ) to the left of the track (**Figure 3.10**).

Figure 3.10 Clicking the Add Keyframe button in the Effect Controls window, for the clip selected in the Timeline panel

Figure 3.11 Changing the speed of the segment between keyframes

2 Repeat step 1 to create another keyframe where you want clip playback speed to change again.

3 Position the pointer over the segment of the rubber band that's between the two keyframes you added, and drag up and down to change the playback speed of just that segment (**Figure 3.11**).

Right now the speed change is instant. To create a smooth transition from one speed to another, you can create a speed ramp.

TIP

You can also edit Time Remapping options and keyframes in the Effect Controls window.

4 Drag either side of a single keyframe to split the keyframe and create a speed ramp. To reposition the entire split keyframe, Alt-drag (Windows) or Option-drag (Mac OS) the keyframe. The speed ramp extends in both directions, centered on the original keyframe time (**Figure 3.12**).

5 To adjust the acceleration or deceleration of the speed ramp, drag the blue point inside the split keyframe or its handles.

Figure 3.12 Creating a speed ramp

Nesting a Sequence and Freezing a Frame

★ *ACA Objective 2.5*

★ *ACA Objective 4.8*

Next you'll create an opening title that includes a video that slows to a freeze frame. You'll do it by combining the video and title in their own sequence and then nesting the sequence inside the highlight video's main sequence.

▶ *Video 3.9 Create a nested sequence*

Practicing Time Remapping

This exercise provides you with a great opportunity to practice the Time Remapping techniques you learned in the previous exercise. This second pass through Time Remapping should make you more comfortable with the following techniques:

- Revealing the controls you need for Time Remapping
- Adding keyframes to the Time Remapping rubber band for a clip
- Creating a speed ramp by splitting a Time Remapping keyframe

The new technique you learn in this lesson is how to freeze-frame a video while using Time Remapping. You do that by Ctrl+Alt-dragging (Windows) or Command+Option-dragging (Mac OS) half of a Time Remapping keyframe as you split it. Remember that you'll see the freeze frame icon (**Figure 3.13**) if you're doing it correctly.

Figure 3.13 The freeze frame icon for Time Remapping

Creating an opening title with video

You've created a title before, but this time you create it from the New Item button (![new item]) at the bottom of the Project panel.

In the Title window, remember that you can move the playhead to find a good background frame from the sequence to use as a guide when designing the title. If the Background Video Timecode is gray (so you can't change it), click the Show Background Video icon (![show bg]) above it to display background video from the active sequence (**Figure 3.14**).

Figure 3.14 Show Background Video button in the Title window

When you're done creating the title, add it to the sequence by dragging it from the Project panel to the Timeline panel. Remember to add it to a track higher than the V1 track that the main video occupies. Make sure the title duration is long enough to play the video and display the text; you can do this by dragging the ends of the title with the Selection tool.

To fade in the title, add a Cross Dissolve transition. Open the Effects panel, find the Cross Dissolve effect in the Video Transitions group, drag it out of the Effects panel, and drop it on the starting end of the title.

Nesting the title sequence into the main sequence

When the title sequence is complete, you can add it to the main highlight video sequence. The sequence you add becomes nested in the main sequence. A nested sequence behaves like any other clip: You can trim the duration of

Figure 3.15 Title sequence nested within the main sequence

the nested sequence and add effects and transitions to it. If you edit the nested sequence, the changes automatically show up in any sequences that use it.

To nest the sequences, do the following:

1 In the Timeline panel, make sure the main sequence is active. If it isn't active but you can see its tab in the Timeline panel, click its tab. If the main sequence isn't in the Timeline panel at all, go to the Project panel and double-click it so that it opens in the Timeline panel.

2 In the Project panel, drag the opening sequence and drop it into the Timeline panel on an empty track higher than the main video track (**Figure 3.15**).

3 Preview the main sequence and make any adjustments that are needed, such as changing the volume of the title sequence so that it merges well with the main video track.

Creating a Lower-Third Title

In this exercise you'll create a *lower-third* title. As you might guess from the name, lower-third titles are conventionally set in the bottom one-third of the screen. The term has become somewhat generic since many lower-third graphics today don't occupy exactly one third of the screen. Now the term tends to describe any title that hangs out near the bottom of the screen, typically used to identify a person, or to provide context such a location in the scene or a date and time.

You've built titles before, so a lot of this will be review and practice for you.

1 Create a new title, this time by choosing File > New > Title. Name it **Lower third** and click OK.

TIP

If you want to drag something so that it snaps to a specific time, position the playhead at that time so that the pointer can snap to it.

TIP

*You can enter time values without colons. For example, you can type 1:46:12 as **14612**.*

★ ACA Objective 2.5

★ ACA Objective 4.4

▶ **Video 3.10** *Add a lower-third*

2 Using the Type tool, add the title text. Format the text as needed.

3 In the Title window that opens, select the Rectangle tool (■) and drag to create a rectangle in the lower third of the preview area.

4 Make sure the rectangle is selected (if necessary, select it with the Selection tool), and then use the Fill option in the Title Properties panel to apply a fill to the rectangle (**Figure 3.16**).

Figure 3.16 Applying a fill using the Title Properties panel

In the video, Joe used a solid black fill, but feel free to experiment with the other fill styles as long as it creates a background on which text will be readable.

5 Adjust the Opacity of the rectangle so that a little bit of the background shows through.

6 With the rectangle selected, choose Title > Arrange > Send to Back to move it behind the text.

As with many commands in Premiere Pro, there's more than one way to find the Arrange commands. Joe chose Arrange > Send to Back from the context menu that appears when you right-click (Windows) or Control-click (Mac OS) the rectangle in the Title window, but you can also use the keyboard shortcuts that you see next to the Arrange commands on their submenu.

7 Choose Title > Graphic > Insert Graphic, locate and select a graphic, and click Open. You can use the file bb-logo-color.ai, which has a transparent background.

8 Use the Selection tool to reposition and resize the graphic as needed (**Figure 3.17**).

Figure 3.17 Resizing a graphic added to a title

9 When you feel your title is complete, drag it from the Project panel and drop it on the sequence in the Timeline panel, superimposing it over the main video.

10 Apply the Cross Dissolve transition to the beginning and end of the title to fade it in and out.

IMPORTING GRAPHICS WITH TRANSPARENT BACKGROUNDS

If you want an imported graphic to have a transparent background, the graphic must meet the following requirements:

- The graphic must be created with areas that are fully transparent, not white. If you create or open the graphic in Adobe Photoshop, transparent areas appear as a checkerboard pattern behind the graphics and text layers. Note that if a graphic in Photoshop has a locked layer named Background at the bottom of the Layers panel, its background is not transparent. In Adobe Illustrator, any area not covered by an object is transparent.

- The graphic must be saved in a file format that allows transparency.

Some of the most popular and highest-quality graphics file formats that support transparency are Adobe Illustrator (with the extension .ai), Adobe Photoshop (.psd), Tagged Image File Format (.tif or .tiff), and Portable Network Graphics (.png). AI format is a vector format, so it scales smoothly to any size.

Graphics Interchange Format (.gif) is capable of only one level of transparency; the other formats can store up to 256 levels of transparency for smooth, anti-aliased edges. For this reason, it's better to use the other formats.

The JPEG (Joint Photographic Experts Group) file format (using the .jpg extension) cannot store transparency; it always has a solid background.

Designing Sound

★ ACA Objective 2.4

★ ACA Objective 4.6

Just as you compose the elements of a video frame to work well together, you should be mindful of how well the different sounds in your audio track work together. For example, if one sound should be dominant, such as a person speaking, you probably want to deemphasize other sounds such as ambient noise or background music by fading down their volume levels.

▶ **Video 3.11** *Sound design*

You've already done a little sound design work earlier in this book when you adjusted the audio levels for clips. Here are a few more tools and thoughts to keep in mind as you refine the sound design of your projects:

- Be sure to listen—not just to the sounds you know about, but to sounds that might be lurking in the mix and surfacing at times when they shouldn't.

- Listen to the relative levels of the different clips on a single track. To hear the audio for only one track, click the Solo button for that track. You've learned how to even out the levels of clips to match each other using the audio level rubber bands on each clip.

- Listen for the relative levels of the various tracks in a sequence. You can adjust the audio level for each track by using the level knobs in the Audio Track Mixer panel.

- If you need to delete the audio track of a video clip or if you want to separately edit the durations of the video and audio tracks of a clip, select the clip and choose Clip > Unlink.

- When working with audio tracks, you may want to make room to see more audio than video in the Timeline panel. You can do this by vertically dragging the thick separator between the video tracks and audio tracks in the panel (**Figure 3.18**).

Figure 3.18 Dragging the separator between video and audio tracks

Creating Rolling Credits

Rolling credits are a great way to end a video Hollywood-style, and they're easy to set up in Premiere Pro.

1 Choose Title > New Title > Default Roll. Name it **Credits** and click OK.

2 If you have a text file containing the credits, open it in a text editing application. You can use the credits text file provided with this project, credits.txt in the Pre-Production folder.

3 Select all of the text and choose Edit > Copy.

4 Switch to the Title window and use the Type tool (T) to click or drag a text object in the title preview area.

5 Choose Edit > Paste. The credits you copied should now appear in the Title window (**Figure 3.19**).

> If you don't see the text or it's hard to read, you may need to change the Title Properties for the text so that it uses a more legible style, size, or color.

6 If the text is so wide it goes off the right side of the title area, click the Title menu and choose Word Wrap. You may also need to remove extra paragraph breaks.

7 To customize how the credits roll, click the Roll/Crawl Options button or choose Title > Roll/Crawl Options. Set options as needed (**Figure 3.20**), and click OK.

> In many cases, especially with long credits, you'll want to select the Start Off Screen and End Off Screen options.

8 Drag the title from the Project panel to the end of the sequence, preview it, and adjust its duration as needed.

> **TIP** You can quickly edit a title by double-clicking it, even when the title is in a sequence in the Timeline panel. It opens in the Title window.

★ ACA Objective 2.5

★ ACA Objective 4.7

▶ **Video 3.12** Add rolling credits

Figure 3.19 Long credits text pasted into the Title window

Figure 3.20 Roll/Crawl Options dialog box

Stabilizing Shaky Clips

Steady footage with smooth camera moves gives a professional look to a production, but in-camera stabilization can do only so much, and high-quality camera stabilization hardware isn't always practical to have on hand when recording. When your clips could benefit from stabilizing in post-production, you can apply the Warp Stabilizer effect in Premiere Pro.

Applying Warp Stabilizer is like applying any other effect. Find it in the Effects panel (it's in the Video Effects > Distort group) and drag it onto a clip in a sequence in the Timeline.

Stabilization is a two-stage process. First, Warp Stabilizer analyzes the footage to determine the degree and direction of instability. Then it applies the precise amount of stabilization necessary to cancel out the instability that was detected. Both the analysis and stabilization stages are processor-intensive and can take a lot of time. Exactly how much depends on the length and resolution of the clip you're stabilizing.

When Warp Stabilizer is in the middle of either of its two stages, it displays a banner across the Program Monitor when the playhead is displaying a clip that Warp Stabilizer is processing (**Figure 3.21**). The banner says either "Analyzing" or "Stabilizing." You can also monitor Warp Stabilizer progress in the Effect Controls panel when the clip is selected. Warp Stabilizer processes in the background, so you can keep working on other parts of your project.

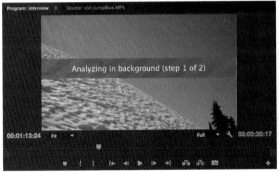

Figure 3.21 Warp Stabilizer processing banners

Although you can simply apply Warp Stabilizer and use the result, there are a few key settings you might want to pay attention to in the Effect Controls panel (**Figure 3.22**):

- **Result:** You should generally leave this option set to Smooth Motion, but if you want to make the shot look like the camera never moved, select No Motion.

- **Method:** If the default Subspace Warp method causes unwanted effects, you can try choosing a simpler method. Position is the simplest.

- **Framing:** Warp Stabilizer can use different methods to handle edges when stabilizing. If the default Stabilize, Crop, Auto-Scale framing causes too much variation in scaling, you can try choosing a simpler framing. Stabilize Only is the simplest. Stabilize, Synthesize Edges will create fill areas for empty areas resulting from shifting and scaling the frame during stabilization; how well this synthesis works depends on the content in the frames.

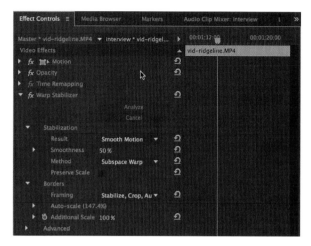

Figure 3.22 Warp Stabilizer settings in the Effect Controls panel

Stabilizing more challenging types of instability is often a balancing act. In general, the more you smooth a clip, the more you have to scale up the clip to crop out the frame-by-frame variations along edges as Warp Stabilizer shifts the content to keep the subject in the same place. In addition to the settings we just discussed, you can explore the Advanced settings to use options that tune the balance between smoothness and the compromises inherent in scaling and edge synthesis.

Exporting Final Video

★ *ACA Objective 5.1*

Before you export a sequence, remember to play back the entire sequence in the timeline to make sure everything's ready for export, and make sure the sequence In and Out points are either cleared or set to the exact duration you want to export.

 *Video 3.14* Fine-
tune and export
your video

When you're ready, make sure the sequence you want to export is active in the Timeline panel and then choose File > Export Media. You've exported video before, so if you need help with the details, refer to "Exporting a Sequence to a Video File" in Chapter 2.

TIP

In the Source Monitor or Program Monitor, you can move one frame back or forward by pressing the Left Arrow or Right Arrow key, respectively.

TIP

The Export Frame button is a quick way to save a still image for use as a poster frame on video sharing websites.

If you set sequence In and Out points because you wanted to export a range of frames instead of the whole sequence, in the Export Settings dialog box you can select Sequence In/Out for Source Range.

The last time you exported video you selected a preset, and it's the same preset you should select here to meet the output requirements specified in preproduction: YouTube HD 720p. But when necessary, you can override a preset by clicking the Export Settings tabs and changing individual settings. You don't need to do that here; after choosing the preset, click Queue or Export.

If you do override a preset and you want to save those changes for future jobs, click the Save Preset button (**Figure 3.23**), name the preset, and click OK. All presets are available in both Premiere Pro and Adobe Media Encoder.

Figure 3.23 Clicking the Save Preset button in the Export Settings dialog box

Challenge: Mini-Documentary

Create a short documentary about an interesting person in your life. Maybe someone in your family has had a fascinating career path, traveled the world, or served with honor. Or do you know a great teacher, or a friend with an unusual hobby?

▶ *Video 3.15*
Mini-documentary
challenge

As you plan your documentary, remember Joe Dockery's Keys to Success (from the video):

- Keep it short.
- Plan. When planning interview questions, keep the questions open-ended. Ask interview subjects to describe and explain their experiences and actions.
- Show good-quality video and record good-quality audio. For video, light subjects in a flattering way. For audio, keep the microphone close to the person speaking and monitor the audio using headphones. Good monitoring helps you catch problems while you can fix them, since you don't want to have to do an interview twice.
- For B-roll, collect and scan photographs, medals, and other media and mementos.
- Share your work with the world!

Conclusion

You've taken a step up in this chapter, learning more about how to build a rough cut, work with audio, add B-roll clips, nest sequences, change the playback speed of clips, and stabilize shaky clips. You also learned more about working with titles, such as how to create rolling titles. You're ready to move ahead and take on more advanced techniques that will make you an even better video editor.

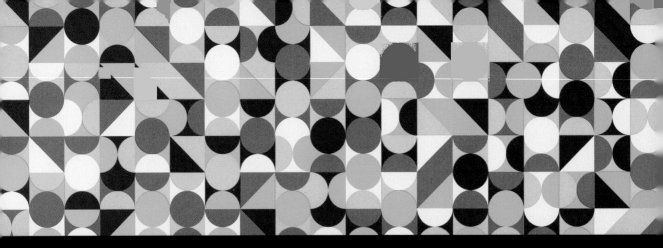

CHAPTER OBJECTIVES

Chapter Learning Objectives

- Create a rough cut.
- Edit on the timeline.
- Understand and edit coverage.
- Edit audio transitions.
- Create a title crawl.
- Use adjustment layers and effects.
- Review and export files.

Chapter ACA Objectives

For more information on ACA Objectives, see pages 235–238.

DOMAIN 1.0
SETTING PROJECT REQUIREMENTS
1.1, 1.2

DOMAIN 2.0
UNDERSTANDING DIGITAL VIDEO
2.4, 2.5

DOMAIN 3.0
UNDERSTANDING ADOBE PREMIERE PRO CC
3.1

DOMAIN 4.0
EDITING A VIDEO SEQUENCE WITH ADOBE PREMIERE PRO
4.1, 4.2, 4.3, 4.4, 4.5, 4.6

DOMAIN 5.0
EXPORTING VIDEO WITH ADOBE PREMIERE PRO
5.1

CHAPTER 4

Editing a Dialogue Scene

In our next training scenario, Anytown High School has hired Brain Buffet to produce a series of short video clips that will help first-year students transition to high school. They will show these videos on their morning announcements and post them on their website. The first video you'll produce for them is designed to let students know about the activity bus.

Preproduction

★ ACA Objective 1.1

★ ACA Objective 1.2

▶ **Video 4.1**
Introducing the activity bus video project

As you've learned, production can't start until the project requirements are clearly understood, so it's time to review those before you begin:

- **Client:** Anytown High School
- **Target Audience:** Anytown High School's target audience is first-year students from 13 to 15 years old.
- **Purpose:** The purpose of producing this video is to inform first-year students that they can still catch the activity bus at 4:30 p.m. if they miss the regular school bus or need to study in the library after school.
- **Actors:** There is a principal and a student.
- **Goal:** The goal is to ensure that first-year students know when the activity bus picks up students after school.
- **Deliverable:** The client expects a 30-to-45-second video featuring two actors, a title, and voiceover. The video should be delivered in H.264 YouTube 720p HD format.

NOTE

If this scene had been shot indoors, you would also have been provided with a WAV file capturing room tone. This is room background noise recorded with no dialogue. A room is not silent, and the background noise of every room has a slightly different character. The uniqueness of room tone lets the audio help the video establish a sense of place and distinguish different locations.

Listing the available media files

In this project, some media has already been acquired for the project. What do you have to work with?

- A photograph of the bus
- Dialogue scene clips with good *coverage* (multiple angles to maintain visual interest by providing variety)

With those items you're ready to start setting up the project.

Listing the preproduction files

There are other planning documents available to you for this project:

- **Project3_activityBus_Storyboard.pdf:** You will get a medium shot, over-the-shoulder shots, close-up shots, and a cutaway. Look at the storyboard for details on how the client sees this scene flowing, and use it as a guide for assembling the rough cut.

- **Project3Script.pdf:** I have provided you with a copy of the script so you can track the dialogue. The actors were allowed to improvise on set, so the dialogue might not be exactly the same as the script. Still, it should cover all the key information.

- **Storyboard_template6panel.pdf:** I provided this blank storyboard template so that you can create your own storyboards.

- **BusDetailsText.txt:** You'll use this text as a title and voiceover at the end of the video.

Setting Up a Project

★ *ACA Objective 4.1*

★ *ACA Objective 4.2*

★ *ACA Objective 4.3*

▶ **Video 4.2** *Access and import your media*

Start the editing stage of production by using the project setup techniques you learned earlier in the book:

1 Unzip the project files using the same techniques you used for the previous project.

2 Start a new project and name it **Anytown HS Activity Bus**.

3 Switch to a workspace that displays the Project panel, such as the Assembly workspace.

4   Import media into the Project panel using the method you prefer, such as drag and drop, the Import command, or its keyboard shortcut.

5   Create a sequence based on a clip.

Creating a Rough Cut

In previous projects the video clips used in the Video 1 track were similar shots. They didn't vary much in terms of field of view, point of view, or camera angle. This project includes more coverage of a scene and uses the traditional filmmaking technique of sequencing a standard set of varied shots to tell a story.

★ *ACA Objective 4.4*

★ *ACA Objective 4.5*

1   Create a new sequence from any of the video clips, but not the audio clip or the photo. Remember that you can create a sequence from a clip by dragging it from the Project panel to an empty Timeline panel.

▶ **Video 4.3** *Edit in the timeline*

It doesn't matter which video clip you use to create the sequence because, at least in this case, they all have the same technical specifications.

2   In the timeline, delete the clip you dragged in since you used it only to create the sequence.

3   In the Project panel, select the sequence you just created.

4   Rename the sequence by clicking the filename of the selected sequence or by choosing Clip > Rename. Type **dialog scene**, and then press Enter (Windows) or Return (Mac OS).

Adding an establishing shot

You'll add a wide-angle shot to establish the scene. Beginning with a wide shot is a traditional way to start a scene because it provides visual context about the location, the time, and sometimes the historical period.

1   In the Project panel, double-click the wide.mp4 video clip so that it opens in the Source Monitor.

2   In the Source Monitor, set the In point to where the principal is approaching the student (about 00:00:04:20), and set the Out point where the principal has turned and is about to speak to the student (about 00:00:08:00).

3   Drag wide.mp4 from the Source Monitor to the V1 track at the beginning of the dialogue sequence in the Timeline panel. This clip doesn't seem to have audio when you listen to it, but it adds an empty audio track to the sequence.

Adding a medium shot and an adjustment

Now you'll add a shot that moves in closer, filling more of the screen with the two characters as the sequence starts to focus more on the story rather than the setting.

1 In the Project panel, double-click the medium.mp4 video clip.

2 In the Source Monitor, set the In and Out points to the range where the principal turns and says "Hi, what's wrong?" Drag the clip to the timeline after the first clip.

Notice that the goal here is to establish and preserve visual and narrative continuity between the two shots. The In and Out points are chosen so that this clip picks up where the previous clip left off and moves the story forward. But if you play back the current sequence, you might notice that the timing of the edit isn't ideal; the action at the end of the first clip repeats a little at the beginning of the second. You'll need to make an edit between the two clips in the timeline.

3 In the Tools panel, select the Ripple Edit tool (⬌).

4 In the Timeline panel, position the Ripple Edit tool just to the right of the edit between the clips so that the tool pointer faces to the right (**Figure 4.1**), because you want to edit the second clip.

Figure 4.1 Preparing to edit the second clip with the Ripple Edit tool

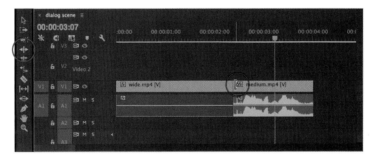

TIP

If both clips are synced but the edit is at the wrong time, use the Rolling Edit tool (⚏) to shift the Out point of the first clip and the In point of the second clip simultaneously.

5 Drag the Ripple Edit tool to the right so that it trims the beginning of the clip until the teacher reaches the bottom step of the stairs. It should now line up much better with when the previous clip left off.

6 Position the Ripple Edit tool just before the edit so that the pointer faces left, and drag to trim the end of the wide shot until it ends precisely when the next clip begins. The Program Monitor dual view of both clips should help you see when the timing is just right.

Editing audio to repair silence

Audio continuity is just as important as video continuity, so it's a problem that the first clip has a silent audio track. You'll extend the background audio that was recorded before the In point of the second clip.

1   In the Timeline panel, select the wide.mp4 clip and choose Clip > Unlink. Then select the audio portion of the clip and press Delete.

2   With the Selection tool (), Alt-drag (Windows) or Option-drag (Mac OS) the In point of the audio portion of the medium.mp4 clip and drag it to the left until it extends all the way to the start of the sequence (**Figure 4.2**).

Figure 4.2 Dragging just the audio portion of the medium.mp4 clip

If you synced the two clips properly on the video track, the sound of steps in the second track should fit perfectly with the steps seen in the video of the first track.

Building the rest of the sequence

At this point you can use the remaining clips to complete the sequence as an exercise. Because this is a dialogue scene, you'll set In and Out points for each clip based on when each character says a line. For reference, follow Project3Script.pdf and Project3_activityBus_Storyboard.pdf in the Pre-production folder. The general idea is to use the clips to visually support the dialogue.

You can add the cutaway_phone.mp4 file where the student mentions that her phone is dead.

After you add all of the remaining clips, play back the entire sequence. You'll probably find that you need to adjust some of the edits in the sequence. Depending on the types of edits to be made, you'll have to use a variety of tools. To learn what each tool does, see the Tools panel overview in Chapter 1.

At the end of the sequence, you can add a Dip to Black video transition to fade it out.

Getting enough coverage

You've probably noticed that the clips in this sequence repeat the same dialogue from different angles and distances. Being able to choose from different shots for a single scene is possible only when the shots were planned this way by the director and the production team. You can achieve similar coverage by specifying them in your shot list. Some productions get their coverage by running multiple cameras at the same time, whereas smaller productions might use one camera and have the actors repeat a scene for each shot that's needed.

Fixing Audio in Adobe Audition

★ *ACA Objective 2.4*

★ *ACA Objective 4.6*

This exercise is a simple example of how you can edit an audio clip by round-tripping between Adobe Premiere Pro CC and Adobe Audition CC. Audition is a powerful audio editing application that's included with your Creative Cloud sub-scription, and it's capable of fixing audio problems that are too challenging for the audio features in Premiere Pro. For example, you can use Audition to clean up audio by removing noise and unwanted sounds such as pops.

▶ **Video 4.4**
Sweeten the audio

To make the fix shown in the video:

1 Make sure that you have installed Adobe Audition CC using the Adobe Creative Cloud desktop application.

2 Back in your Premiere Pro project, select the medium.mp4 clip in the dialogue scene sequence in the Timeline panel.

3 Choose Edit > Edit in Adobe Audition > Clip.

Audition opens and displays the audio clip with its waveform.

> **TIP** *You can also right-click (Windows) or Control-click (Mac OS) and choose Edit Clip in Adobe Audition.*

4 In the heads-up display (HUD), scrub the audio level value to the right until it maxes out at +15. This value is relative to the starting audio level of the clip.

You're trying to boost the level until it reaches about –6 dB on the scale along the right side, but because the HUD is limited to +15 dB per adjustment, you'll have to scrub it a second time.

5. Scrub the HUD level to the right again until the waveform peaks at about –6 dB on the scale along the right side (**Figure 4.3**). Many video editors use –6 dB as a guideline for a good level for dialogue.

6. Save your work in Audition, and switch back to Premiere Pro.

   In the Timeline panel, the waveform for medium.mp4 should now be higher.

   In the Project panel, note that there is a new audio file called medium Audio Extracted.wav. This is the audio from the medium.mp4 clip that's currently used in the sequence. It was extracted from the video clip, edited in Audition, and automatically replaced the original audio clip in the timeline.

Figure 4.3 Scrubbing the audio levels HUD in Audition

Audition is also professional multitrack audio workstation software, so you can mix a video's soundtrack with much more control and precision than you can in Premiere Pro. You could say that Audition is as optimized for audio editing as Premiere Pro is for video editing.

Audition and Premiere Pro are integrated, so you can move clips between them without having to manually import and export. For example, you could bring in all of the audio tracks from a video project, use the advanced audio production features in Audition to create the mixes for each of your final formats (such as stereo and surround sound), and then use those sound mixes for the final version of your Premiere Pro project.

Applying Video Adjustments

Just like still photos, video clips often need a little work after they come out of the camera. Even if your shots are technically correct, they might require additional adjustment when lighting conditions aren't ideal or the camera wasn't set correctly.

▶ **Video 4.5** Make tonal range adjustments

Adjusting video levels

Just as audio clips sometimes need a levels adjustment, video clips may need to be made lighter or darker. The Levels video effect is a common way to lighten or darken a clip. As you've already learned, you can apply an effect to a clip by simply dragging it from the Effects panel and dropping on a clip.

NOTE

Although the Level Settings dialog box is not available in Mac OS, you can immediately see the results of your Effect Controls adjustments in the Program Monitor.

1   In the Anytown HS Activity Bus project, open the Effects panel.

2   Find the Levels video effect (by typing **levels** in the Search field or choosing it in the Video Effects > Adjust group). Drag Levels from the Effect Controls panel and drop it on the overShoulder.mp4 clip in the dialogue scene sequence in the Timeline panel.

3   In the Effect Controls panel, do one of the following:

   ▪ In Windows, click the Settings button (🔧). In the Level Settings dialog box, under the histogram, drag the black slider to 33, drag the middle gray slider to 0.73, and drag the white slider to 251.

   ▪ In Windows or Mac OS, set (RGB) Black Input Level to 33, (RGB) White Input Level to 251, and (RGB) Gamma to 73 (**Figure 4.4**).

4   Disable the effect by clicking the fx button (*fx*) next to the Levels label in the Effect Controls panel. Click the fx button again to enable the effect. Toggling the fx button is a good way to get a before/after view of an effect.

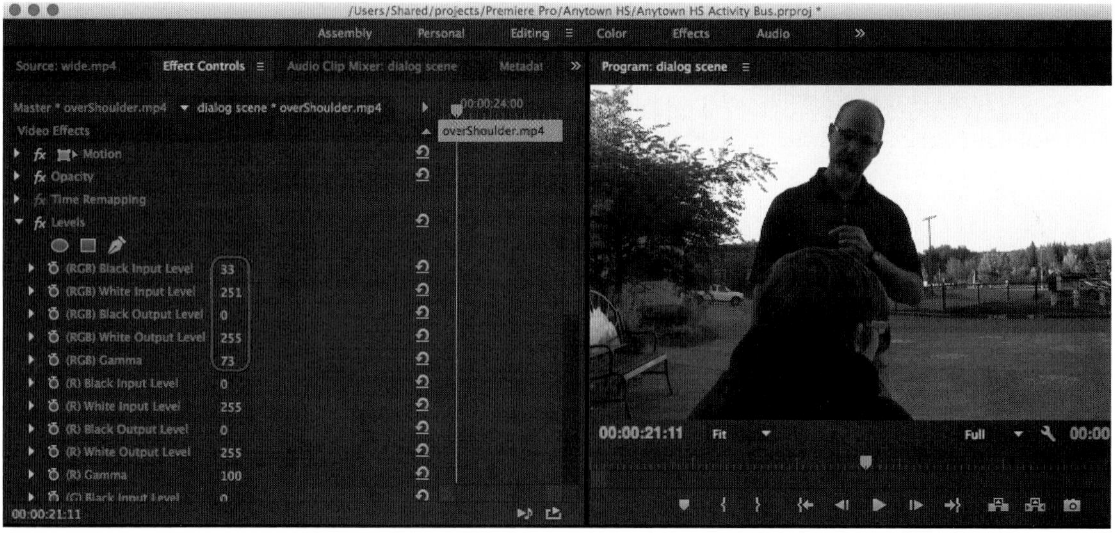

Figure 4.4 Adjusting the Levels effect in the Effect Controls panel

The Levels effect is a good place to start, and it should be familiar if you've used Adobe Photoshop. Premiere Pro includes other effects that can adjust levels in ways you might find more intuitive, such as the Three-Way Color Corrector in Chapter 5.

Applying an adjustment layer

By now you're familiar with how to apply an effect to a clip. But what if you want to apply the same effect to many clips in a sequence? Although there is a way to cut and paste effects from clip to clip, even that can be tedious if you have an hour-long program with hundreds of clip instances.

In Premiere Pro you can apply an effect to an entire track by using an *adjustment layer*. If you've used adjustment layers in Photoshop, you already have an idea about how it works: An adjustment layer is like a clip in that it appears in the Project panel after you create it, but it contains only an effect and no content. If you add an adjustment layer to a sequence, any effects you apply to the adjustment layer also apply to all clips in lower tracks.

1   In the Project panel, click the New Item button () and choose Adjustment Layer. Accept the default settings by clicking OK. A new item named Adjustment Layer is added to the Project panel.

If you want to change its name, you can rename it in the same way you renamed other Project panel items earlier.

2   Drag Adjustment Layer and drop it on track V2 in the Timeline panel. Drag its ends so that its duration matches the entire sequence (**Figure 4.5**).

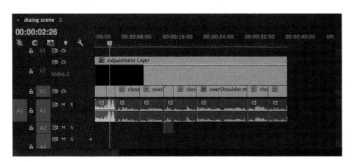

TIP

You can also choose File > New > Adjustment Layer if the Project panel is active.

Figure 4.5 An adjustment layer added to the timeline

3   In the Timeline panel or Program Monitor, move the playhead to a frame inside the second clip.

4   Find the Fast Color Corrector video effect (either by typing part or all of its name in the Search field or by choosing it from the Video Effects > Color Correction group). Drag Fast Color Corrector from the Effect Controls panel and drop it on the adjustment layer on track V2 in the Timeline panel.

5   In the Effect Controls panel, scroll to find the Fast Color Corrector effect.

6   In the Fast Color Corrector effect, select the White Balance eyedropper; then in the Program Monitor, click the eyedropper on a white area of the sign near the left edge of the frame. This samples the white as the reference for shifting the clips' white balance to neutral (**Figure 4.6**).

    Notice that in the Fast Color Corrector, the Balance Magnitude handle (the small circular handle near the center) has moved out along the color wheel to indicate which hues it has boosted and by how much.

7   Check your work by using the Fast Color Corrector fx button (*fx*) to disable and enable the effect.

Figure 4.6 Using the Fast Color Corrector

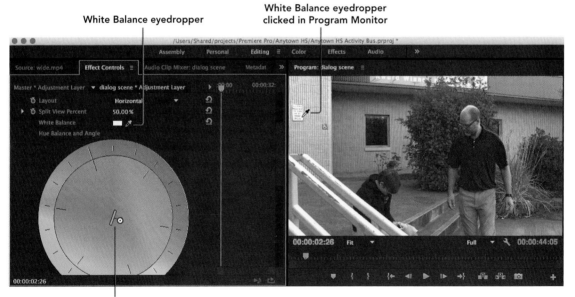

White Balance eyedropper

White Balance eyedropper clicked in Program Monitor

Balance Magnitude handle

As with other clips you've worked with on the timeline, the default rubber band for an adjustment layer is Opacity. For an adjustment layer, reducing its opacity reduces the strength of the effect. And as with rubber bands in general, you can add keyframes to the Opacity rubber band to vary the strength of the effect over time. For example, if you need to make multiple white balance corrections throughout a single clip because the camera moved among different-colored light sources (such as from daylight into a room lit by fluorescent lightbulbs), you can add a keyframe at each time where you need to make a color balance change and adjust the Fast Color Corrector values at each keyframe.

Recording a voiceover

To help drive home the message that this video needs to deliver, it ends with a voiceover and title based on the same text. You'll create the title soon, but right now it's time to record the voiceover. You've recorded a voiceover earlier in this book, so use this exercise to practice what you've learned. This time, though, you'll be using a script that's provided with the media files for this project. Record the voiceover according to these requirements:

1   Before recording, make sure your microphone is set up correctly in the Audio Hardware pane of the Preferences dialog box in Premiere Pro.

2   Record the voiceover to audio track A2 in the sequence.

3   Read from the script BusDetailsText.txt that's included with the media files for this project.

4   After the voiceover is recorded, make any adjustments that are necessary to merge it smoothly with the preceding clips, such as trimming the ends or adding an audio transition.

Add a Still Image to the Sequence

★ ACA Objective 2.5

★ ACA Objective 3.1

▶ **Video 4.7** Add a photo and title

You just recorded a voiceover at the end of the sequence, but the video track is currently empty. To provide a visual background for the voiceover, you'll add a photograph of a bus and also add a title that reflects the voiceover and animates into the scene for additional visual interest and emphasis.

Create a title to superimpose over the image

Create a new title using the text of the script. It will appear over the image of a bus that you'll add soon. Because you've created several titles by now, this should be a familiar task:

1 Name the title **bus time**.

2 Paste the title text into the title, and format it to fit within the Safe Title margins.

3 Use the Title window tools and settings to format the text for readability.

When you're done (**Figure 4.7**), close the Title window so that you can prepare the image that will display under the title.

Figure 4.7 Preparing the bus time title

Add a still image

You can add a still image to a sequence the same way you've added video, audio, and titles: by dragging it from the Project panel or a bin into the Timeline panel. As with most photos, the aspect ratio of the image is different from the 16:9 video frame. Fortunately, it's easy for you to resize and reposition the image anywhere in the frame.

1 Drag the file bus.jpg to the end of the sequence in the Timeline panel.

   The still image comes in using the Still Image Default Duration specified in the General panel of the Preferences dialog box in Premiere Pro, so you'll need to adjust the duration.

2 Drag the Out point of the bus image to make its duration match the voiceover audio.

3 In the Program Monitor, double-click the bus image. Handles should appear on a bounding box around the image.

4 Drag a handle to resize the image so that it fills the frame without any black bars on the sides (**Figure 4.8**).

Figure 4.8 Handles for resizing a still image in the Program Monitor

If you don't see bounding box handles and you see only the middle of the bus, the image is probably much bigger than the frame and its handles are probably outside the frame. This is normal because digital camera images usually contain many more pixels than even an HD video frame. To fix this, go to the Program Monitor and choose a low magnification such as 25% or 10% so that you can see the area outside the frame. This should make the clip handles visible. Now you can drag a handle to fit the image in the frame.

Some digital cameras record frames with a 3:2 aspect ratio; others record frames with a 4:3 aspect ratio. Images with those aspect ratios will need to be recomposed to fill a 16:9 HD video frame without black bars on the sides. A few cameras let you select a 16:9 aspect ratio.

Set up the title to crawl left and hold

Now it's time to add the title over the bus image.

1 In the Project panel, find the bus time title you created and drag it to the Timeline panel into a track above the bus image.

2 Adjust the title's In point so that it starts a couple of seconds after the bus image, and drag its Out point to end when the voiceover and bus image end.

Figure 4.9 The Roll/Crawl Options dialog box

3 Double-click the title to open it.

4 Choose Title > Roll/Crawl Options. Select the Crawl Left and Start Offscreen options, enter **150** in the Preroll option (**Figure 4.9**), and click OK.

The options you see in the Roll/Crawl Options dialog box operate as follows:

- The **Crawl Left** option animates the title from right to left

- The **Start Offscreen** option positions the title beyond the right edge of the frame so that the crawl brings it into the frame

- The **150-frame postroll** finishes the crawl 150 frames before the end of the title duration so that it holds for 5 seconds (5 times 30 frames per second).

Play back the sequence and see if your results match the example in the tutorial video; make any adjustments as needed.

Blur the background at a specific time

Although the title works, it's hard to read over the visually busy bus photo. You'll fix this problem by blurring the bus photo. You can apply video effects to still images.

1 Find the Fast Blur video effect by searching for it or choosing it from the Video Effects > Blur and Sharpen group. Drag Fast Blur from the Effect Controls panel and drop it on the bus.jpg image in the Timeline panel (**Figure 4.10**).

Figure 4.10 Applying Fast Blur to the bus image

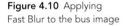

2 Move the playhead to the time when the title is about to come to a stop.

3 In the Effect Controls panel, make sure the bus.jpg tab is active, and expand the Camera Blur options.

Toggle Animation   Blurriness   Add Keyframe
stopwatch   value   button   Keyframe

Figure 4.11 Adjusting the
Blurriness value

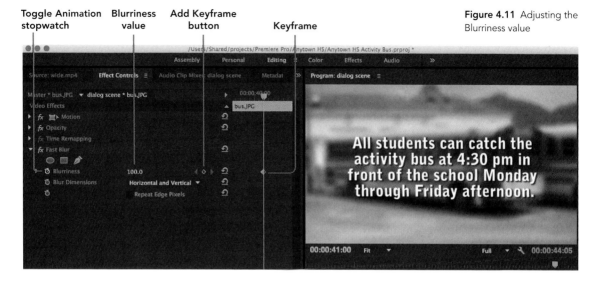

4 Immediately to the left of the Blurriness option, click the Toggle Animation
   stopwatch so that it's blue.

5 In the Blurriness option, type **100** and press Enter or Return (**Figure 4.11**).
   You can apply a little more or less blurriness if you like (the value can go
   above 100).

   Notice that the Add Keyframe button becomes selected, because changing a
   value when the Toggle Animation stopwatch is on automatically adds a keyframe at the playhead.

6 Move the playhead to the beginning of the bus.jpg image. In the Effect
   Controls panel, set Blurriness to 0.

Play back this part of the sequence. The title should slide in from the right as the
bus image becomes blurry, and the title should stop and hold in the middle of the
frame 5 seconds before the bus image ends.

Reviewing with Your Clients
and Exporting the Final Video

★ *ACA Objective 5.1*

Video 4.8
Preview and review

At some point your clients are going to want to see what you've been working
on for them, maybe even before you're finished with the project. You don't need
to export video to show the client a full-screen presentation; you can do it from
Premiere Pro itself.

Reviewing a project using Cinema mode

Cinema mode can help you and your clients review a project while you're still working on it in Premiere Pro. In Cinema mode you can present full-screen playback of a clip or a sequence.

1 Do one of the following:

   ▪ To present the active clip in the Source Monitor, click it.

   ▪ To present the active sequence in the Program Monitor, click it.

2 Press Ctrl-` (the tilde key) in Windows or Control-` in Mac OS. The monitor you clicked expands into full-screen mode.

3 If you want, you can use the keyboard shortcuts for navigating the timeline, such as pressing Home or End to go to the start or end, respectively, or pressing the Up Arrow or Down Arrow key to go to the previous or next edit, respectively.

4 Press the spacebar to start or pause playback.

5 To exit Cinema mode, press Ctrl-` (Windows) or Control-` (Mac OS) or the Esc key.

Exporting the final video

Before you export final video, remember to play it back all the way through and make sure there are no more adjustments or corrections to be made. You may want to play it back several times to focus on different aspects of the production. For example, you might spend one pass just watching the timing of edits and another pass just listening to the audio. Pause playback whenever you notice something that needs attention, and add it to a checklist. Rendering final video can take a long time, so it's more efficient to take care of problems before you export.

After you choose File > Export Media, double-check specifications such as the source range, the format, the preset, the output name, and the folder location.

Challenge: Create Your Own Dialogue Scene

Now that you've built a dialogue scene by using the media provided and completing these exercises, create your own dialogue scene. You can try a variation on the theme of this chapter's project of orienting new high school students. Provide directions to important rooms or buildings such as a cafeteria or gym, show the students what to do in an emergency, or explain how to use the library.

▶ **Video 4.9** *Dialogue video challenge*

As you plan your documentary, remember Joe Dockery's Keys to Success (from the video):

- Keep it short.
- Plan. Write a good script and storyboard. You can use the storyboard_template6panel.pdf file in the Pre-Production folder for this chapter, which contains a grid of six blank storyboard panels.
- Shoot good-quality video and record good-quality audio. For video, light subjects in a flattering way. For audio, keep the microphone close to the person speaking and monitor the audio using headphones. Good monitoring helps you catch problems while you can fix them, since you don't want to have to do an interview twice.
- Get complete coverage. Shoot the entire scene from multiple angles.
- Share your work and continue to build your portfolio.

Conclusion

In this chapter you've had a chance to spend more practice time on valuable basic skills such as editing video, editing audio, and creating titles. You've added some new abilities such as working with still images, editing audio in Adobe Audition CC, and keyframing effects. Keep practicing with your own ideas and projects, and let's continue on to the next chapter.

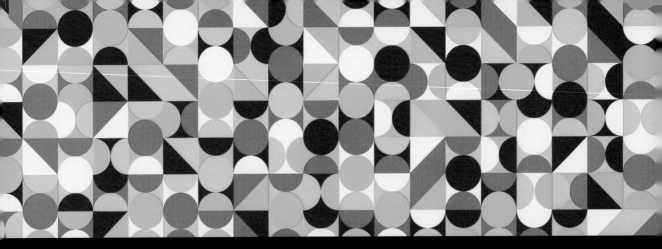

CHAPTER OBJECTIVES

Chapter Learning Objectives

- Apply special effects.
- Draw a simple opacity mask.
- Use the Ultra Key effect to remove a green screen.
- Animate effects with keyframes.
- Add video layers.

Chapter ACA Objectives

For more information on ACA Objectives, see pages 235–238.

DOMAIN 1.0
SETTING PROJECT REQUIREMENTS
1.1, 1.2

DOMAIN 2.0
UNDERSTANDING DIGITAL VIDEO
2.3

DOMAIN 4.0
EDITING DIGITAL VIDEO USING ADOBE PREMIERE PRO
4.1, 4.2, 4.3, 4.8

CHAPTER 5

Compositing with Green Screen Effects

In this project's scenario, our editor for Brain Buffet TV is out today, so we need you to edit the weather report. This will give you some great practice compositing the footage shot on our green screen with the weather graphics. You'll learn how to "key out" a background, import a layered Photoshop file, and light for green screen. The entire scene is only about 25 seconds long.

Preproduction

As you've learned, production can't start until the project requirements are clearly understood. Let's review them before you begin:

- **Client:** Brain Buffet TV

- **Target Audience:** Brain Buffet TV is broadcast at the Happy Old Retirement home, so your target audience is 70–90 years old, mostly female.

- **Purpose:** The purpose of the weather report is to let the people living in the retirement home know what type of weather to expect if they go outside.

- **Deliverables:** The client expects a 20-to-30-second video featuring the weather report layered over the map and motion graphics illustrating the weather-related facts. The video should be delivered in H.264 720p. The client also requires an audio file that can be used to create a written transcript for the deaf. The audio should be delivered in MP3 format with a bitrate of 128 Kbps.

★ *ACA Objective 1.1*

★ *ACA Objective 1.2*

▶ *Video 5.1*
Introducing the weather report project

Listing the available media files

In this project, some media has already been acquired for the project. What do you have to work with?

- A master video clip shot in front of a green screen
- A weather map still image in Adobe Photoshop format with separate layers for sunshine, temperatures, and thunder and lightning
- A TV station logo still image in Photoshop format
- Hiking photo

With those items you're ready to start setting up the project.

Setting Up a Project

★ *ACA Objective 4.1*

★ *ACA Objective 4.2*

★ *ACA Objective 4.3*

▶ **Video 5.2**
Organize your project

Start the editing stage of production by practicing the project setup techniques you learned earlier in the book:

1 Unzip the project files using the same techniques you used for the previous project.

2 Start a new project and name it **weather report**.

3 Switch to a workspace that displays the Project panel, such as the Assembly workspace.

4 Import the two files weatherReport.mp4 and hiking.jpg into the Project panel; leave the other files alone for now.

Importing layered Photoshop documents

★ *ACA Objective 4.2*

Now you'll import the two Photoshop files, and you'll see that they import slightly differently than the other files.

1 Import the BBLogo.psd file.

The Import Layered File dialog box appears. It lists the layers inside the document along with options for how to import them. You can import the layers as a single image or as individual images (**Figure 5.1**).

Layered Photoshop files are useful for video graphics because it's possible to animate each layer independently in Adobe Premiere Pro. You'll soon see how this works.

2 Click the Import As menu and choose Merge All Layers to import the file as a single image.

3 Import the weatherMap.psd file.

4 In the Import Layered File dialog box that appears, click the Import As menu and choose As Separate Files; then click OK.

   Check boxes let you choose which layers to import, but in this case you want all of the layers, so leave all of them selected.

5 Click OK. Notice that the weatherMap.psd file was imported as a folder, with separate images inside the folder that were derived from each layer in the Photoshop file (**Figure 5.2**).

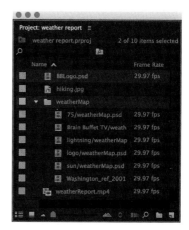

Figure 5.1 Images from the layered weatherMap.psd file imported into a bin inside the Project panel, shown in List view

White balancing a clip using a gray target

Now create a new sequence based on the weatherReport.mp4 clip, using whichever technique you prefer.

The weatherReport.mp4 clip begins with someone holding up a target with three shades of neutral gray on it. Why does this clip start this way? It's a *green screen* clip, which features a subject against a solid green backdrop that you will soon replace with a different background. The process of removing a solid-colored background from a shot is called *chroma key compositing*, or "keying out" the background. Chroma refers to the color that's keyed out.

Figure 5.2 Importing the layered PSD file as individual layers

In a natural scene, the camera can usually find some neutral areas to use as a reference for white balancing the video. In a green screen clip, there are neither neutral colors nor natural colors. If the camera is set to automatic white balance, it has no reliable way of deciding what the proper white balance should be. The gray target provides the necessary neutral reference in the clip when you want to use the White Balance eyedropper in the color correction tools in Premiere Pro, such as the Fast Color Corrector you used Chapter 4 or the Three-Way Color Corrector demonstrated in the tutorial video for this chapter.

Why is the green color so unnatural? That color will make it easier for Premiere Pro to isolate the color so that it can remove it cleanly while not removing anything you want to keep visible. If you use a backdrop with a color that appears in nature, such as an earth tone, a background replacement feature might accidentally remove natural areas you want to keep visible, such as a person's face or clothing.

The target in the video has three strips representing highlights, midtones, and shadows. If you applied a color correction effect that has just one eyedropper, it may be best to click middle gray or white. If you applied a color correction effect with eyedroppers for different tonal ranges (**Figure 5.3**), you'll want to do the following:

- Click the White Level eyedropper on the white stripe in the handheld target in the Program Monitor.
- Click the Gray Level eyedropper on the middle gray stripe.
- Click the Black Level eyedropper on the black stripe.

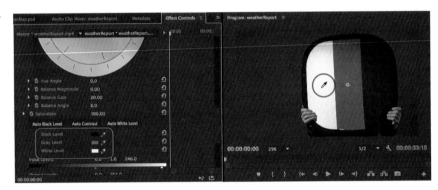

Figure 5.3 The Fast Color Corrector is an effect that uses three eyedroppers for more precise white balancing by sampling highlights, midtones, and shadows.

Preparing to shoot green screen clips

▶ **Video 5.3** *Video lighting*

A background replacement feature works best when the area to be replaced is cleanly defined so that it's easy to isolate. The background you're replacing must have consistent color and consistent lighting.

Follow these guidelines for successfully shooting a scene on a green screen background:

- Light the background evenly. If you have "hot spots," you may need more lights to cover more of the background area, or you may need to add diffusers to the lights.
- Make sure the green screen is clean and not wrinkled. It should be solid, not any kind of a pattern or gradient. This is easy to achieve because you can buy rolls of green screen background or use green screen paint.
- Position the talent several feet away from the background. This will help prevent shadows from falling on the green screen and prevent green reflections (spill) on the talent. It will also make it more likely that the background will be out of focus so that stains or wrinkles on the green screen will be less visible.

- Use a standard key light and fill light to make sure the talent is well lit. (A key light is about lighting the subject, not about chroma keying.)

- Add hair lights so that the rim light effect helps separate the outline of the talent from the background.

- Dress the talent in colors that are not similar to the green screen so that keying software can easily distinguish the background color that needs to be removed.

Compositing a Green Screen Clip with a New Background

★ ACA Objective 2.3

★ ACA Objective 4.8

▶ **Video 5.4** *Key weatherman over weathermap*

Now you're ready to remove the green screen, revealing the weather map underneath.

Drawing a garbage matte

The first phase of green screen compositing is to draw an *opacity mask*, which is traditionally called a *garbage matte*. Although it is possible to simply have Premiere Pro remove the background based on the green color, using an opacity mask quickly masks off the areas that never need to be shown at any point in the clip, reducing the amount of potential variation in the green screen color and making background removal easier to define and perform.

1   In the weatherMap bin in the Project panel, drag the green screen clip, weatherReport.mp4, to a higher track than the new background in the Timeline panel. For example, put a green screen clip on V2 so that you can put the new background under it on track V1.

2   Drag the weather map graphic, Washington_ref_2001/weatherMap.psd, to track V1 at the beginning of the clip.

3   With the Rate Stretch tool, stretch Washington_ref_2001/weatherMap.psd to match the duration of weatherReport.mp4 (**Figure 5.4**). You need to use the Rate Stretch tool because Premiere Pro sees the PSD file as more of a video clip than a still image.

Figure 5.4 The weatherMap graphic set up with the correct position and duration in the Timeline panel

4 Make sure the weatherReport.mp4 clip is selected in the Timeline panel.

5 Scrub through or play back the sequence and note how far out weather reporter Joe's hands extend during the presentation.

6 In the Effect Controls panel, expand the Opacity setting.

7 Select the Free Draw Bezier tool (**Figure 5.5**).

Figure 5.5 The Free Draw Bezier tool selected in the Effect Controls panel and positioned over the Program Monitor

8 In the Program Monitor, click the Free Draw Bezier tool around Joe to draw a rough mask that stays outside the furthest reach of Joe's hands during the presentation (**Figure 5.6**).

The mask doesn't have to follow Joe's outline tightly or precisely; leave a bit of margin between Joe and the mask path. Click only in the green areas; don't click any points inside Joe, and don't let any path segments cross over Joe.

9 When you're ready to close the path, click the tip of the Free Draw Bezier tool on the first point you drew.

The path automatically closes. The area outside the mask becomes transparent (**Figure 5.7**).

Figure 5.6 Drawing the path of an opacity mask

Figure 5.7 A completed opacity mask path

10 Play back the sequence and see if any part of Joe's body crosses over the mask at any time.

11 If you need to move a path point or make other adjustments to the path, use the Selection tool () to reposition any points on the mask path. If you need to move a point outside the frame, zooming out will let you see outside the frame.

12 If you want to convert any straight segments to a curved segment, Alt-drag (Windows) or Option-drag (Mac OS) a point to extend *Bézier handles*. These handles curve the segments extending from a point (**Figure 5.8**).

Figure 5.8 Creating curved segments by extending Bézier handles

KEYING OUT THE GREEN BACKGROUND

With the garbage matte in place, now you can have Premiere Pro concentrate on isolating and removing the green screen color that remains.

1 In the Effect Controls panel, find the Ultra Key video effect (it's in the Video Effects > Keying group). Drag Ultra Key from the Effect Controls panel and drop it on the weatherReport.mp4 clip in the Timeline panel.

2 In the Effect Controls panel, scroll down to the Ultra Key settings and select the Key Color eyedropper (**Figure 5.9**).

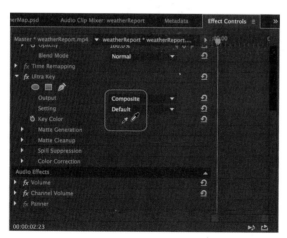

Figure 5.9 The Key Color eyedropper selected in the Ultra Key settings

3 Click the Key Color eyedropper on the green screen in the Program Monitor.

This samples the green color that Ultra Key should remove, and what was the green screen color should now be transparent (**Figure 5.10**).

TIP *You may get better results if you click the Key Color eyedropper in a darker area of the green screen.*

Figure 5.10 Before and after clicking the green screen color with the Key Color eyedropper

4 In the Effect Controls panel, go to the Ultra Key settings, click the Output menu, and choose Alpha Channel. This displays the mask created by Ultra Key so you can see whether it is clean enough (**Figure 5.11**).

There is a saying that can help you remember how to read an alpha channel: "White reveals, black conceals." White mask areas allow the clip to display because they represent opaque areas, whereas black areas are part of the mask that makes those areas of the clip transparent. Gray areas are partially transparent, so dark gray areas are mostly transparent but still let through some of those clip areas.

5 Scrub through the sequence to see if the mask is clean for the entire sequence.

Figure 5.11 After choosing the Alpha Channel setting

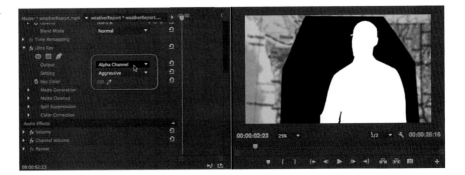

6 If the mask is not clean at times (there are gray areas), in the Effect Controls panel go to the Ultra Key settings, click the Settings menu, and choose a different option to see which one works best. Each option is a preset for the advanced settings below the Key Color option (**Figure 5.12**). If the advanced settings are expanded, you can see how they change when you choose a Settings preset.

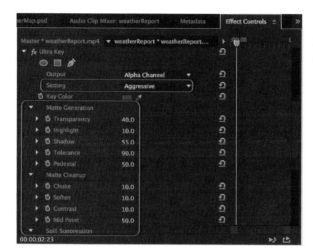

Figure 5.12 Settings presets change the values in the advanced settings.

If you're feeling adventurous or already have a technical familiarity with keying, you can expand the Matte Generation, Matte Cleanup, Spill Suppression, and Color Correction settings and try adjusting them. But if no Settings options work well enough, the fastest fix may be to sample a different Key Color by repeating steps 3–5.

7 Scrub through the sequence to see if the mask is now clean for the entire sequence. If it isn't, try step 6 again.

8 In the Effect Controls panel, go to the Ultra Key settings, click the Output menu, and choose Composite.

This displays the composite result of the two tracks plus the mask applied to the upper track.

9 Play back the sequence to make sure it looks right. Watch out for irregularities in the keyed-out area, and keep an eye out for green spill on the subject.

TIP

You can address green spill using the Matte Cleanup options in the Ultra Key effect, especially the Choke and Soften settings.

TIP

It might be worth playing back the sequence with the lower track hidden. Then you can preview the mask against a black background.

Adding and Animating More Graphics

▶ **Video 5.5** *Add graphics*

With the weather presentation composited over the weather map, it's time to add some more graphics to help round out the weather report.

Adding a track

You'll soon add graphics on another track. If your sequence doesn't have an empty track above the sequence, add one.

Right-click (Windows) or Control-click (Mac OS) the Timeline panel just to the left of where the highest video clip starts, and choose Add Track (**Figure 5.13**). Premiere Pro adds a new video track above the track where you clicked.

> **TIP** *When you want to add more than one video or audio track, choose Add Tracks from the same context menu or choose Sequence > Add Tracks.*

Figure 5.13 Adding a track above the pointer

Adding an animated logo

You need to add the Brain Buffet logo so that it enters the frame at the bottom-left corner while rotating and stops at the bottom-right corner of the frame.

1 In the weatherMap bin in the Project panel, drag BBLogo.psd to the beginning of the sequence, onto an empty track above the others.

2 Use the Rate Stretch tool ( ) to display the logo during the entire duration of the sequence.

3   Select the logo and resize and reposition it in the bottom-left corner of the frame, in one of the following ways:

- In the Program Monitor, double-click the logo, drag to reposition it, and drag its handles to resize it. Be careful not to accidentally drag the anchor point.

- In the Effect Controls panel, with the Motion settings expanded, make sure Uniform Scale is selected and scrub the Position and Scale values.

4   In the Effect Controls panel, adjust the Opacity value to around 70% to make the logo semitransparent (**Figure 5.14**).

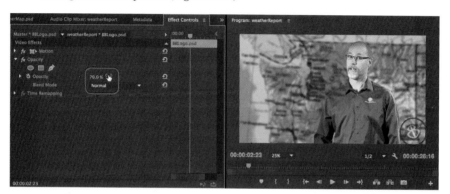

Figure 5.14 The Brain Buffet logo with its final position and appearance

5   Move the playhead to the time when the logo should stop at the bottom-right corner, when Joe finishes saying "Welcome to Brain Buffet TV!"

6   In the Effect Controls panel, enable the Toggle Animation button for the Position and Rotation options so that it adds Position and Rotation keyframes at the current time (**Figure 5.15**).

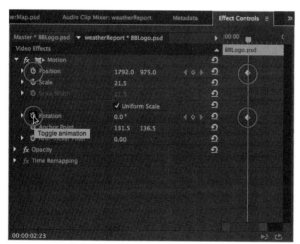

Figure 5.15 Position and Rotation keyframes added at the playhead

7　Move the playhead to the beginning of the sequence.

8　Click the Add Keyframe button for the Position setting.

9　Scrub the Rotation setting to the left to "wind up" the rotation in a counter-clockwise direction to its starting point. Because Toggle Animation is on for Rotation, a keyframe is added at the playhead (**Figure 5.16**).

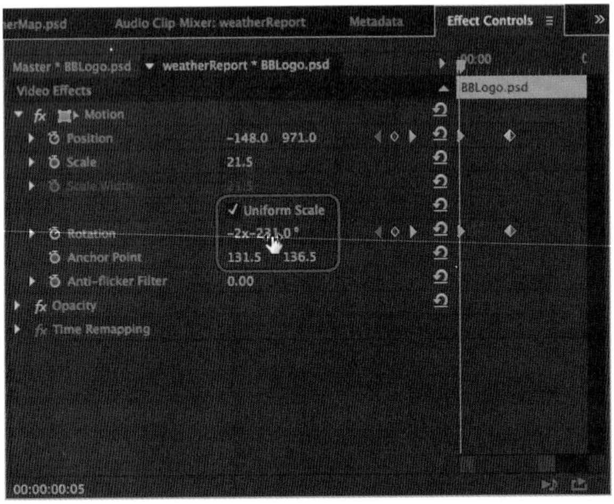

NOTE

Because you rotated counterclockwise, it's normal for the Rotation angle to be a negative value.

TIP

When editing a key-frame, make sure the playhead snaps to it before editing the key-frame value. You know you're on it when Add Keyframe is blue.

TIP

As you add tracks to a sequence, you might want to drag the horizontal dividers between tracks and the audio/video track sections so that you can see what you want to work on.

Figure 5.16 Scrubbing to set the Rotation angle

10　To make the logo slow to a stop instead of suddenly stopping, right-click (Windows) or Control-click (Mac OS) the second Position keyframe, and choose Ease In from the context menu that appears (**Figure 5.17**).

11　Play back the sequence and evaluate both the movement and rotation. Make any additional adjustments that are needed.

Figure 5.17 Applying the Ease In command to the end of the motion

Adding weather graphics to the map

With the presenter now composited over the weather map, it's time to add the weather graphics that appear over the map: a lightning icon and a sun icon. They don't need to move, so to help keep them organized you'll first create a sequence that contains them both.

▶ *Video 5.6 Create picture-in-picture*

1 In the weatherMap bin in the Project panel, create a new sequence based on the sun/weatherMap.psd file.

2 Rename the new sequence **sun and 75**.

3 From the weatherMap bin, drag the 75/weatherMap.psd file to the Timeline panel. In the Project Monitor, the 75 should appear just below the sun (**Figure 5.18**).

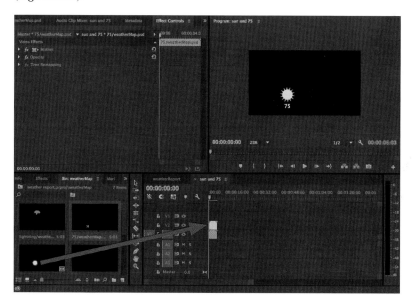

Figure 5.18 Adding the temperature to the sun

4 Click the weatherReport tab in the Timeline panel to make it active.

5 Play the weatherReport sequence so that you can identify where Joe says "sunshine and 75 degrees" and position the playhead to the time where he starts saying that phrase, because that's where you're about to add the sequence you just created.

6 Drag the "sun and 75" sequence from the weatherMap bin and drop it in the Timeline panel, in the empty space just above the top track so that it begins at the playhead (**Figure 5.19**).

Figure 5.19 The "sun and 75" sequence nested within the weatherReport sequence

Dropping an item into the empty space above tracks automatically adds a track for the item you drop, so you don't have to use the Add Track command in advance.

7 Add cross-dissolve video transitions to the start and end of the "sun and 75" clip to fade it in and out.

8 Play the weatherReport sequence so that you can identify where Joe says "thunder and lightning" and position the playhead to the time where he starts saying that phrase, because that's where you're about to add the lightning graphic.

9 Drag the lightning/weatherMap.psd graphic from the weatherMap bin and drop it in the Timeline panel to the top track so that it begins at the playhead.

10 With the lightning/weatherMap.psd graphic selected in the Timeline panel, in the Effect Controls panel scrub the two Motion values (X and Y) to position the lightning graphic over Joe's hand (**Figure 5.20**). This is another way to position a clip.

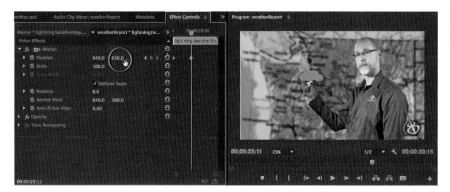

Figure 5.20 Adjusting the Position keyframe values for the lightning graphic

11 Animate the lightning graphic so that it slides down into the frame from the top to follow how Joe's hand comes down when he mentions thunder and lightning.

You did this earlier in this chapter with the Brain Buffet logo, and you can use a similar technique here by using the Effect Controls panel to set Position keyframes at the start and stop of the animation. But this time the primary movement is along the y-axis (the second Position option).

12 Play the weatherReport sequence so that you can identify where Joe says "camping" and position the playhead to the time where he starts saying that phrase, because that's where you're about to add a hiking photo.

13 From the Project panel, drag the hiking.jpg file to the top track.

14 Resize and reposition the hiking.jpg so that it appears to sit on Joe's hand.

15 In the Effect Controls window, find the Drop Shadow video effect (it's in the Video Effects > Perspective group). Drag Drop Shadow from the Effect Controls panel and drop it on the hiking.jpg clip in the Timeline panel.

TIP

This sequence contains more tracks and effects than you've worked with so far, which is more work for your computer's processor. If playback isn't smooth, click the Select Playback Resolution menu and choose a resolution lower than Full, such as 1/2.

TIP

If scrubbing requires dragging a long way to reach the values you want, press Shift while scrubbing.

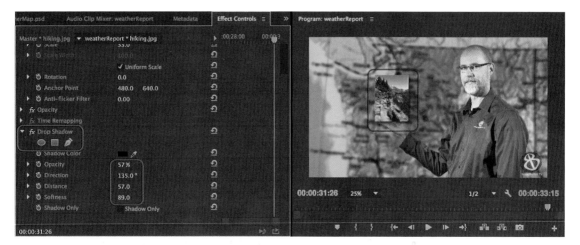

Figure 5.21 Drop Shadow settings in the Effect Controls panel

16 In the Effect Controls panel, find the Drop Shadow settings until you like how it looks (**Figure 5.21**).

17 Play back the weatherReport sequence and clean up any loose ends that you find.

When you're satisfied with how the sequence looks, export the final video using the H.264 YouTube 720 HD preset for easy online delivery and playback to the audience at the retirement home.

Exporting Final Video

As you did in Chapter 2, export the sequence to the Adobe Media Encoder queue for final rendering. But before you click the Render button, remember that one of the deliverables is an MP3 audio file that can be used to create a transcript for the hard of hearing. You can easily create the audio file from the same sequence in Adobe Media Encoder, so you don't have to export twice from Premiere Pro.

To set up creation of the MP3 audio file:

1 In Adobe Media Encoder, select the weatherReport sequence you exported from Premiere Pro, and click the Duplicate button (**Figure 5.22**).

Figure 5.22 Duplicating the weatherReport sequence

2 In the Preset Browser panel, expand the System Presets list and then expand the Audio Only list.

3 Drag the MP3 128Kps preset from the Preset Browser, and drop it on the duplicated sequence (**Figure 5.23**). The Format and Preset for the duplicate sequence change to indicate the new settings.

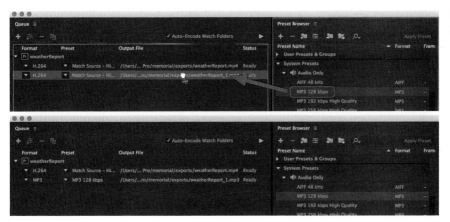

Figure 5.23 Dropping a preset onto a sequence

When you click the green Start Queue button in the Queue panel, Media Encoder will process the items in the queue, producing H.264 video and MP3 audio versions of the sequence for you.

Challenge: Create Your Own Composited Video

▶ **Video 5.7** *Special FX challenge*

Now it's time for you to come up with your own special effects video.

As you plan your project, remember Joe Dockery's Keys to Success (from the video):

- Keep it short, around 30–60 seconds long.
- Determine the background media. It can be a different part of your city, a picture or video of an exotic location, or even another planet.
- Determine the background that you'll remove. It can be a large sheet of paper or a painted wall, as long as it's a distinct color that won't be confused with any colors in the content that you want to keep visible.
- Shoot good-quality video and record good-quality audio.
- Frame actors tightly, such as from the waist up, to simplify keying.
- Plan the timing of the talent's lines and movements to coordinate them with other elements you want to composite into the scene.
- Set the white balance of the camera with the gray target.
- Follow the other guidelines for lighting and shooting green screen clips earlier in this chapter.

Conclusion

In this chapter you've gotten a taste of how Hollywood and television can make any idea look real by conceiving sequences as visual composites of live action video clips, backgrounds, and digital graphics. Let your own imagination run free!

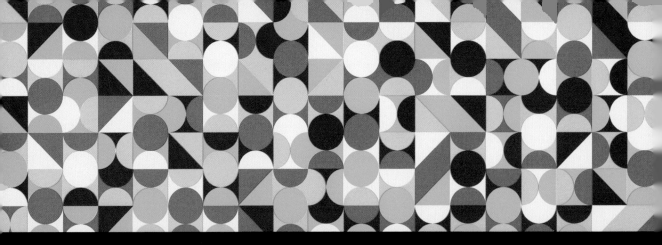

Chapter Learning Objectives

- Review file management and project organization.

- Organize files.

- Open and save a project.

- Set preferences for importing multiple still images.

- Set up Automate to Sequence to accelerate sequence creation.

- Set up variations of a job in Adobe Media Encoder.

Chapter ACA Objectives

For more information on ACA Objectives, see pages 235–238.

DOMAIN 1.0
SETTING PROJECT REQUIREMENTS
1.1, 1.4

DOMAIN 2.0
UNDERSTANDING DIGITAL VIDEO
2.3, 2.5

DOMAIN 4.0
EDITING DIGITAL VIDEO USING ADOBE PREMIERE PRO
4.1, 4.2, 4.3, 4.8

DOMAIN 5.0
EXPORTING VIDEO WITH ADOBE PREMIERE PRO
5.1

CHAPTER 6

Creating a Video Slide Show

Your latest assignment is something that Brain Buffet is often asked to do: create a short memorial video of a deceased loved one or community member from photographs provided by family and friends. Using tools in Adobe Premiere Pro CC, it doesn't take long to set many photos to music and add motion effects. The result is a moving presentation that tells the story of why and how the deceased should be remembered.

Preproduction

As you've learned in previous chapters, production can't start until the project requirements are clearly understood, so let's review those before you begin:

- **Target audience:** Family and friends of the deceased, from 10 to 80 years old.
- **Goal:** Celebrate the life of a family or community member who recently passed away.
- **Deliverable:** The client expects a 1-to-3-minute video of photographs set to music, in two versions: one version optimized for fast online delivery, and another version optimized for high-quality playback on a computer at the memorial service.

The available media files are photographs of the departed and background music for the slide show.

★ ACA Objective 1.1

★ ACA Objective 1.4

▶ *Video 6.1*
Introducing the memorial slideshow project

Setting Up a Slide Show Project

★ *ACA Objective 4.1*

★ *ACA Objective 4.2*

★ *ACA Objective 4.3*

▶ *Video 6.2*
Organize your project

Because this slide show contains many images, it's a good idea to decide on the default duration for still images so that you need to set it only once. For this project you want each slide to display for 4 seconds, and the place to set that duration as the default is in the Premiere Pro Preferences dialog box.

1 Open the Preferences dialog box and select the General pane.

2 For Still Image Default Duration, choose Seconds and then enter **4** (**Figure 6.1**).

3 Click OK.

Figure 6.1 Setting the Still Image Default Duration value

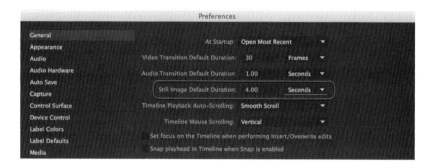

Start the editing stage of production by practicing the project setup techniques you've been using throughout the book:

■ Unzip the project files and store them in a folder you create for this memorial project.

■ Start a new project; you can name it **memorial**.

■ Save the project into the memorial project folder you created.

■ Switch to a workspace that displays the Project panel, such as the Assembly workspace.

■ The images are all in a single folder, and that makes them easy to import all at once. Import the Photos folder using your favorite import method. Because you imported a folder instead of one file, the folder is added as a bin within the Project panel.

■ Import the Memorial.wav file into the Project panel, not inside the Photos bin. Memorial.wav is the music for the slide show.

Creating a Sequence from Multiple Files Quickly

There are 50 images in the Photos folder for this project. To drag each of them individually to the Timeline panel, adjust their durations, and add transitions to each clip could take a long time. Fortunately, Premiere Pro has ways to speed up adding multiple items to a timeline and adding transitions to them.

★ ACA Objective 2.3

★ ACA Objective 2.5

★ ACA Objective 4.2

Creating a sequence based on a preset

Up to this point most of the new sequences you've created have been based on one of the source video clips. You won't be able to set up this project's sequence that way, because there are no source video clips: they're either still images or audio. You'll need to start a new sequence from scratch and specify what sequence settings it should use.

▶ **Video 6.2** *Organize your project*

1 Start a new sequence by doing one of the following:

   ■ Choose File > New > Sequence.

   ■ Click the New Item button in the Project panel, and choose Sequence from the menu that appears.

   ■ Right-click (Windows) or Control-click (Mac OS) an empty area in the Project panel and choose New Item > Sequence.

2 In the New Sequence dialog box, name the sequence **memorial slide show**, but don't click OK yet.

   You'll choose a preset that's closest to the high-definition frame dimensions and high level of quality that the slide show should have when it's played off a computer, which is the higher-quality deliverable in the preproduction requirements.

3 In the Available Presets list, expand the Digital SLR group; then expand the 1080p group and select DSLR 1080p30 (**Figure 6.2**).

   The DSLR 1080p30 preset uses the popular and high-quality standard of 1080p video (1920 x 1080 pixel frame size, progressive scan) at 30 frames per second.

Figure 6.2 Choosing a preset to define the sequence settings

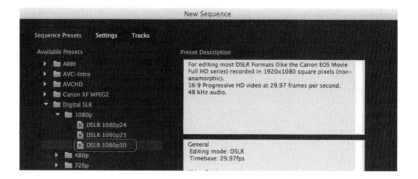

4 Add the Memorial.wav audio file to the Timeline panel, beginning at the start of the sequence.

You'll need two copies of the sequence for later, so you'll duplicate one of them now.

5 In the Project panel, select the memorial slide show project and choose Edit > Duplicate.

6 Click the filename of the duplicate and name it **markers**. You'll work with this sequence later.

Next you'll try two ways to add media to a sequence that are much faster than adding and editing them one by one. You'll practice these techniques with photos, but keep in mind that they'll work with video too.

Arranging multiple items before adding them to a sequence

▶ *Video 6.3*
Organize your photos in the Project panel

One way to save time is by using the Project panel or bin as a sort of storyboard pad for getting clips in the right order before you add them to a sequence.

1 Position the pointer over the Project panel or opened bin that contains the media you want to arrange, and press the tilde (~) key. You don't have to do this, but maximizing the panel lets you see the most items at once as you arrange them.

2 Drag image thumbnails to put them in the order that tells the story best.

3 When you're done arranging, position the pointer over the Project panel or opened bin that contains the media you were arranging, and press the tilde (~) key to restore the panel to its original size.

4 The next steps will use the order of media you've arranged here.

Adding multiple items to a sequence at a regular interval

Use this technique when you want to add selected media items to the timeline with the same interval between the start of each item. In this case the interval is based on the Still Image Default Duration value you set earlier in Preferences.

1   Make sure the memorial slide show sequence is active in the Timeline panel and that the playhead is at the beginning of the sequence.

2   Make sure the Photos bin is active, and choose Edit > Select All.

3   Click the Automate to Sequence button().

4   In the Automate to Sequence dialog box, set the following options (**Figure 6.3**):

   ■ Click the Ordering menu and choose Sort Order.

   ■ Click the Placement menu and choose Sequentially.

   ■ Make sure the Clip Overlap option is set to 30 Frames. This ensures that clips overlap enough that you can apply a transition.

   ■ Make sure Apply Video Transition is selected.

5   Click OK.

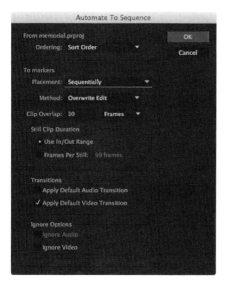

Figure 6.3 Setting up the Automate to Sequence dialog box for sequential placement

▶ *Video 6.4*
Automatically add photos to the timeline

TIP

If you want to change the default transition that's applied between items on the timeline, do that before you start these steps. In the Effects panel, expand the Video Transitions, right-click (Windows) or Control-click (Mac OS) the transition you want, and choose Set Selected as Default Transition.

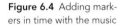

TIP

As Joe has demonstrated often in the video, many commands are available both from the menu bar and on a context menu. For example, the Replace with Clip > From Bin command is also available if you right-click (Windows) or Control-click (Mac OS) an item in the Timeline panel.

The clips are added to the sequence using the Still Image Default Duration value specified in Preferences, using the sort order you used, and applying the default transition between each item. That entire sequence took only a few moments to set up.

If you want to adjust any of the edits or transitions, you can do that using the editing techniques you've learned in earlier chapters.

You may find that you want to replace an item in the sequence with another item. Here's how you do that:

1   In the Project panel or bin, select the item you want to use.

2   In the Timeline panel, select the unwanted item in the sequence.

3   Choose Clip > Replace with Clip > From Bin.

Adding multiple items to a sequence at markers

▶ **Video 6.5** Use markers to place photos

If you want more control over where Automate to Sequence adds items to a sequence, you can use markers. For example, if you want to pace the slide show images to music, you can add sequence markers at key moments in the music.

1   Move the playhead to the beginning of the Timeline panel.

2   Position a finger over the M key.

3   Play back the sequence.

4   When you hear a point in the music where a new image should appear in the slide show, press the M key. A marker appears on the timeline.

5   Continue dropping markers until the music ends (**Figure 6.4**). If you think you might have missed a time when you should have dropped a marker, feel free to replay any part of the sequence and add missing markers.

    Although there is a button you can click to add a marker, it's often easier to use the M key shortcut instead.

Figure 6.4 Adding markers in time with the music

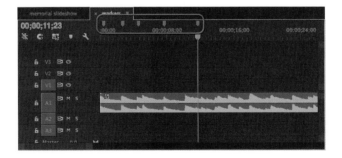

6   If a marker is not exactly at the correct frame, simply drag it left or right until it's at the correct time.

Now you're ready to add the photos to the sequence.

7   Make sure the markers sequence is active in the Timeline panel and that the playhead is at the beginning of the sequence.

8   Make sure the Photos bin is active, and choose Edit > Select All.

9   Click the Automate to Sequence button.

10 In the Automate to Sequence dialog box, set the following options (**Figure 6.5**):

    ■ Click the Ordering menu and choose Sort Order.

    ■ Click the Placement menu and choose At Unnumbered Markers.

    Many other options aren't available because they apply only when Placement is set to Sequentially.

11 Click OK.

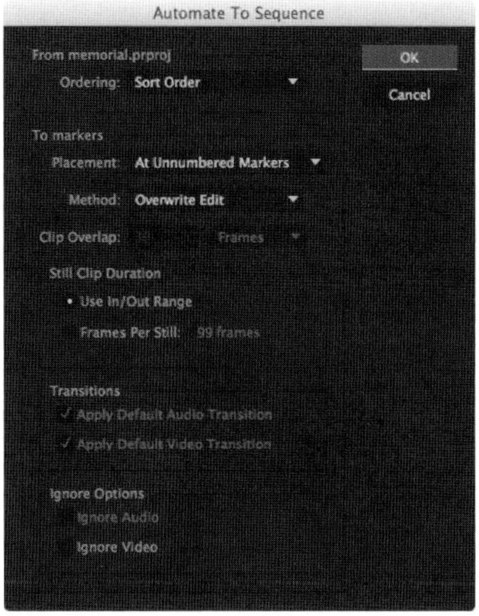

Figure 6.5 Setting up the Automate to Sequence dialog box to place stills at markers

The clips are added to the sequence using the Still Image Default Duration value specified in Preferences and in the sort order you used. Each clip is added to the sequence at the next available unnumbered marker.

You may see gaps between items. This can happen for photos when the Still Image Default Duration value specified in Preferences is shorter than the time between markers. You can easily fill those gaps by dragging one end of a photo with the Selection tool to extend is duration until it snaps to the adjacent clip.

If you want to add the default transition between items, you still can do that quickly, although it's a manual process:

1   Navigate to the next edit by pressing the Down Arrow key.

2   Press Ctrl+D (Windows) or Command+D (Mac OS).

    That's the keyboard shortcut for the Sequence > Apply Video Transition command. Although it's usually easier to use menu commands when you're learning, in this case it's going to be a lot easier and faster to keep your hands on the keyboard pressing the Up Arrow key and the transition shortcut than it would be to keep going up to the menu bar every time you want to add a transition.

3 Repeat steps 1 and 2 to add the default transition (**Figure 6.6**) at any other edit where it's needed. (If you want to go to the previous edit, press the Up Arrow key.)

Figure 6.6 Adding the default transition at each edit

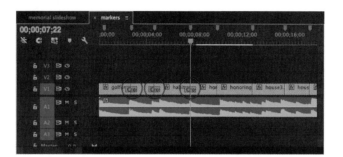

TIP

You can add a note to a marker by double-clicking it.

Adding a Ken Burns motion effect

★ *ACA Objective 4.8*

The Ken Burns effect refers to panning and zooming the camera over a still image so that it produces a more dynamic effect than a motionless image on the screen. The effect is named after the documentary filmmaker Ken Burns. He did not invent the technique, but it was noted as an effect he frequently used with old photos and artifacts in his historical documentaries.

▶ *Video 6.6 Add motion to your images*

Now that you know that the Ken Burns effect is about panning and zooming, hopefully you have already guessed how you can easily achieve that effect in Premiere Pro. You can pan and zoom by setting keyframes for the Motion options in the Effect Controls panel when a clip or still image is selected in the Timeline panel—a technique you've practiced in earlier chapters. You control panning with Position keyframes, and you control zooming with Scale keyframes (**Figure 6.7**).

Choose a few images in the Markers sequence to practice Ken Burns–style panning and zooming. As you do this, the following guidelines will help:

- For panning across a photo, you need only two Position keyframes if you want to move the camera in a straight line. You can add more keyframes if you want to move the camera in different directions.

- For zooming a photo, you usually use only two Scale keyframes.

- Avoid sudden changes in scale or position unless there's a reason.

- When you right-click (Windows) or Control-click (Mac OS) a keyframe, the Temporal Interpolation commands can help smooth changes in speed. The Ease In and Ease Out commands smooth stopping and starting, respectively. The Spatial Interpolation commands can help smooth changes in position.

Figure 6.7 The frame starts showing the package being handed to the veteran and ends after panning his head closer to the center and scaling up the frame to zoom in on his reaction. The keyframes used are shown in the Effect Controls window.

- If you plan to zoom into an image by a high magnification, use a frame size larger than the video frame size. For example, if you want to zoom in by 2x for a 1920 x 1080 pixel video frame, you should use a version of that image with twice the width and height of the video frame (3840 x 2160 pixels) if available, so that the image maintains maximum detail when zoomed in.

If you plan to use similar Motion effects on multiple photos, you can copy and paste the effect to use as starting point for next photo:

1. Apply the effect to the first photo.

2. With the photo selected, choose Edit > Copy.

3. Select another clip and choose Edit > Paste Attributes.

4. In the Paste Attributes dialog box, select the Motion option under Video Attributes (**Figure 6.8**), and click OK.

5. Customize the effect for that photo.

   TIP *Copying and pasting attributes and effects works for video, still images, and audio.*

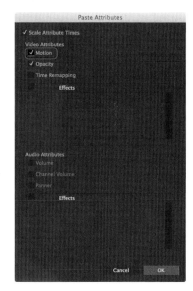

Figure 6.8 Pasting a motion effect to another clip

Exporting Multiple Versions with Adobe Media Encoder

★ ACA Objective 5.1

▶ **Video 6.7** *Export your slideshow*

The requirements for this project specify two versions: one version optimized for fast online delivery, and another version optimized for high-quality playback on a computer at the memorial service. And you have two different versions of the sequence to provide in both formats. But you don't have to export from Premiere Pro four times, because you can use Adobe Media Encoder CC, a tool you first met in Chapter 2.

You'll set up the initial export in Premiere Pro. This first export will use the same settings as the sequence, which will produce a high-quality version.

1   Open the memorial slide show sequence.

2   Choose File > Export > Media.

3   Click the Format menu and choose H.264.

4   Click the Preset menu and choose Match Source - High Bitrate.

5   In the Video tab, click the Bitrate Encoding menu and choose VBR, 2 pass (**Figure 6.9**).

Figure 6.9 Customizing export settings

Two-pass encoding usually produces higher quality than one-pass encoding, so it's being used here for the high-quality slide show. However, two-pass encoding takes more time to process and results in a larger file size than one-pass encoding.

6 Click Output Name and make sure this first export will be saved to the location and filename that you want. Add **HQ** to the end of the filename to signify that this will be the high-quality version.

Keep in mind that you'll be rendering multiple versions of this sequence. Have a plan for where to store them all (should they be in a new folder of their own?) and what to name each of them so that you can tell them apart.

7 Click the Queue button to send the sequence to Media Encoder.

8 Open the markers sequence, and repeat steps 1–7.

Now you'll switch to Media Encoder and set up the other versions of those two sequences there, because it will be less work than doing two more exports from Premiere Pro.

9 Switch to Adobe Media Encoder.

10 In the Queue panel, select one of the sequences and then Ctrl-click (Windows) or Command-click (Mac OS) the other sequence so that they're both selected (**Figure 6.10**).

NOTE

If you change any settings after choosing a preset, the Preset menu will change to Custom because you have altered settings away from how the preset is defined. You can save your customizations as your own preset.

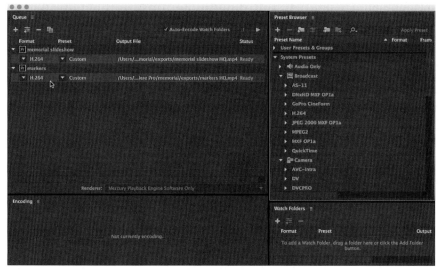

Figure 6.10 The two original sequences selected in Queue panel

TIP

When selecting items in the Media Encoder queue, aim for blank spaces between text and buttons. Clicking an item's text or buttons will open a menu or dialog box for editing export settings or the export's filename and location.

11 Click the Duplicate button (**Figure 6.11**). Both sequences are duplicated; note the filenames to identify the duplicates.

12 Make sure both duplicates are selected (the files with names ending in _1).

13 Click the Preset menu (not the text) for either selected sequence and choose YouTube 1080p HD. The applied preset changes for both selected sequences (**Figure 6.12**).

Figure 6.11 The four sequences after clicking the Duplicate button

Figure 6.12 After choosing the YouTube 1080p HD preset for both selected sequences

TIP

If you just need to change the preset, choose it from the Preset drop-down menu for an item. If you want to customize specific settings, click the Preset text.

14 Deselect the items, and click the Output File text for the first duplicate and edit it so that the filename ends with **LQ** (for Low Quality); then click Save. Repeat for the other duplicate.

15 Click the Play button to start the rendering queue (**Figure 6.13**).

Figure **6.13** Queue processing in progress

Media Encoder shows you which sequences are processing, the progress of all sequences, and the progress and thumbnail of each sequence that's currently processing.

Challenge: Your Own Slide Show

▶ *Video 6.8*
Memorial challenge

Now it's time for you to come up with your own slide show. You can create one for a memorial, a birthday, a wedding, a sports team's season, or a special event.

As you plan your slide show, remember Joe Dockery's Keys to Success (from the video):

- Keep it short.
- Allocate plenty of time for collecting photographs and other special objects, and scanning or photographing items that aren't already digital.
- Find appropriate music for the background.
- Add a little movement to the images to maintain visual interest.
- Share it with the world.

Conclusion

A project like a slide show can be effective with little or no video at all, especially because you can add motion by animating the images. Being able to transform still images into a compelling slide show is another tool that you can use to tell stories with Premiere Pro.

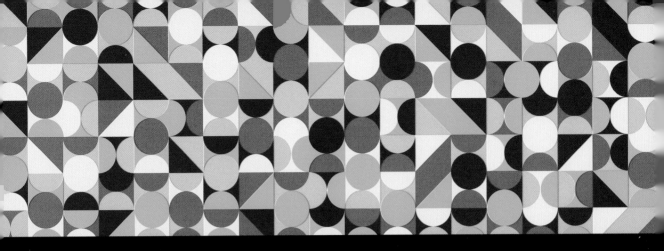

CHAPTER OBJECTIVES

Chapter Learning Objectives

- Import numbered still images as a single clip.
- Navigate and zoom the timeline.
- Use tools to select, arrange, and trim clips, including Slip and Slide tools.
- Change clip speed and duration.
- Split a clip.
- Edit keyframes with the Pen tool.

Chapter ACA Objectives

For more information on ACA Objectives, see pages 235–238.

DOMAIN 3.0
UNDERSTANDING ADOBE PREMIERE PRO CC

3.1 Identify elements of the Premiere Pro user interface, and demonstrate knowledge of their functions.

DOMAIN 4.0
EDITING A VIDEO SEQUENCE WITH ADOBE PREMIERE PRO

4.1 Create a new project.

4.2 Import media and assets into a project.

4.3 Demonstrate knowledge of how to set up and navigate a sequence in Premiere Pro.

4.4 Organize and manage video clips in a sequence.

4.5 Trim clips.

4.8 Add and manage effects and transitions in a video sequence.

CHAPTER 7

Reviewing Tools
and Shortcuts

To round out this course, you'll review some of the key tools and techniques that you've learned from the tutorial videos. You'll concentrate on the Adobe Premiere Pro CC tools that are fundamental to video editing. The more familiar you become with the functions and shortcuts for those tools, the more efficient and faster you'll be as a video editor.

Setting Up a Project

★ ACA Objective 4.1

★ ACA Objective 4.2

★ ACA Objective 4.3

▶ Video 7.1
  Introducing final
  review

Start the editing stage of production by practicing the project setup techniques you've been using throughout the book:

- Unzip the project files for this chapter (project6_review.zip) and store them in a folder you create for this memorial project.

- Take a quick look through the unzipped folders, because they don't contain typical video, audio, and still image files. They contain numbered frames that help clarify what happens when you use different tools.

- Start a new project; you can name it **Numbers**. Save it into the folder you created for this project.

Now import a series of still images as an image sequence so you can follow the tutorial videos:

1 Press the keyboard shortcut for the File > Import command (Ctrl+I in Windows or Command+I in Mac OS).

2 In the Import dialog box, navigate to the folder where you stored the files for this project. Open the Numbers folder and then open the Blue folder and select the first image, BlueNumber-001.jpg.

3 Select the Image Sequence option, and click Import.

Premiere Pro imports the entire folder as a single clip.

4 Import the red and yellow image sequences too.

5 To practice with the demonstrations in the tutorial videos, create a sequence from any of the imported clips, name it **master sequence**, and then add the other two clips (**Figure 7.1**). The order of the colors doesn't matter.

Figure 7.1 Project setup with a sequence

NOTE

For the Import Sequence option to work properly, the file-names of every image in the folder should be numbered sequentially in the correct order.

Importing a folder containing a numbered series of still images as a single clip is often useful. For example, you can create a clip out of a folder of frame files that were exported from animation software, and you can create a single clip from hundreds of time-lapse frames from a still camera. After you import a folder of still images using the Image Sequence option, it behaves like a video clip: You can add it to a sequence, adjust its speed and duration, and apply effects.

Working in the Timeline Panel

★ *ACA Objective 3.1*

★ *ACA Objective 4.4*

 *Video 7.2 Manage sequences in the timeline*

In earlier chapters you practiced various ways of setting up and customizing the Timeline panel. Review what you've learned, and practice using the sample project.

- To align the pointer precisely with the playhead, the In point and Out point of clips, and other useful times such as markers, the Snap feature is on by default. You can disable or enable it by clicking the Snap button in the Time-line panel (**Figure 7.2**) or by choosing Sequence > Snap.

- To adjust the height of a track in the Timeline panel, drag one of the hori-zontal video track dividers immediately to the left of the timeline. Dragging up shows the track in more detail, revealing thumbnails, the fx icon, and the rubber band (Figure 7.2).

- To make all tracks taller in one step, click the wrench icon and choose Expand All Tracks.

- Take a minute to explore the other Timeline panel display options in the menu that appears when you click the wrench icon (**Figure 7.3**). For example, the first three commands let you customize how thumbnails display in the timeline.

- Although you can drag and drop to add media to the timeline, you might also want to use keyboard shortcuts or buttons such as Insert or Overwrite to add media to the timeline without dragging. When you add media that way, Premiere Pro needs to know the track on which new media should be added. You indicate that by setting *target* tracks. To toggle whether a track is targeted, click its track targeting icon (**Figure 7.4**).

When multiple tracks are targeted, Premiere Pro adds media to the lowest targeted track.

Snap button   Track divider dragged up to expand track V1

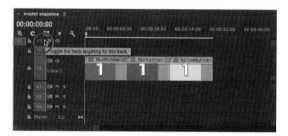

Figure 7.2 Key components of the Timeline panel

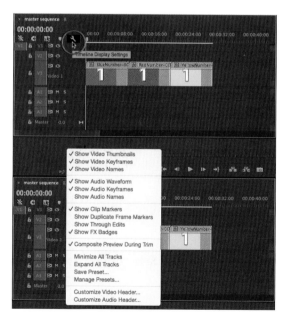

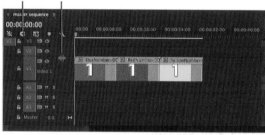

Figure 7.4 Toggling the target setting for track V3

Figure 7.3 The Timeline display settings menu

TIP

Track targeting also tells Premiere Pro which tracks it should follow when you use the Up Arrow or Down Arrow key to move among edits.

- There are additional display settings in the Timeline panel menu, including options that let you display more thumbnails in a track (**Figure 7.5**). There is a trade-off: On a slow computer or in a project with many clips, the additional processing required to update all thumbnails may make Premiere Pro less responsive.

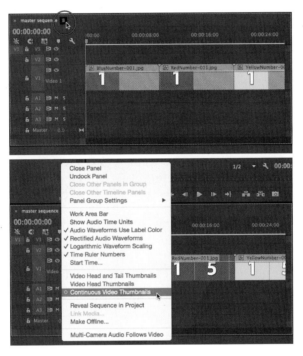

Figure 7.5 Clicking the Timeline panel menu

Navigating in the Timeline Panel

★ *ACA Objective 3.1*

★ *ACA Objective 4.3*

▶ *Video 7.3*
Navigate the timeline

In the projects you've completed so far, you've practiced how to move forward and back in time in the Timeline panel. Review what you've learned and practice using the sample project.

To make more detailed edits, you'll need to magnify the timeline, and to edit larger chunks of a project, you'll need to reduce the timeline. Because you'll be constantly changing the timeline magnification, Premiere Pro provides several ways to do this:

- To magnify the timeline click it with the Zoom tool, and to reduce the timeline Alt-click (Windows) or Option-click (Mac OS) it with the Zoom tool.

- To change the timeline magnification with keyboard shortcuts, press the + (plus) key to magnify and press the - (minus) key to reduce.

- To zoom the timeline continuously, drag either end of the magnification scroll bar at the bottom of the Timeline panel. When you're zoomed in, you can move an earlier or later range of frames into view by dragging the middle of that scroll bar (**Figure 7.6**).

- To toggle the timeline view between the current magnification and seeing the entire sequence, press the \ (backslash) key.

Moving to a different time in a sequence is also something you'll do constantly while editing, so Premiere Pro provides several ways to do that in the Timeline panel (**Figure 7.7**):

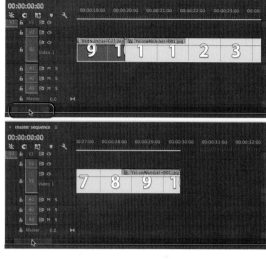

Figure 7.6 Dragging the magnification scroll bar to move later in time

- To search the timeline for the correct frame, drag the playhead horizontally; this is called *scrubbing* the timeline. You can also scrub the playhead time display.

- To immediately move the playhead to a specific time, click that time in the time ruler. You can also click the time display and type the time value; you don't have to type colons or semicolons.

- To control playback, use the Play/Stop Toggle button in the Source Monitor or Program Monitor, or press the spacebar. You can also use the JKL keyboard shortcuts: Press J to play in reverse, K to stop, and L to play forward. Pressing L more than once increases the forward playback speed; pressing the J key multiple times does the same thing but in reverse.

- To move one frame back or forward, press the Step Back One Frame or Step Forward One Frame button in the Source Monitor or Program Monitor, respectively. You can also press the Right Arrow or Left Arrow key, respectively.

- To go to the beginning of a clip or sequence, press the Home key. To go to the end, press the End key.

Figure 7.7 Timeline navigation controls

A **Step back one frame**

B **Play/stop toggle**

C **Step forward one frame**

D **Playhead time display**

E **Playhead**

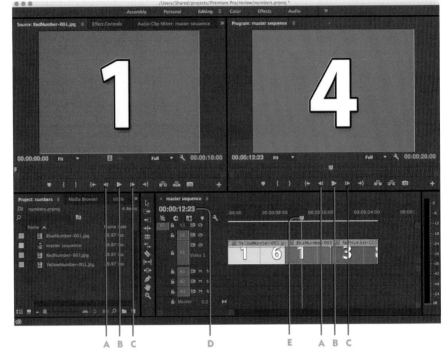

★ *ACA Objective 3.1*

★ *ACA Objective 4.4*

Selecting and Moving Clips in the Timeline Panel

▶ **Video 7.4** *Select, arrange, and trim your clips*

As you refine a sequence, you'll often need to select clips and change their position or order. If you're already familiar with the selection techniques used on your computer desktop—such as clicking to select, selecting multiple items by dragging a selection marquee across them, and selecting multiple items by Shift-clicking—you're ahead of the game. Review the techniques you've learned and practice using the sample project.

■ To select a clip, click it with Selection tool (🔓). A clip selected in the timeline is highlighted, displaying different colors than the clips around it.

■ To select multiple clips, Shift-click each of them or drag a selection rectangle around them.

- To move selected clips, drag them with the Selection tool. When you drop the clips, they'll overwrite other clips that they overlap.

- To move a clip and ripple-move any clips you drop them on, Ctrl-drag (Windows) or Command-drag (Mac OS) the clip (**Figure 7.8**). This is great when you want to move a clip to another position in the sequence while protecting any clips you might drop it on.

- To remove empty space on a track, right-click (Windows) or Control-click (Mac OS) the empty space and choose Ripple Delete from the context menu that appears.

- To select all clips at or before the time you click, click with the Track Select Backward tool (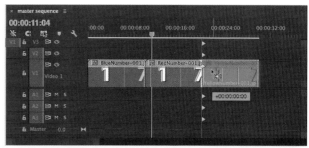). To select all clips at or after the time you click, click with the Track Select Forward tool ( ). Both tools affect all unlocked tracks.

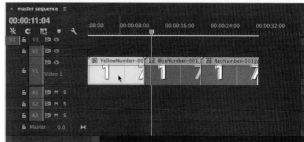

Figure 7.8 Ripple-moving the last clip so that it becomes the first clip, shifting the other two clips forward

Trimming Clips

★ ACA Objective 3.1

★ ACA Objective 4.5

Trimming clips is an essential editing task; you'll do it many times with every project. Review what you've learned and practice using the sample project.

- To trim a clip, drag either end with Selection tool. Notice the pointer's edit icon color is red when you're about to do a simple Selection tool edit.

▶ Video 7.4 *Select, arrange, and trim your clips*

- To trim without leaving a gap, use the Ripple Edit tool ( ) to drag either end of a clip. Notice the pointer's edit icon color is yellow when you're about to do a ripple edit. When closing a gap, a ripple edit also shifts all following clips to keep them together.

- To shift the time at which the edit happens, use the Rolling Edit tool ( ) to drag an edit. A rolling edit shifts the Out point of the clip before the edit and the In point of the clip after the edit.

▶ Video 7.5 *Use the Slip and Slide tools*

- To change which frames of a clip are visible between two adjacent clips, use the Slip tool ( ) to drag a clip. A Slip edit changes the In point and Out point of the clip you drag without changing the adjacent clips. Dragging a clip with the Slip tool is like slipping the dragged clip behind adjacent clips (**Figure 7.9**).
- To change how a clip overlaps the two adjacent clips, use the Slide tool (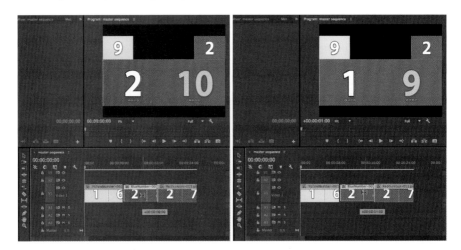) to drag a clip. Dragging a clip with the Slide tool changes the Out point of the preceding clip and the In point of the following clip and does not change the In and Out points of the clip you drag. A Slide edit is like sliding the dragged clip over adjacent clips (**Figure 7.10**).

Figure 7.9 Slip edit

Figure 7.10 Slide edit

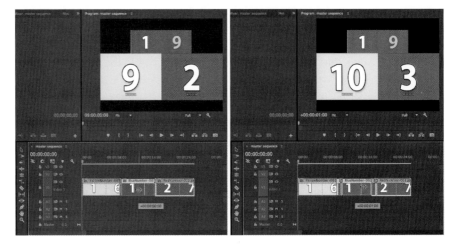

Keep in mind that trimming is nondestructive; every frame in the clip is available for you to trim or restore at any time. But if you're going to apply a transition, remember that your edits have to leave enough extra frames to accommodate the transition duration you want. A one-second transition needs a half a second of additional frames on both sides of the edit.

> **NOTE** *Remember that a clip in a sequence has two sets of In and Out points: Clip In and Out points, which mark the range of source clip frames that are played, and sequence In and Out points, which mark the sequence times when the clip starts and stops playing.*

Changing Clip Speed and Duration

★ *ACA Objective 4.8*

▶ *Video 7.6* *Use the Rate Stretch tool*

When you change the playback speed or duration of a clip without changing the number of frames in the clip, the playback speed and duration change together because they're linked. For example, if you shorten the duration of a clip, it plays back faster, because the frame rate goes up.

Review what you've learned about manipulating clip speed and duration, and practice using the sample project.

- To adjust speed and duration interactively, use the Rate Stretch tool () to drag either end of a clip.
- To adjust speed and duration by entering a new speed or duration value, select the clip in the timeline and choose Clip > Speed/Duration.

You can alter the relationship between speed and duration using related features in Premiere Pro:

- To vary speed changes during a clip so that it plays back faster, slower, or even backward at any time during the clip, use Time Remapping.
- To make a clip stop and hold on one frame, you can edit the Time Remapping rubber band to create a freeze frame effect.

TIP
Premiere Pro also has Frame Hold commands on the Clip > Video Options submenu; they are useful for some types of edits.

Splitting a Clip

★ *ACA Objective 4.5*

▶ *Video 7.7* *Use the Razor tool*

You've used the Razor tool ( ) once or twice earlier in the book, so it's a good idea to review it and practice using the sample project. As its name implies, you use the Razor tool to slice a clip wherever you click it.

There are two ways to slice a clip. You can use the Razor tool to click within a clip, splitting it into two instances. You can also position the playhead at the time where you want to cut a clip, select the clip, and choose Sequence > Add Edit. The Add Edit command can be more efficient if you want to slice clips on multiple tracks, because you can control which tracks the Add Edit command slices at the playhead:

- To slice clips based on which tracks are targeted, don't select any clips.
- To slice clips on different tracks than those that are targeted, select the clips (**Figure 7.11**).
- To slice clips on all tracks no matter which tracks are targeted or which clips are selected, choose Sequence > Add Edit To All Tracks.

Figure 7.11 Applying the Add Edit command when clips on two of three tracks are selected

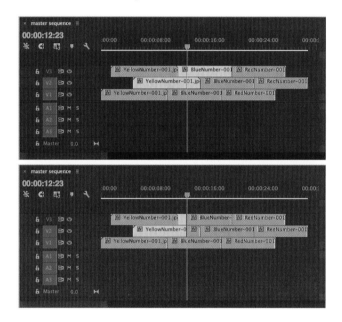

Editing Keyframes with the Pen Tool

★ ACA Objective 3.1

★ ACA Objective 4.8

▶ *Video 7.8* Use the Pen tool

Editing keyframes on clip or track rubber bands is a fundamental skill when you want to animate options in Premiere Pro. For example, you edit keyframes on rubber bands to vary clip opacity or audio levels over time. Review what you've learned and practice using the sample project.

- To display a clip's rubber band, right-click (Windows) or Control-click (Mac OS) the fx icon on a clip and choose which setting you want the rubber

Figure 7.12 Choosing which setting a rubber band will edit

Figure 7.13 Extending a Bézier handle to add an acceleration curve to the graph

band to represent (**Figure 7.12**). If you still can't see the rubber band, try expanding the track (increasing the track height).

- To add a keyframe, click a rubber band with the Pen tool ( ), or Ctrl-click (Windows) or Command-click (Mac OS) a rubber band.

- To adjust how quickly a value changes between keyframes, use the Pen tool to Ctrl-drag (Windows) or Command-drag (Mac OS) a keyframe to extend a Bézier handle (**Figure 7.13**). This adds a curve to the rubber band; the curve represents how a value's rate of change accelerates or decelerates as it leaves one keyframe and approaches another.

You might notice that the Pen tool is similar to the pen icon that appears when you draw an opacity mask. Both an opacity mask and a rubber band are drawn using Bézier paths and curves, and the Pen tool is a standard way of drawing and editing Bézier paths. Creating Bézier paths with the Pen tool is also the basis for drawing shapes in applications such as Adobe Illustrator and Adobe After Effects.

Finding Shortcuts That Make You More Efficient

Just about all of the tools, buttons, and commands you've reviewed here have keyboard shortcuts. If you tend to work faster with the keyboard than with a mouse or trackpad alone, be sure to look up the shortcuts for the tools, buttons, and commands you use the most. Remember that shortcuts are shown in the tool tips that appear when you hold the pointer over a tool in the Tools panel or a button, and shortcuts for commands appear next to each command in the menus (**Figure 7.14**).

★ *ACA Objective 3.1*

Figure 7.14 Finding keyboard shortcuts for tools and commands

Keyboard shortcuts next to menu commands

Tool tips next to tools

Figure 7.15 Opening the context menu for a clip

TIP

You can edit the Premiere Pro keyboard shortcuts. Choose Edit > Keyboard Shortcuts (Windows) or Premiere Pro > Keyboard Shortcuts (Mac OS)

Also keep in mind that you can right-click (Windows) or Control-click (Mac OS) almost anything in the Premiere Pro workspace to access a context menu with relevant commands (**Figure 7.15**). This often gives you more convenient and immediate access to the command you want compared to looking through all of the commands in the menu bar.

If you watch a lot of expert Premiere Pro video editors, you might think that you should use every keyboard shortcut or use only context menus. But that's not the case at all. The variety of ways to do any task exist so that you can choose which combination fits your working style. Mix and match different types of shortcuts depending on what makes you comfortable and efficient.

Conclusion

Congratulations! You've completed all of the exercises in this book, and in this chapter you have reviewed many essential tools and techniques for video editing. Continue to practice with your own projects so that the basics of editing become second nature and so you can discover your most productive working style and creative voice with Premiere Pro.

CHAPTER OBJECTIVES

Chapter Learning Objectives

- Hone your creativity.
- Prepare your mind for design.
- Apply the design hierarchy.
- Discover the elements of art.
- Understand the element of shape.
- Learn how color works.
- Explore typography.
- Understand the principles of design.

Chapter ACA Objectives

For more information on ACA Objectives, see pages 235–238.

DOMAIN 2.0
UNDERSTANDING DIGITAL VIDEO

2.2 Demonstrate knowledge of basic principles and best practices employed in the digital video industry.

2.3 Demonstrate knowledge of how to use transitions and effects to enhance video content.

2.4 Demonstrate knowledge of how to use audio to enhance video content.

CHAPTER 8

Leveling Up with Design

Now that you have a good grasp on the tools in Adobe Premiere Pro, you'll start learning how best to use them. Much like any other skill, understanding how a tool works and becoming a master craftsperson are two completely different levels of achievement. In many ways, they're distinct ways of thinking about the tools you've learned to use.

As an example, think about carpenters. Their initial level of learning covers tools such as a saw, hammer, and drill. They learn how to use the tools correctly and when to apply specific techniques, including cutting with or against the grain and joining the wood at the joints. Using the right techniques, carpenters can theoretically build anything.

You're now at the point at which the only way to get better is to practice and to learn the thought processes that a master craftsperson goes through to create amazing, creative, and unique work. The beauty of this stage is that it's when you start to become an artist. Being good at using any tool is not just about knowing how it works and what it does. It's knowing *when* to use it and what techniques to apply to create something new.

▶ *Video 8.1 Design School: Introduction*

Creativity Is a Skill

Video 8.2 *Design School: Creativity is a skill*

We discussed creativity in the introduction to this book, and I'd like to share a little more about it. First, let's refer to a highly scientific and statistically accurate diagram that I've created to help illustrate the point (**Figure 8.1**).

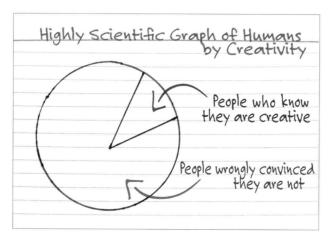

Figure 8.1 Graph of human creativity

Okay, so perhaps the diagram isn't *exactly* statistically accurate and maybe my methods weren't scientific, but it's still true. Creativity is a skill that you can learn and improve with practice. But there's only one way to guarantee that you'll never be more creative than you are now: giving up.

The biggest creative problem some people have is that they give up. Some give up before even making their first effort. Others give up after their fifth effort or after 15 minutes of not creating a masterpiece. Nobody creates a 15-minute masterpiece. A big difference between a great artist and a terrible artist is that a great artist has tried and failed, made some adjustments, and tried again. The next try may also lead to failure, but the artist pushes forward. The artist isn't deterred by bumping into a problem because it's all part of the learning and creative process.

Of course, you can't know how far you can take your creative skills until you start practicing and expanding those skills. But if you never use them, they'll only grow weaker. Remember that every effort, every new attempt, and every goof-up builds strength.

Getting a creative workout

This chapter is about developing your creative skills and flexing your creative muscles. It's about turning the craft of being an interactive media designer into a natural ability. Even if you take the big step of becoming an Adobe Certified Associate, you need to realize that passing the test is just getting through the tryouts. When you get that credential, it's like being picked to be on a professional football team. It's certainly something to be proud of, but the real goal is the *Super Bowl!* You have a lot more work ahead, but it's fun and rewarding work.

This book introduces you to exercises that help you explore and enhance the skills you already have. Getting beyond the basics of creativity and design is just a matter of applying your existing skills in ways you've never tried. That's all there is to creativity.

Prepping your mind

Preparing your mind is the most important part of increasing your creative skills. For most of us, it's also the hardest because today's culture is so focused on instant success and efficiency that people learn to fear the essence of creativity: failure.

Failure—and more specifically, the ability to take failure in stride—is the key ingredient in developing your artistic skillset. This is especially true if you're a beginner and aren't entirely happy with your current abilities. Just face that you're a design baby—and start acting like one!

Yes, I just encouraged you to act like a baby. But I mean an actual infant, not a grown person who is throwing a fit. Babies are fearless and resilient when they fail. They keep trying. They don't give up. Most of the time, they don't even realize that they're failing because they haven't yet learned that concept.

That's what you need to tap into. In art, there are no failures—there are only quitters. Tap into your inner infant! Try and fail, and try and fail, and try and fail. Eventually, you'll take your first step. You may quickly fail again on your second step, but don't give up. Babies don't know that they've failed. They just know that they got *a little bit closer*. They know what every true artist knows and what the rest of us need to remember but have forgotten along the way: *Failure is the path.*

The Design Hierarchy

▶ **Video 8.3** *Design School: The Design Hierarchy*

Most of us recognize art when we see it, but nobody can agree on how to create it. In an attempt to provide a framework, artists have developed a list of elements, the building blocks of art, and principles, the essential rules or assembly instructions of art. While every artist understands the importance of the elements and principles of art, there is no official list of those elements and principles that all artists agree on. This can be incredibly frustrating. How can you study and learn about something that nobody can fully identify?

Celebrate this fact—the lack of an "official" list means that you can't be wrong. A sculptor and a painter see and approach their art in different ways. A movie producer approaches her art differently than a costume designer approaches his. But all of these artistic people still study and embrace some elements and principles to guide their art.

Applying the design hierarchy

The design hierarchy shown in **Figure 8.2** is one way to understand and think about the artistic elements and principles. This isn't the *ultimate* approach to understanding and interacting with the artistic elements and principles. (An "ultimate" approach probably doesn't exist.) It is more of an organized starting place that might help you focus your design skills.

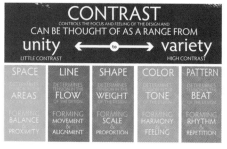

Design, unlike art, generally has a purpose. It's often about creating or accomplishing something specific, rather than simply enjoying or exploring an artistic impulse. A design task might require that you advertise a product, communicate an idea, or promote a cause or specific issue. I find it much easier to think about artistic elements and principles in terms of design, and you can use a design task as a framework on which to "hang" your creative quest when those vague artistic elements and principles seem confusing or muddled.

Figure 8.2 The design hierarchy

Thinking through these building blocks can also serve as a great little exercise when you're looking at a piece of work that you're not happy with but can't quite figure out why. Sometimes, just rolling through the following elements and principles in your mind can be an excellent creative checklist.

START WITH A FOCAL POINT

The focal point is what your design is all about. In an advertisement, it's your "call to action" phrase that will motivate the consumer. For a cause, it's the primary message that your cause is trying to get across. In interactive media design, it could be the navigation elements or the major interactive elements. It's the primary idea that you want people to take with them, like the title of a book or a chapter. It's the "sales pitch" of your design.

The focal point should be the most memorable aspect of the design. In a symmetrical or radial design, center the focal point for the most emphasis. In an asymmetrical design, let it fall on one of the natural focal points, which you'll learn about shortly when you study space.

Critical Question: *Do people know where to look in my design?*

CREATE FOCAL POINTS USING CONTRAST

Contrast creates a focal point by generating "tension" in the image (**Figure 8.3**). Place one red golf ball in a pile of 10,000 white golf balls, and you'll notice it immediately. The most dramatic way to create contrast is to vary the most common characteristic of the elements in the design. If you have a number of multicolored circles that are the same size, then varying the size of one circle, regardless of its color, will create a contrast that draws the eye. Keep the shape the same size, but make it a star instead of a circle to generate the same tension.

Establishing unity in a design is essential to allowing you to create tension. Without a degree of unity, you cannot create a focal point and the eye struggles to find something to focus on. Design is about forcing a focal point to be where you want it. When too many different, unrelated elements are present in your design it makes chaos, and the viewer will not know where to look.

Critical Question: *Does my design lack sufficient contrast to see the important features clearly?*

Figure 8.3 A focal point is created with contrast: Make one thing different and it stands out.

Figure 8.4 Keep the contrast in your image low toward the unity side unless you're trying to make something stand out.

RANGING FROM UNITY TO VARIETY

Imagine that contrast can be described as the "tension" in the image, and that contrast is a range from low contrast, which we call unity, to high contrast, which we call variety. Compositions with very low contrast have very little tension, and these designs are generally perceived as peaceful and calm but can sometimes feel emotionless, cold, and lifeless. Compositions with very high contrast have a lot of tension; they're generally perceived as energetic, lively, active, and hot, but sometimes they feel unpredictable or emotional (**Figure 8.4**).

A FRAMEWORK FOR CONNECTING THE DOTS

The following framework connects artistic elements and principles to help you at the onset of the creative journey. They're good starting points. Remember that with any design, you're not trying to *define* the artistic elements and principles as much as trying to *embrace* and apply them. As with every study of the artistic elements and principles, you won't arrive at a destination. Rather, you'll embark on a journey. These connections should help you make sense of the elements and principles long enough to find your way to understand and apply them.

- **Create balance and proximity by arranging the elements in your compositional space:** Tension develops among the various areas of your composition; unify the design with symmetry and equal spacing, or vary it using asymmetry and grouping elements.

Critical Question: Does my design use space to help communicate relationships?

- **Create movement and alignment by arranging your elements along lines:** Tension is created with the direction or flow of your composition; unify the design with strict alignment or movement along straight or flowing lines, or vary it with random, chaotic movements away from any single line or flow.

Critical Question: Does my design use lines to communicate order and flow?

- **Create scale and proportion by carefully designing shapes in your composition:** Tension is created among the sizes of elements in your composition; unify the design with similar or related sizes of elements, or vary it with a mix of unrelated sizes. Keep in mind that a paragraph has a shape, and a group of elements has a shape. Look at areas as well as objects in your design.

Critical Question: Does my design consider the message sent by the size of shapes I create?

- **Create themes and feeling by using typography, colors, and values in your composition:** Tension is created among elements of different type, value, or color. Unify the design with related type, colors, and values, or vary it with clashing colors or extreme difference in values or type.

Critical Question: Does my design consider the message sent by the typography, color, and value I used?

- **Use repetition and rhythm to create patterns and texture in your compositions:** Tension is created among elements with different texture or patterns. You can unify design with simple repetition to produce predictable patterns and rhythms, or vary it using complex, irregular, or chaotic patterns and rhythms.

Critical Question: Does my design consider the message sent by the patterns and textures I designed?

WRAPPING UP THE DESIGN HIERARCHY

If you're familiar with the basic artistic elements and principles, this hierarchy might be a framework you can use. But the goal of art is to continually explore the elements and principles. The next section covers them all, along with some challenges designed to help you dig a little deeper.

The Elements of Art

★ *ACA Objective 2.2*

The elements of art (**Figure 8.5**) are the building blocks of creative works. Think of them as the "nouns" of design. The elements are space, line, shape, form, texture, value, color, and type. Many traditional artists leave type off the list, but for graphic designers it is a critical part of how we look at design (and besides that, type is really fun to play with).

▶ *Video 8.4 Design School: The Elements of Art*

Figure 8.5 The elements of art

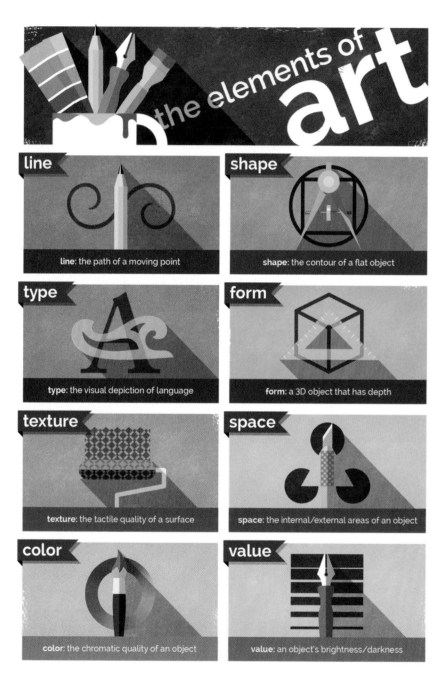

The element of space

Space is the first element of art to consider. It also happens to be one of the most abused, overlooked, neglected, and underrated elements in design. You can look at and consider space in multiple ways.

▶ *Video 8.5* *Design School: The Element of Space*

SPACE AS YOUR CANVAS

The most basic way to look at space is as your canvas or working area. In Premiere Pro, you start a new sequence and specify a frame size to create your space. Sometimes the dimensions are specified and provided to you, such as when you're designing for a specific project size or screen resolution. But sometimes you can create a fun way to work by giving yourself an uncommon space to design in.

SIDE QUEST: A PENNY IN SPACE

Here's a fun challenge:

1 Grab a piece of blank paper, and simply place a coin on it. Don't pick a random place to put it; *design* the spot where it should go.

2 Look at the paper with the coin on it and get a sense for the "feeling" it creates.

3 Fold the paper any way you want, except directly in half, so that you have a differently shaped space, and repeat the process.

Can you see how simply using different sizes and dimensions of space—with the exact same content—can change the way your art "feels"?

And did it enter your mind to fold the paper in a way that wasn't rectangular? Not all spaces have 90-degree corners. Think outside the box...*literally*!

SPACE AS A CREATIVE TOOL

Another important way to look at space is as a design element (**Figure 8.6**). The inability to use space well is an obvious sign of a new designer. A crowded design practically *screams* "newbie"! It takes a while to use space well, and it requires some practice. Start learning to use space as a creative element and you'll see a drastic increase in the artistic feel of your designs.

TIP

Using masks in Premiere Pro is a great way to experiment with non-rectangular compositions within a rectangular video frame.

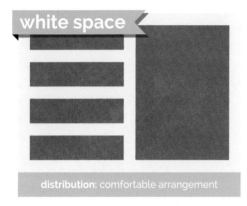

white space

distribution: comfortable arrangement

Figure 8.6 Use space to create comfortable arrangements of elements for your design.

When used properly, space can provide the following benefits to your designs:

- **Creating emphasis or focus:** When you have space around an object, it tends to give it emphasis. Crowding things makes them seem less important.

- **Creating feeling:** Space can be used to create a feeling of loneliness, isolation, or exclusivity. It can also be used to create a feeling of seriousness or gravitas.

- **Creating visual rest:** Sometimes space is needed to simply create some visual "breathing room" so that the other elements in your design can speak as intended.

THE RULE OF THIRDS

TIP

Beginning designers center everything, which can contribute to a static look and boring feeling. One way to get started with the rule of thirds is to simply stop centering things. You'll notice that you tend to move elements quite naturally to a focal point suggested by the rule of thirds.

The rule of thirds (**Figure 8.7**) is critical in photography and video, and it also applies to all visual arts. To visualize it, think of the rule of thirds like a tic-tac-toe board overlaid onto your design. Two horizontal and two vertical divisions create nine equal boxes on your design. The basic rule is that major elements of your design should fall on the dividing lines, and the areas of emphasis for the design should fall on the intersections. Using this rule in your designs creates compositions that have much more interest, tension, and visual strength.

Figure 8.7 Use the rule of thirds to determine where major elements should fall to create a visually appealing layout.

NEGATIVE SPACE

In the design industry, people use the term negative space, or "white space," to refer to blank areas in the design, even if you're working on a colored background. Negative space (**Figure 8.8**) is one of my favorite creative uses of the element of space. It can be fun to explore using negative space to create clever logos or designs.

Figure 8.8 Negative space

TIP

You can see an awesome collection of updated examples of negative space online at www.brainbuffet .com/design/ negative-space.

Sometimes you can place a boring idea in negative space to get moving in a new, creative direction. It can be tough for beginners to even "see" negative space, but once you look for it, you'll start to see creative uses of it everywhere. Begin to use it, and your design skills will jump up a level.

From here on out, the elements get much easier to understand because we can think of them as things (whereas we tend to think of space as the absence of things, or "nothing"). Learn to use space well. The ability to do so is the mark of an experienced and talented artist.

NOTE

For many people, the terms negative space and white space are interchangeable. If you're unclear about what someone is asking for, seek clarification. Art and design are not entirely technical, accurate, and organized processes, so you'll need to get used to lots of "mushy" terms that are used in multiple ways.

SIDE QUEST: SKETCHING NOTHING

This simple exercise will help you start to see negative space and learn how to create it.

Place a chair on a table, and then sketch everything you see *except* the chair. Don't worry if your sketch is messy—this is not about your artistic skill; it's about learning to see. Just focus on learning to see the space around things rather than the things themselves. When you're done, you'll have a chair-shaped hole in your drawing. Notice that the space where you drew nothing has the most visual impact. Space is powerful!

The element of line

▶ *Video 8.6* Design School: The Element of line

The meaning of line is pretty obvious. Although technical definitions such as "a point moving through a space" exist, we are all aware of what a line is. A line is exactly what you think it is: a mark with a beginning and an end (**Figure 8.9**). Don't overthink the basics. We're going to dig deeper than that, but let's start with the basic idea and then build the new understanding on it.

Figure 8.9 The element of line

SIDE QUEST: LINE 'EM UP!

On this fun side quest you'll experiment with lines. See how many ways you can think about the concept of a line. You'll explore more of these ideas later in this chapter, but first let's see how many different kinds of lines you can draw.

Here are some quick ideas to get you started:

- **Level 1:** Short, long, straight, wavy, zigzag, geometric, organic
- **Level 2:** Angry, lonely, worried, excited, overjoyed
- **Level 3:** Opposition, contrast, politics, infinity

Try to create as many different kinds of lines as you can and find a word to describe each one. There are no wrong answers here; this is art.

Remember, you're just drawing lines, not *pictures*. So to indicate sadness, don't draw an upside down "u." The goal is to draw a line that, in itself, represents sadness. It's a little challenging as you move away from descriptions and closer to abstract ideas, but that's the point. The best artists learn to "hint" at feelings and concepts in their art. Explore!

COMMON LINE DESCRIPTORS

The following adjectives are often associated with lines, and thinking about the ways lines are used or drawn can help you determine the meaning that your lines are giving to your design.

TIP

Having a hard time remembering horizontal and vertical directions? "Horizontal" (like the horizon) has a crossbar in the capital "H" that is a horizontal line itself. Vertical starts with the letter "V," which is an arrow pointing down.

- **Direction (Figure 8.10):** A common way to describe lines is to express the direction in which they travel. Lines can be horizontal, vertical, or diagonal. Sometimes the way a line is drawn can even express movement in a particular direction. Think about this and make sure that the lines of your art are moving in the directions you want. Vertical lines tend to express power and elevation whereas horizontal lines tend to express calm and balance. Diagonal lines often express growth or decline, and imply movement or change.

- **Weight (Figure 8.11):** Another common descriptor is the weight of a line, which describes its thickness. Heavy or thick lines generally represent importance and strength, and they tend to feel more masculine. Light or thin lines generally communicate delicacy and elegance, and they tend to represent femininity. Using a variable line width implies natural, artistic, flowing feelings and often suggests an intentional grace or natural beauty.

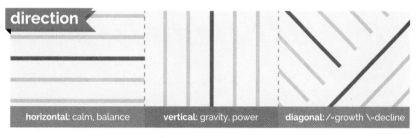

Figure 8.10 Line direction

Figure 8.11 Line weight

- **Style (Figure 8.12):** A line style is an effect, such as a double line or dotted line. Words used to describe popular line effects *include varying-width, hand drawn*, and *implied*. Varying-width lines are useful for expressing flow and grace. Hand-drawn lines look as if they were created with traditional media such as paints, charcoal, or chalk. Implied lines are lines that don't really exist—like dotted or dashed lines, or the lines we create when we line up at the grocery checkout. **These implied lines are powerful tools for designers; individual things can feel unified or grouped together when they are aligned.**

- **Flow:** We've created this word for the category that is related to the energy conveyed by lines and shapes. Geometric lines tend to be straight and have sharp angles; they look manmade and intentional. Geometric lines communicate strength, power, and precision when used in design. Curved lines express fluidity, beauty and grace. Organic lines are usually irregular, and imperfect— the kind of lines you find in nature or as the result of random processes. Organic lines represent nature, movement, and elegance. Chaotic lines look like scribble and feel very unpredictable and frantic. They convey a sense of urgency, fear, or explosive energy (**Figure 8.13**).

If you look at the leftmost line of these paragraphs, you can see a "line" formed by the beginning of each line of type. Pay attention to the implied lines you create using the design elements in your artwork. Think of creative ways to use and suggest lines, and pay attention to what you might be saying with them. Make sure that the message all your lines send matches the intent of your work.

Figure 8.12 Line style

Figure 8.13 Line flow

The element of shape

The next element needs little introduction: Shapes are boundaries created by closed lines. Shape (**Figure 8.14**) can be defined as an area enclosed or defined by an outline. We're familiar with shapes such as circles, squares, and triangles, but there are many more shapes than that. Those specific shapes are created in geometry, but what about the shape of a hand or cloud? These are shapes too, and we often use the same descriptors for shapes as we do lines.

▶ *Video 8.7* *Design School: The Element of Shape*

Figure 8.14 The element of shape

COMMON SHAPE DESCRIPTORS

The next element needs little introduction: Shapes are boundaries created by closed lines. Shape (**Figure 8.15**) can be defined as an area enclosed or defined by an outline. We're familiar with shapes such as circles, squares, and triangles, but there are many more shapes than that. Those specific shapes are created in geometry, but what about the shape of a hand or cloud? These are shapes too, and we often use the same descriptors for shapes as we do lines.

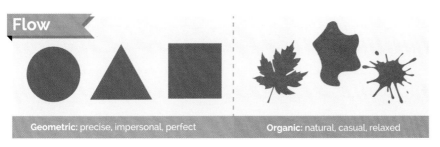

Figure 8.15 Shape flow

REPRESENTATIVE SHAPES

A pictograph (or pictogram) is a graphic symbol that represents something in the real world (**Figure 8.16**). Computer icons are pictographs that often suggest the function they represent (like a trash can icon to delete a file). Other examples of pictographs are the human silhouettes often used to indicate men's and women's restrooms. They're not *accurate* representations of the real objects, but they are *clear* representations of them. Ideographs (or ideograms) are images that represent an idea. A heart shape represents love, a lightning bolt represents electricity, or a question mark represents being puzzled. Representative shapes are helpful in communicating across language barriers and can be valuable when you are designing for multicultural and multilingual audiences.

Figure 8.16 Representative shapes

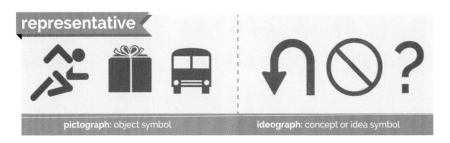

SIDE QUEST: SHAPING UP!

This quest is designed to get you experimenting with shapes. I've provided the same list of words you used to inspire line drawings.

- **Level 1:** Short, long, straight, wavy, zigzag, geometric, organic
- **Level 2:** Angry, lonely, worried, excited, overjoyed
- **Level 3:** Opposition, contrast, politics, infinity

Draw shapes that represent these same words. Try to avoid any common representative graphics—that's too easy. Develop new shapes or just try to create shapes that seem to represent emotions or ideas that aren't normally communicated using shapes.

This is also a fun exercise to do with a friend. Have your friend pick a word for you to draw, or draw something and see how your friend describes it. You'll learn a lot about the different ways that people understand and express ideas. Remember, there are no wrong answers. Just explore, see what happens, and have fun with it.

The element of form

Form (**Figure 8.17**) describes three-dimensional objects or, at least, objects that look 3D. The best way to visualize form clearly is to consider that circles, squares, and triangles are shapes, whereas spheres, cubes, and pyramids are forms. Like shapes, forms are basically divided into geometric and organic types. Geometric forms, such as a cube, are common to us. We are also familiar with organic forms such as the human form or the form of a peanut. When you work with 3D in applications, these forms are often referred to as "solids."

▶ Video 8.8 *Design School: The Element of Form*

Figure 8.17 Form

3D LIGHTING

In art and design, we place a special focus on the techniques that make images appear 3D in a 2D work of art. You have some standard elements to consider when you want to create a feeling of depth and form. **Figure 8.18** explains the standard elements of a 3D drawing.

- **Highlight:** The area of a form directly facing the light; appears lightest.
- **Object shadow:** The area of the form that is facing away from the light source; appears darkest.
- **Cast shadow:** The shadow cast on the ground and on any objects that are in the shadow of the form. One thing to remember is that shadows fade as they get farther from the form casting the shadow. Be sure to take this into account as you're creating shadow effects in your art.
- **Light source:** The perceived location of the lighting in relation to the form.
- **Reflected highlight:** The area of the form that is lit by reflections from the ground or other objects in the scene. This particular element of drawing a 3D object is most often ignored but provides believable lighting on the object.

Figure 8.18 Elements of 3D design

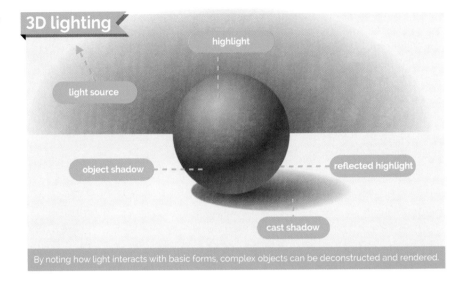

By noting how light interacts with basic forms, complex objects can be deconstructed and rendered.

SIDE QUEST: FORMING UP

This is a standard art exercise. You might ask a friend in an art class or an art teacher to help with this one, or find a tutorial online. You'll draw a sphere with lighting and shadow on a flat plane. Imagine a cue ball on a white table. Be sure to include the elements mentioned in this section and shown in the example of 3D lighting.

Your sketch might not be great. In fact, it may be horrible. If it's your first time and it looks better than you could do in kindergarten, you're doing well. Although you've got digital tools to help with this stuff, learning to draw and doodle activates a different part of your brain, and you want to wake up that part. I'm more concerned with you learning the ideas than mastering 3S drawing on paper.

Focus on learning how things *look* and how to represent them in art and design. And look at some real 3D objects in the light. Put a tennis ball on the sidewalk and just stare at it. It's amazing how much of the real world you never pay attention to! Art is more about learning to *see* than learning to draw or create.

The elements of texture and pattern

Pattern (**Figure 8.19**) can be defined as a repetitive sequence of colors, shapes, or values. Pattern is technically a different concept from texture, but in graphic design it's often regarded as the same thing. Let's face it: all of our "textures" are just ink on paper or pixels. Any repetitive texture might also be considered a pattern. (Think of "diamond plate" or "tile" textures. They're just a pattern of Xs or squares.)

Texture (**Figure 8.20**) can describe an actual, tactile texture in real objects or the appearance of texture in a 2D image. It's important to use texture to communicate feeling and authenticity in your art or designs. If you want to depict something elegant, soft, or comfortable, you could use a texture that resembles fabric or clouds. To represent strength or power, you might choose textures that represent stone or metal. And you could represent casual, informal, or nostalgic feelings using a texture that represents weathered wood or worn paint.

As you work more as a designer, you'll start to notice the nuances and subtle differences between textures and patterns. For now, just think of them as the visual qualities of your shapes and forms that can't be described by color and/or value alone.

▶ **Video 8.9** *Design School: The Element of Texture and Pattern*

Figure 8.19 Pattern and texture

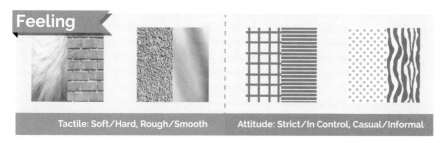

Figure 8.20 Texture and feeling

The element of value

Video 8.10
Design School: The Element of Value

Value (**Figure 8.21**) describes the lightness or darkness of an object. Together with color, value represents all of the visible spectrum. You can think of value as a gradient that goes from black to white. But remember that value applies to color as well, and you can have a spectrum that fades from black, through a color, and then to white. This also introduces the idea of a "red black" or a "blue black" that introduces a hint of color to your blacks. You'll explore that concept later in this chapter.

Figure 8.21 Value

Values range from light to dark through gray and through all colors.

Professionals in the art and design industry often use the term value, but clients rarely use it. Clients will just ask you to lighten or darken a graphic or text, or sometimes use tint, shade, or tone in place of value. Technically, these terms are different, but many people use tone, shade, tint, and value interchangeably. As always, when clients use a term and you're not exactly sure what they mean, ask for clarification. Sometimes clients don't know exactly what they mean, so asking ensures that everyone is on the same page.

The element of color

★ ACA Objective 2.4

▶ *Video 8.11* Design School: The Element of Color

When you think about it, color is hard to define. How would you define color without using examples of colors? Check out its definition in a dictionary and you'll find that defining color doesn't help you understand it. Color is best *experienced* and *explored*.

We have so many ways to think about color and so many concepts to dig into that exploring color is a lifelong pursuit for most artists and designers. Color theory is

SIDE QUEST: VALUE VISION

Value is an interesting element to work with, and you've already experimented with it. Remember the "Forming Up" side quest? That was a great exercise in controlling your pencil to draw a believable sphere. Honestly, there's no better exercise for learning to control your pencil and properly use value than to create 3D forms. But this experiment is going to take you a little further.

Pencils afford you the ability to create different values pretty easily, but what about a pen?

The challenge is to create a set of values while experimenting with monochromatic (no gray) textures. Learn about hatching, cross-hatching, and stippling, all created using a fine point marker. I prefer to use the thin-line Sharpies or an ultra-fine roller ball (.05 or less). Experiment with making different values using purely black and white duotone (no gray) methods.

- **Level 1:** Create three levels of gray across a spectrum.
- **Level 2:** Generate seven layers of gray across a gradient using mixed methods.
- **Level 3:** Generate a 3D sphere using purely duotone methods.

a deep and complex study. You'll explore the basics here, but remember that this is just the on-ramp to understanding color. Grasp these concepts and you'll still have a lot more to learn.

Color psychology is a relatively new discipline and an interesting study that focuses on the emotional and behavioral effects that colors have on people. The colors you choose really do matter. For our purposes, we'll define color as the perceived hue, lightness, and saturation of an object or light.

HOW COLOR WORKS

Color is created in two ways: combining light to create additive color and subtracting light to create subtractive color (**Figure 8.22**).

Additive color is created by combining light. This is how your monitor works, and the most common color mode for additive color is RGB. The letters RGB stand for red, green, blue, which are the three colors used to create digital images. Monitors and electronic devices are dark when turned off, and you create colors by adding light to the screen.

Subtractive color is created by subtracting light. This is the color system you learned in early art classes in which red, blue, and yellow were the primary colors. For print, we use CMYK, which is cyan, magenta, yellow, and black. We start with a white surface (the paper) that reflects all the light back to us. Then we subtract color by using paints or inks that limit the light that is reflected back to the viewer.

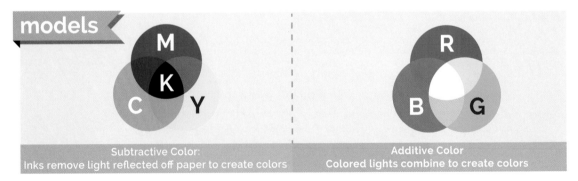

Figure 8.22 Subtractive and additive color

THE COLOR WHEEL

Sir Isaac Newton first invented the color wheel (**Figure 8.23**) in the mid-17th century. The color wheel offers a way to display and build all the colors possible using paint. It's a common exercise in beginning art classes to create a color wheel when learning to mix and experiment with colors. In digital imaging, it's not as important to go through this exercise, but if you have a chance, give it a try. It's interesting to see how all of the colors can mix to obtain the infinite colors and shades the human eye can perceive.

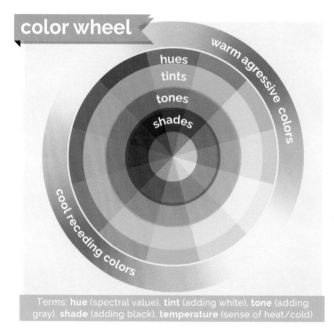

Figure 8.23 The color wheel

The color wheel is important because many color theories we use are named after their relative positions on the color wheel. They're a lot easier to remember if we use the color wheel to illustrate.

The first thing to realize is that some colors are classified as primary colors. These colors can be combined to create every other color in the visible spectrum. For subtractive color used in traditional art, the primary colors are red, blue, and yellow. For additive colors, the primary colors are red, blue, and green.

The colors that are created when you combine primary colors are called secondary colors because you can create them only by applying a second step of mixing the colors. When we mix secondary and primary colors, we get another set of colors known as tertiary colors. **Figure 8.24** illustrates how these colors are built.

Figure 8.24 How secondary and tertiary colors are built

color mixing

Primary Colors- cannot be created by mixing
Secondary- Mix 2 primary colors
Tertiary- Mix primary and secondary colors

SIDE QUEST: ROLLIN' WITH COLOR

Creating a color wheel is a staple project in art classes. Any experienced traditional artist or art teacher can help you with this task. You can find a ton of information about this online, but this is a valuable project to help you get in touch with color and understand how colors are related.

- **Level 1:** Create a traditional color wheel using paint on paper.
- **Level 2:** Create a color wheel in Premiere Pro using basic shape tools.

BASIC COLOR RULES

Color rules (also called color harmonies) are a great way to start picking colors for your projects in Premiere Pro. The color rules (**Figure 8.25**) are all named for their relative locations on the color wheel. When you're choosing colors and exploring

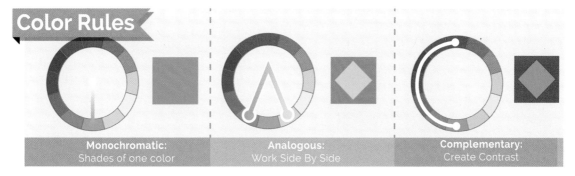

Figure 8.25 Color rules

other ways to join colors to create contrast or harmony, these color rules are where you should begin. We're going to cover some of the basic color rules and the impressions they tend to communicate.

The three most common ways of thinking about colors (and, really, the basis of all color rules) are monochromatic, analogous, and complementary color schemes.

- **Monochromatic:** Monochromatic colors, as you've probably guessed, are based only on different shades and tints of the same color. They tend to communicate a relaxed and peaceful feeling, and you'll create little contrast or energy in art using these colors.

- **Analogous:** If you want to add a little more variation while maintaining a calm feeling, consider analogous colors. Analogous colors sit side by side on the color wheel, and they tend to create gentle and relaxing color schemes. Analogous colors don't usually stand out from each other; they seem to work together and can almost disappear together when overlaid.

- **Complementary:** Complementary colors are opposite each other on the color wheel. Complementary color combinations are high in contrast and normally very vibrant, so use with caution. When overused, complementary color can be very "loud" and can easily cross over into visually obnoxious if you're not careful. You can remember this rule with the alliterative phrase "Complementary colors create contrast."

If you want to explore color combinations, visit http://color.adobe.com and explore the Adobe Color CC website (**Figure 8.26**). It's an amazing way to browse other people's color collections, or grab colors from an image you like and create a color set to use for your projects. When you register with your free Adobe ID, you can save the color themes you find or create and bring them into your Adobe apps to use and share with others.

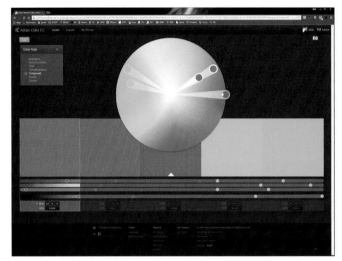

Figure 8.26 Use the Adobe Color CC website to explore color harmonies and save combinations to your Creative Cloud account.

Figure 8.27 The Adobe Capture app lets you capture colors from photos you've taken or grab them live using the camera.

Adobe Color is also part of a free app for iOS and Android. Open the Adobe Capture CC app (**Figure 8.27**) and select Colors, open an image or point your phone camera at something, and create a color theme. Experiment with creating custom themes from your favorite blanket, a sunset, your goldfish, or your crazy uncle's tie-dyed concert shirt from Woodstock.

COLOR ASSOCIATIONS

We tend to associate different things with different colors. Whether this is learned behavior or instinct can be debated. But as a designer you must learn to recognize and properly use the right color for the right message. Again, this isn't a science, and you'll need to consider more than this chart when developing your color-picking strategies. But understanding colors and their associations (**Figure 8.28**) can be useful to produce the right "feel" in your images. You can evoke interesting feelings and contrasts by capitalizing on these associations in your interactive design work.

The element of type

Type (**Figure 8.29**) is generally not considered a traditional element of art, but it can be a critical part of your work as a designer. Typefaces carry a lot of emotional meaning, and choosing the proper typefaces for a job is a skill that every designer needs (yet many don't have). Like color, this area of design is so deep and has so many aspects that entire books and college courses are focused only on typography. We can't reduce it to simple rules such as "Use three typefaces, maximum. When in doubt use Helvetica. And never use Chiller." (Even though that's not a bad starting point!)

associations

sky, water, peace, cold

nature, growth, money

sunlight, joy, energy

fire, warmth, attention

blood, passion, danger

flowers, creativity

Color associations can depend on: culture, profession or experience.

Figure 8.28 Color associations

Figure 8.29 The element of type

Working with type is often like being a marriage counselor or matchmaker. Every typeface has a personality and you need to carefully match the type in your design work so it has a compatible relationship with the overall feeling of the piece. The typefaces you use also need to work together. It takes time and experience to master this balance, but over time you can become a skillful typeface matchmaker. Most artists have a few fonts they tend to lean on heavily, and that's okay—especially at the beginning.

★ ACA Objective 2.3

▶ *Video 8.12* Design School: The Element of Type

SIDE QUEST: PUZZLING TYPOGRAPHY

A popular jigsaw puzzle style right now (often available in bookstores) has a strong typographic focus that lists "Family Rules" or "Life Lessons" in various fonts. However, any puzzle with lots of larger text in multiple typefaces will work great. As you're doing the puzzle, notice the subtle differences between fonts and the letterforms of each font. You'll learn to pay attention to the subtle differences between the different styles of type.

- **Level 1:** Do a puzzle like this with a group of friends and discuss your observations.
- **Level 2:** Do a puzzle like this by yourself.

TYPOGRAPHY

Typography is the art of using letterforms and type arrangement to help the language communicate a message. As mentioned earlier, type can be its own topic of study and can easily get overwhelming. We'll skim the surface here but hope that as you move forward in your design, you'll dig a little deeper. Let's get some vocabulary out of the way first.

Technically, a typeface (**Figure 8.30**) is the letterform set that makes up the type. Helvetica, Arial, Garamond, and Chiller are examples of typefaces. In brief, it's the "look" of the letters. Fonts are the whole collection of the typeface in each of its sizes and styles. So 12 pt. Arial Narrow and 12 pt. Arial Bold are different *fonts* of the same *typeface*. The same is true for two different sizes of the same typeface.

Figure 8.30 Many of today's typography terms were created in the days of movable type and have changed as publishing technology has evolved.

From now on, let's use the term font, because that's also the name of the file you'll install when you add typefaces to your computer, and it's the most common term. Few people will bother splitting hairs in these differences that really don't exist anymore for computer-generated type.

TYPE CLASSIFICATIONS

There are many different ways to classify typefaces, but we'll rely on the Adobe Typekit classifications for the purpose of this chapter. Generally, people divide fonts into two main categories of type that should be used for large areas of type: serif and sans-serif (**Figure 8.31**).

- Serif fonts are often associated with typewritten documents and most printed books. Generally, serif fonts are considered to be easier to read in larger paragraphs of text. Because so many books use serif fonts and early typewriters produced them, serif text often feels a bit more traditional, intelligent, and classy.

- Sans serif fonts do not include serifs. "Sans" is a French word that migrated to English and simply means "without." Sans serif fonts are often used for headlines and titles for their strong, stable, modern feel. Sans serif fonts are also preferred for large areas of text for reading on websites and screen reading.

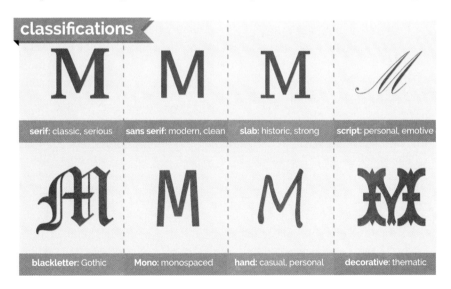

Figure 8.31 Serif and sans serif fonts

Beyond these basic types of text we use in our documents, designers use other typefaces that are not appropriate for large areas of type because they're not easy to read in a long paragraph. Most designers consider the following fonts to be "decorative" for that reason.

- Slab serif fonts (also called Egyptian, block serif, or square serif) are a more squared-off version of a typical serif font. These fonts bridge the gap between serif and sans serif fonts and generally feel a bit more machine-built. The simple design tends to make them feel a bit rougher than their serif counterparts.

- Script fonts (also called formal or calligraphical) have an elegant feeling. These fonts are great to use for invitations to formal events, such as weddings, and in designs where you want to convey a feeling of beauty, grace, and/or feminine dignity. If you are designing for a spa, for a beauty shop, or for products or services, script fonts will carry a feeling of relaxed and elegant beauty.

- Blackletter fonts (also called old English, Gothic, or textura) feature an overly ornate style and are often used to title formal documents such as certificates, diplomas, or degrees, as well as old German Bibles and heavy metal bands. It conveys a feeling of rich and sophisticated gravitas, often hinting at a long history of tradition and reliability.

- Monospaced fonts (also called fixed-width or nonproportional) use the same amount of horizontal space for each letter. Typically, fonts use a variable spacing technique called kerning. (You'll learn more about kerning later in this chapter.) Monospaced fonts, in contrast, use the same width for every character. Monospaced fonts are good to use when you're trying to make something look impersonal, machine-generated, or retro-geeky because typewriters and early computers used monospaced fonts.

- Handwritten fonts (also called hand fonts) simulate handwriting. They are popular for adding a personalized, casual, or human touch to your designs and are often used on junk mail to try to trick you into opening that "Special limited time offer just for you!" (don't fall for it). Handwritten fonts are prefect for communicating casual and friendly feelings, but they can be tough to read in a larger block of text.

- Decorative fonts (also called ornamental, novelty, or display) don't fall into any of the other categories. They also tend to convey specific feelings. Decorative fonts should be used sparingly and very intentionally. Never use a novelty font just because you think it looks cool; that's a typical newbie move. Make sure you are striving to convey something very specific when using decorative fonts.

TIP

Want to create a font based on your own handwriting? Go to www.myscriptfont.com to create a font from your handwriting for free.

- Dingbat fonts (also called wingdings) are a special type of font that doesn't have an alphabet but instead consists of a collection of shapes or objects.

NOTE

Each character of a font, whether it's a letter, number, symbol, or swash, is called a glyph.

TYPE TALK

You'll need to learn a lot of jargon concerning type when working in the design industry. Some of it is commonly used in discussion about design, and some of it will help you discuss fonts when you're trying to find the perfect typeface for your design.

TYPOGRAPHIC ANATOMY

Figure 8.32 illustrates many of the anatomical terms used when discussing typography. Software has no settings for these options, so we won't go into detail about them. When you start to study typography and learn these terms, you will more easily discern the differences between typefaces. It's easiest to understand these terms by simply looking at the illustration. You will hear these terms in the industry, and when you're looking for a specific font, knowing these terms will allow you to more easily describe what you're looking for. Let's face it: you can't get too far professionally if you're always using words like "doohickey" and "little hangy-downy thingy." These terms are descriptive like ascenders and descenders; anthropomorphic like arms, shoulders, and tails; or architectural like counters and finials.

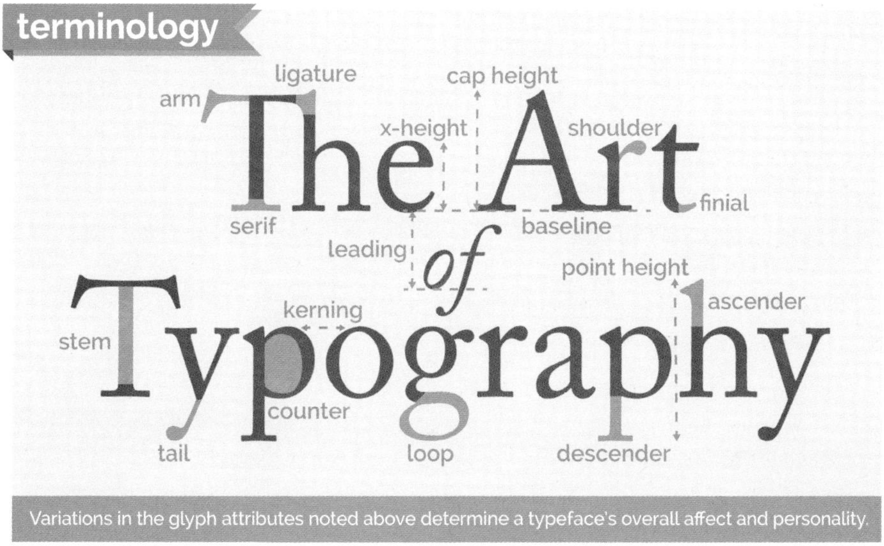

terminology

The Art of Typography

ligature · arm · cap height · x-height · shoulder · serif · finial · baseline · leading · point height · kerning · ascender · stem · counter · tail · loop · descender

Variations in the glyph attributes noted above determine a typeface's overall affect and personality.

Figure 8.32 Many key typographical terms are illustrated in this image.

THE HOLY TRINITY OF TYPOGRAPHY

Three main concepts of typography exist: kerning, leading, and tracking, known as "The Holy Trinity of Design" (**Figure 8.33**). As a designer, you need to master these concepts. The terms defined here affect the ways that the letters are spaced from each other vertically or horizontally.

- Kerning is the space between specific letter pairs. For example, the first two letters in the word "Too" are closer than the first two letters in the word "The" because the letter "o" can tuck under the crossbar of the "T." A high-quality font file will have a good set of kerning pairs for specific letter combinations, but for some professional work (and with poorly designed fonts) you might need to get in there and tweak the kerning. Adjusting the kerning between specific letters can help you perfect your type presentation in logos and headlines.

- Tracking is the overall space between all the letters in a block of text. It allows you to compress or expand the space between the letters as a whole, rather than just between specific pairs as you do with kerning. Adjusting tracking can greatly affect the feeling that text conveys. Experiment with tracking to help create various feelings in headlines and titles.

- Leading is the amount of space between the baselines of two lines of text. The baseline is the imaginary line that text sits on. Whereas word processing applications tend to limit you to single and double-line spacing, professional design software lets you manipulate the leading to set a specific distance between multiple lines of text. Doing so can create great-looking space in a design or even overlap with your paragraph text. Experiment with this option in your work. You can change the mood of text by adjusting only the leading of a paragraph.

Figure 8.33 Kerning, tracking, and leading

SIZE, SCALE, AND SMALL CAPS

The terms that appear in **Figure 8.34** are available in the character panel of the interface for most Adobe design applications. However, even though Premiere Pro does not include certain aspects discussed here, you should still familiarize yourself with them.

- Type size is traditionally the height from the highest ascender to the lowest descender in a font, expressed in points (1/72 of an inch). Today, it's more of a guideline than a firm definition, so most designers set the appropriate type size by eye. Different fonts of the same point size can appear to be much different in physical size if the ascenders and descenders are different from each other.

- Vertical and horizontal scale are terms that describe the function of stretching letters and distorting the typeface geometry. Because they distort the typeface, use them with caution. They should be used only when you are trying to express a specific feeling and should not be used in blocks of type because readability can suffer with either of these adjustments.

- All caps and small caps are similar in that they both use only the uppercase letterforms for each letter, but **ALL CAPS** makes all the letters the same size, whereas SMALL CAPS sets the letters that would normally be capitalized at a larger size. Small caps tend to increase readability compared to all caps, but both cap formats should be avoided in large blocks of text because they are more difficult to read than standard text.

> **TIP** *Higher-end typefaces may provide a small caps face that is much nicer than using the setting in software. If this is critical for your design, look for a font that supports this feature.*

Figure 8.34 Size and special characters

- Ligatures and swashes are special alternative settings offered with some fonts to combine letters or add stylized touches to certain letter combinations or letters. For example, when the "Th" combination touches in a headline, you can replace it with a single ligature that looks much better. Swashes add flowing and elegant endings to letters with ascenders and descenders. Both of these are normally reserved for type that is expressing an especially elegant or artistic feel.

SIDE QUEST: GAMES OF A CERTAIN TYPE

You can find a lot of great online resources for exploring typography, and you can also find some that are not that great but are worth visiting at least once or twice. A frequently updated list of typographic resources is available at www.brainbuffet.com/design/typography, and we hope you'll take the time to explore some of them to dig a little deeper into your understanding of type and typography.

- **Level 1:** Experiment with at least three typographic games online.
- **Level 2:** Achieve a high score on at least one typographic game online.
- **Level 3:** Achieve a high score on five or more typographic games online.

Wrapping up the elements

As you've seen in this chapter, the elements are the building blocks or the raw materials of design. But what turns these elements into art is applying the principles of design to the way you arrange these elements on your workspace. In the next section, you'll explore these principles, which are a framework that help you arrange your work in an artistic way.

The Principles of Design

Video 8.13
Design School:
The Principles of
Design

Much like the elements of design, different artists and schools of thought will generate different ideas about what makes up the principles of design (**Figure 8.35**). For a young artist, this can be frustrating. Sometimes you just want someone to tell you the answer.

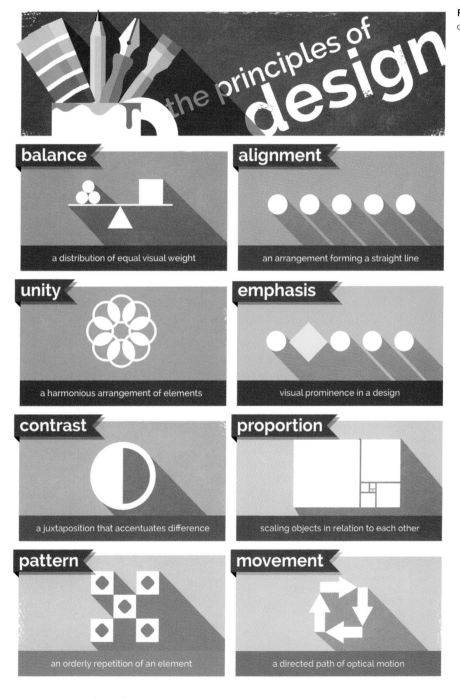

Figure 8.35 Principles of design

But after you understand the principles, you'll appreciate that no one can point to a universal list of artistic principles. If there's no correct answer, there's also no *wrong* answer either. Creatively, you always have another way to approach your art, and becoming an artist doesn't mean that you learn to see any one approach. Becoming an artist means that you learn to *see*.

Until you explore design principles, you will not be ready to understand them. Therefore, definitions are not as helpful as hands-on work. But truly grasping the principles and experiencing them is the only way to grow as an artist. This is the beginning of a lifelong exploration of beauty and creativity.

The bottom line is this: Don't get hung up on names or descriptions. Try to engage with each idea as a loosely formed concept that remains fluid and flexible rather than defining boundaries. By studying principles, you're trying to do just the opposite—moving in directions that have no boundaries. The goal of all good art and design is to explore new ways to use the elements and principles, and not to repeat what's been done in the past. You'll examine these principles to start your understanding of something, not to limit it.

The principle of emphasis or focal point

▶ *Video 8.14*
Design School:
The Principle of
Emphasis

Emphasis (**Figure 8.36**) describes the focal point to which the eye is naturally and initially drawn in a design. Some art has a focus that's obvious. Most marketing and advertising is that way. Other art invites you to step in and explore. It might encourage an exploration of color or texture, but it has no specific point other than the color or texture.

Figure 8.36 Emphasis creates the focal point— a place where the eye is naturally drawn when encountering the image. Use this to your advantage when designing.

Think of emphasis as the main point or primary idea in a piece of art. You can move the viewer's eye to a specific point in the design by making something *different*. You can easily find examples right on the pages of this book. Chapter headings are larger than the rest of the type. Glossary terms are a different color. Even the simple process of *italicizing* words or putting them in **boldface** makes text stand out. The human eye is naturally drawn to unique things. So if you want to make something stand out, make it different.

Careful use of contrast is critical to master because a typical design newbie tries to make everything special and unique. As a result, nothing stands out. The design looks *random*, not cool. Give a piece some unity, and it will feel right. You can then emphasize what's truly important.

The principle of contrast

Contrast generally creates visual interest and a focal point in a composition. If you think about it, a blank canvas is a canvas with no contrast. As soon as you begin to alter the surface and create contrast, you also start to create a focus. The principle of contrast can be defined as a difference in the qualities of the elements in an image. To use contrast is to create something different from the surrounding pieces of the composition.

▶ *Video 8.15*
Design School: The Principle of Contrast

Many artists limit their understanding of contrast by confining it to color or value. But contrast is much more than that. Any difference between one thing and another creates contrast. You can have contrast in size, texture, value, color, or any of the defining characteristics you learned about in exploring the elements.

The most important thing to remember about contrast is that all contrast creates some emphasis, and if you have too much emphasis, you will have no focal point.

The principle of unity

Unity generally communicates calm, peaceful, or cool feelings in your art. The principle of unity (also called harmony) requires that the things that go together should *look* like they belong together (**Figure 8.37**). The elements in your design should feel like a family. This doesn't necessarily mean that everything needs to be the same—just that they should share some similar traits. When you have no unity, you can have no focal point and, therefore, no emphasis.

▶ *Video 8.16*
Design School: The Principle of Unity

Figure 8.37 The similar
lines, colors, and even
values of this image give
it a unified feeling.

Note the headings of the different sections in this chapter. They make it easy to find the content you are looking for when skimming the book. Even the breaks between paragraphs help distinguish one concept from another. But all of the words in this paragraph belong together because they share a unity of typeface, spacing, color, and so on.

Unity is important in your compositions so that when you create contrast it draws the viewer's eye where you want it to go. In design, more than in art, we are interested in guiding a viewer's perceptions. Design generally tends to be much more intentional than art. Both are important, however, and beginning with design can make your experimentation with artistic elements and principles much more effective and productive.

The principle of variety

▶ *Video 8.17*
Design School:
The Principle of
Variety

Variety tends to communicate energy, heat, and high emotion in a design. When applying the principle of variety, you use different elements in an image to create visual interest. In many ways, it is the exact opposite of unity. You can think of unity and variety as being at the opposite ends of contrast. Unity is establishing a low degree of contrast in a composition. Variety does the opposite and brings a higher amount of contrast to the composition.

Variety is a principle that normally needs to be used sparingly. Too much variety quickly moves your art from interesting to chaotic and disorganized (**Figure 8.38**). Beginning artists and designers sometimes have a hard time properly using variety. They get a little bit carried away and lose all sense of focus or unity. Beware of that tendency!

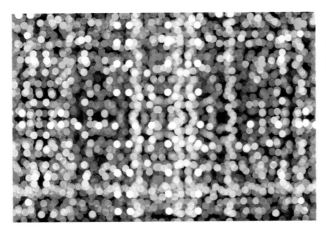

Figure 8.38 When everything is different in an image like these colored lights are, nothing stands out.

The principle of balance

Balance suggests the arrangement of things in an image should not be evenly distributed. This is not to say that everything should be centered, and that placing something in the top right means you should mirror it with something similar in the top left. That's how a nondesigner lays out a composition. Experienced artists learn to properly balance all of the elements—including space—in their compositions.

Balance comes in many forms: symmetrical, asymmetrical, or radial.

- **Symmetrical:** Symmetrical balance is what most students latch on to at first. It occurs when you can divide an image along its middle and the left side of the image is a mirror image of its right (or the top reflects the bottom). Using a seesaw analogy, a symmetrical balance would have two equally sized people equally distant from the fulcrum. This is the easiest balance to execute, but it conveys a very intentional, formal, and mechanical feeling.

- **Asymmetrical:** Asymmetrical balance (**Figure 8.39**) achieves balance with different elements on each side (or the top and bottom) of an image. Imagine an adult on a seesaw with a child. They can balance, but only if the adult is closer to the fulcrum and the child is farther away. To achieve asymmetrical balance, you need to use space to counterbalance the different weights on each side.

Video 8.18
Design School: The Principle of Balance

TIP

Many artists and designers characterize pieces that are out of balance as "leaning to the left," "leaning to the right," or "top-heavy." Over time, you'll develop these feelings too and be able to spot when art seems like it might physically tip over.

Figure 8.39 This image, though asymmetrical, is well balanced. The bright sun is offset by the visual weight of the rocks in the lower right.

- **Radial:** Radial balance (**Figure 8.40**) is a circular type of balance that radiates from the center instead of the middle of a design. Many artists get the feeling that they're viewing a radially balanced image from above. This kind of balance is almost always circular. An excellent example of radial balance is a kaleidoscopic image, which can feel balanced and unified but also typically feels more static than the other types of balance.

Figure 8.40 This image has a radial balance.

The principle of proportion or scale

Proportion, sometimes called scale, describes the relative sizes and scale of things. If you've ever seen a drawing and observed that "the head is too small" or "the body is too fat," you're evaluating the proportion. It's simply the sense that things seem to be the proper size relative to each other.

You can manipulate proportion and scale to create emphasis. Things that are larger than they should be appear stronger, more important, or more powerful. Take the chapter headings in this book. By making the headings disproportionately large, we've indicated importance and emphasis. You can also reduce the perceived value, strength, or importance of something by reducing its scale.

▶ *Video 8.19*
Design School:
The Principle of
Proportion or Scale

The principles of repetition and pattern

The two principles of repetition and pattern—along with movement and rhythm—seem to be the most confusing and difficult to grasp. As a matter of fact, some artists and writers more readily connect pattern and repetition with rhythm than with movement. In this introductory look at these concepts, think about the simplest and most concrete uses of them here. As always, you're encouraged to explore these areas much more deeply on your own.

▶ *Video 8.20*
Design School:
The Principles of
Repetition and
Pattern

Repetition is a principle that is pretty easy to grasp: repeating an element in your design. Repetition can convey many things, but it often represents importance, movement, or energy. Think of an illustration of a ball moving or a cartoon of a bird flapping its wings. Just repeating a few lines can convey a sense of motion.

Pattern happens when different objects repeat in a sequence. The best way to think about the difference between repetition and pattern is that repetition is done with a single element (such as pinstripes on a suit), whereas pattern happens with a collection of elements (such as a floral pattern on fabric). Pattern also happens when elements are repeated consistently and, at some point, eventually move past repetition and become a pattern.

Another important way to think about repetition is to share certain traits of the elements in your design. Doing so brings some unity to those elements and lets the viewer know they're related. For example, you could repeat the colors of the logo in headers and bold type or repeat the same colors from a photo into the header text of an associated article in a magazine. Repetition of this kind conveys a sense of unity in the design.

The principles of movement and rhythm

▶ *Video 8.21*
Design School:
The Principles of
Movement and
Rhythm

Movement and rhythm are similar, much like repetition and pattern. They modify an image much the way an adverb modifies an adjective. They explain a feeling that the elements create, rather than making specific changes to the elements.

Movement refers to the visual movement in an image. Depending on the context, it can refer to the movement the eye naturally follows across an image as it moves from focal point to focal point, or the perceived movement or flow of the elements in the image.

Movement can also refer to the "flow" of an image, and is a critical principle to consider in your work. It's more of a feeling than a concrete visual aspect of your design. When something "doesn't feel right," it may be that the flow is uncertain or contradictory. If you haven't considered the flow of your design, analyze it and create a flow that guides the viewer through your design. The more linear your flow, the more your design will convey a sense of reliability, consistency, and calm. A more complex flow can convey a sense of creativity, freedom, or even chaos.

Rhythm refers to the visual "beat" in the design, a sense of an irregular but predictable pattern. Just as a rhythm is laid down by a drummer, a design's rhythm is creative and expressive, rather than a consistent pattern or repetition. Depending on the design you're working on, rhythm may or may not be a critical principle to consider. A predictable rhythm can convey a sense of calm and consistency, whereas an erratic or complex rhythm can convey a sense of urgency or energy.

These two principles tend to be the most subjective, so be sure to clarify anything you're unsure about when discussing these principles with a client. Because they're more of a feeling than a specific element or technique, it takes a little experience to get a handle on them. But these are just like all of the principles: once you start looking for them, you'll start to see them.

Wrapping Up the Design Concepts

As an interactive media designer, you must understand the elements and principles so that your work can communicate clearly to your audience. Learning the technical basics of Premiere Pro is fairly easy, and they can be mastered by people who will never "make it" in the industry.

Take the time to develop your design skills set and to remember that it *is* a skills set. You've got to practice and continue to develop your craft to level up those skills. Using Premiere Pro without having a design sense is like starting up a jet engine without the jet. It's powerful, but you won't be able to fly it to a destination. The artistic elements and principles are the wings and controls that let you harness that power and get your art to go where you want it.

Invest the time and effort to practice and refine your design sense. You'll find that your personal art not only grows more impressive over time, but that the entire world opens up and becomes much more interesting, beautiful, and detailed.

Premiere Pro is about learning to create effective videos with exceptionally high quality, but becoming an artist and refining your skills is about learning to *see*.

Open your eyes… and enjoy the beauty you've been missing that's all around you!

▶ *Video 8.22* Design School: Wrapping up Design School

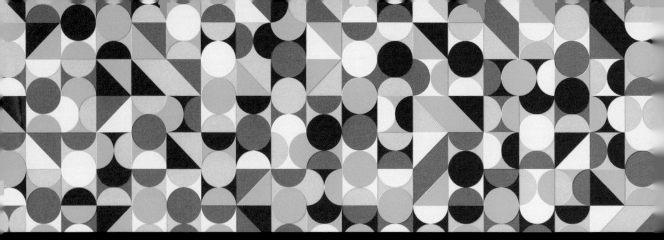

CHAPTER OBJECTIVES

Chapter Learning Objectives

- Understand your client's needs.
- Familiarize yourself with copyright and licensing basics.
- Explore project management.
- Avoid project creep.

Chapter ACA Objectives

For more information on ACA Objectives, see pages 235–238.

DOMAIN 1.0
SETTING PROJECT REQUIREMENTS

1.1 Identify the purpose, audience, and audience needs for editing video.

1.2 Summarize how digital video professionals make decisions about the type of content to include in a project, including considerations such as copyright, audience needs, permissions, and licensing.

1.3 Demonstrate knowledge of project management tasks and responsibilities.

1.4 Communicate with others (such as peers and clients) about editing plans.

DOMAIN 2.0
UNDERSTANDING DIGITAL VIDEO

2.2 Demonstrate knowledge of basic principles and best practices employed in the digital video industry.

CHAPTER 9

Working with Outsiders

As a video editor, you're going to work with others. Being a designer and being an artist are two different careers, but most people who do creative work for a living find a need to do both. It's similar to the way a lot of photographers shoot weddings to pay the bills. It may not be their favorite type of photography, but it pays well and makes people happy. However, if you love to shoot old, crumbly walls and rusty farmhouse doors, you will find that you simply can't pay the bills with your "rusty hinge" photo collection.

Aside from the money, you will probably learn to develop an immense passion for creating designs for others. The secret to this part of the job is twofold: really listen and really care.

▶ Video 9.1
*Introduction To
Project Planning*

Who You're Talking For
and Who You're Talking To

★ *ACA Objective 1.1*

The first step in designing for a particular project is to understand the client's needs. This is critical because, among other things, the client pays the bills. Most of all, the client is hiring you to speak for them. As a video editor, that's a weighty responsibility. You're being trusted to communicate for an entire company or cause. First and foremost, you need to address that client's needs and goals for the project. This will be the guiding principle when answering design questions. You must constantly remember your goals and focus narrowly on them to streamline your workflow and minimize distractions.

Let's look at a few example scenarios:

- Rockin' Zombies is a metal-opera-jazz-bluegrass fusion band that wants to promote an upcoming free concert at the local farmer's market.

- Hoi Polloi Church needs a video for their website highlighting their project to solicit volunteers and donations to help orphaned children recover from Hurricane Sally.

- OfficeHome Custodial Services wants to share with businesses about their upscale, environmentally friendly office cleaning services.

- Zak's Bulldozer wants to promote their tree removal for residential homes using low-impact tools.

- The city's Health Department wants a campaign to promote healthy eating and active lifestyle changes and to inform and warn people about common bad habits.

- Pop-Lite is a new, collapsible photo light, and the inventors need a promo video for their Kickstarter campaign.

Each project has different goals, right? Some want to give away something for free. Some want to make money. Some want to solicit help from others. It's important to help the client pin down their project goals—and that can be hard to do.

Single voice, single message

▶ *Video 9.2*
Discovering Client Goals

Here's a brainteaser. You have 20 close friends, and you can no longer understand what they say. Why? They're close enough to talk to one another. They are all speaking your language. They are all speaking loud enough for you to hear clearly. They have no health or physical impairments. What's the problem?

They're all talking at once!

If a video says too much, it says nothing. It becomes "noisy" and makes it hard for the viewer to focus on the main idea. This reality is similar to the design concept of focal point. All creative projects have a kind of focal point. It's important to clearly define and pin down the most important goals of a project. Sometimes, clients are trying to clearly define their purpose, vision, or dreams for their organization. The overall goals and dreams for the business are helpful in the design process and should be heard so that you understand your client. But to get a project done efficiently—and create a project that communicates well—you must work with the client to establish and narrow down the goals for this project.

This short version of a campaign's goals is often called the "elevator pitch" because it summarizes the project in the time that it would take for an elevator ride. It's communicating your purpose in a short, simple sentence. Normally, I push a client to shoot for seven words or less. The aim is to clearly define the goals for this particular design project.

Here are some elevator pitches related to the scenarios listed earlier:

- Come to our free concert.
- Help child victims of a disaster.
- Get safe cleaning services for your office.
- Trees removed without damaging your yard.
- Get healthy and avoid hidden dangers.
- Our little photo lights are fun and functional.

Admittedly, these pitches are not elegant or enticing. There's no "pop" to the message. But they're the very core of what you're trying to communicate. It is the reason your client is paying you to produce the video. You'll need more detail than this to deliver an effective video, but focusing on this core goal can help you rein in the insidious forces of project creep (which we'll talk about later in this chapter). But first, let this sink in: Your client's goals are your number-one priority.

If the goal is unclear, the finished product will be unclear. Figure out the goal, and you can always come back to it as a "home base" when the project starts to grow or lose its focus. Sometimes the goal isn't obvious, or it turns out to be different than it first appeared. But it's always critical, and one of your first jobs is to help the client focus on the primary goal of the project. Nonetheless, at the end of the day you work for the client, so the client calls the shots, has the final say, and makes the decisions—even if you disagree.

Now we'll talk about the second-most important person on the project—the one who doesn't really exist. I'm talking about the ideal audience viewer of the piece.

Identifying your client's ideal customer

★ *ACA Objective 1.2*

In life, we shouldn't judge people, make assumptions, and lump them together. But we do. And as creative producers, we *must*. This means developing a demographic for the project and identifying the target audience. It's a critical step in helping your clients bridge the gap to the audience they want to reach. You do this by identifying the common characteristics of that audience and creating an image in everyone's minds of the typical customer. Some clients will say "Everybody needs my product," but those clients will still need to focus on a target demographic specific to the project at hand. As the old saying goes, "Aim at nothing and you'll hit it every time." Those are wise words, especially when identifying a target audience.

▶ *Video 9.3*
Finding the Target Audience

Identifying a target demographic for your project is a critical step, second only to defining the client's goals. And generally, it's also a part of the client's goals. For example, when you want to create a new fishing pole, you can easily picture your target audience: fishermen. So you're probably not going to use the same graphics, words, images, or feel as you would to reach a punk rock audience. At the same time, expectant mothers probably wouldn't be drawn to images that would reach your fish or punk target.

Identifying a demographic helps you focus on who you want to get your message. Understand the goals of your viewer as well as the speaker, your client. Make sure you share information in a way that will connect or resonate with that audience. And if you understand what your audience needs and feels, you can show how what you're sharing meets those needs.

The easiest way to do this is to create imaginary "perfect fits" for your client's project. Here are some things to consider:

- **Income:** Determine if you want to focus on quality, exclusivity, or price.
- **Education:** Establish the vocabulary and complexity of the design.
- **Age:** Dictate the general appeal, attitude, and vocabulary.
- **Hobbies:** Help in choosing images, insider vocabulary, and attitudes.
- **Concerns, cares, and passions:** Identify core beliefs, trigger points, and so on.

It's easy to see how different audiences will need different images. You don't want images of extreme sports in an ad aimed at expectant mothers. You wouldn't use a crowded nightclub image in a promo video for a camping and canoe outfitter company. Inexperienced editors sometimes try to make a production to please themselves, and that isn't always what pleases the target audience.

What makes your audience unique? Who has the problems that this product solves? Have those pictures in your mind. Work these ideas over with your client and help them envision their typical customer. Then look for clips that will appeal to that ideal customer, this project's target demographic.

Think of yourself as a matchmaker. You're trying to introduce your client to the perfect customer or consumer. Speak in the language that the ideal client would want to hear, and use images that will bring their lifestyle and outlook together with your client.

The golden rule for client projects

Effective video helps someone else convey their vision. It communicates a message. When you're starting a new edit, use the business version of the golden rule: He who has the gold makes the rules.

▶ **Video 9.4** *The Golden Rule for Client Work*

Ultimately, you work for your clients. Help them see what you regard as the most effective way and identify the right questions to ask, but don't fight with them. They might have insight or perspective about their target audience that you don't have. Even when you disagree with a client about a design decision, you still need to help them realize their vision for their project. If you don't like it, you don't have to put the final piece in your portfolio, but you'll still get to put their check in the bank. If it comes down to what the client wants versus what you think their audience will respond to, do what the client asks. It's their project, their audience, and their money.

There's one exception to this rule that you need to follow at all times. When your client asks you to skirt copyright law, you're still responsible for respecting the law and your fellow producers. Often the clients are just confused and you can help them understand that you can't copy other designs or employ copyrighted materials without authorization. Along those lines, let's take a moment to talk about copyright.

Copyrights and Wrongs

★ ACA Objective 1.2

Copyright is an amazing set of laws designed to protect and promote artists along with their art, creativity, and learning. It's gotten a really bad rap, and you should can set aside any preconceived ideas for a bit and think through the copyright concept (**Figure 9.1**).

Figure 9.1 Copyright can be a complex issue, but the basics are straightforward.

Copyright law is generally misunderstood by the public, so understanding it is an awesome way to score high at trivia night. A solid understanding of copyright law will also enable you to help your struggling author and artist friends realize that they don't have to pay an attorney tons of money to "make sure they get their stuff copyrighted." You can do it for them or show them how to do it themselves. It's free and easy. As a matter of fact, it's probably already been done.

Keep in mind that I'm a producer, editor, and instructor, not a lawyer. This chapter does not constitute legal advice; it's just intended to help you understand the law and the reasons it exists so you can appreciate it. It's easier to obey a law that you understand and appreciate, and copyright laws protect your rights. So get on board.

Here's something to remember: **Copyright law promotes freedom and creativity**. Let's explore how.

Copyright happens

The first thing to know about copyright in the United States is that it just happens. If something can be copied, then it's copyrighted. You needn't fill out any special forms, report to a government office, or do anything extra to put it in place. The law is written so that copyright happens as soon is something original and creative is recorded in a "fixed form." This means that as soon as you write something down, sketch it out, or click the shutter on your camera, whatever you just created is copyrighted. The only reason you might do anything additional is to establish verifiable proof of when a creation was copyrighted, because the person who can prove that she recorded it first owns the copyright.

▶ **Video 9.5** *About Copyright*

Imagine that you're in a restaurant talking with a friend. During this conversation you make up a song on the spot. A famous singer in the booth behind yours hears you and writes it down. He claims the copyright to the lyrics and melody and makes a million bucks with your spontaneous song, and there's little you can do about it. However, if you recorded it on your phone when you sang it, you recorded it in fixed form *first*. So, *you* own the copyright on the lyrics, and the artist now owes you a truckload of money.

Why does the law have this quirky little rule? Because the courts have to decide who owns copyright when its ownership is contested in court. And courts rely on tangible proof. So the law makes it simple by stating that she who first records something in fixed form wins. This way, you're not going to sue someone if you have no proof that you were first. But even if you were, and you can't prove it, you're out of luck.

TIP

While your original work is automatically copyrighted without registering it with the US Copyright Office, you can potentially collect much higher monetary damages from an infringer if you do register the work.

So why do we have a copyright notice on music, DVDs, and one of the first pages of this book? If we don't need it, why do we display it?

Simply put, it reminds people who owns this copyrighted material. When no date and copyright symbol are displayed, people may think they can legally make photocopies of this book for their friends. Most people assume if no copyright notice appears, then no copyright exists. (They're totally wrong.) The presence of a visible copyright statement discourages this conclusion and behavior.

So it certainly can't cause any harm to scratch a copyright symbol on your art when you're done with it, but it's more to remind *the public* than to protect *you*. You're already protected by law. Adding the copyright symbol to your work is like putting one of those security system signs in your front yard. It won't stop a determined thief, but it can deter less committed offenders. Still, if you think it makes your front yard look cheap, you don't need it for protection. The system already protects you.

Placing a copyright notice in digital content

Video 9.6 *Digital Tools for Tracking Copyright*

The beauty of digital files is that they have the ability to contain hidden information that never compromises the enjoyment of the document itself. As a result, you can add copyright information to digital content without having a visually distracting copyright notice on the artwork (**Figure 9.2**). You do this by adding information called metadata into your digital files.

Metadata is information that doesn't show up on the document itself but is hidden inside the file. This is a perfect way to store copyright information, contact details, and so on. On some digital cameras, metadata can record the lens information, the location via GPS, whether a flash was attached and fired, the camera settings, and more. In digital files, metadata can share the computer on which it was created, the time, and even the name of the creator. (This is how good technology teachers catch cheaters.) Be sure to make use of metadata when you're sending your work out over the web, and always check files that your clients give you to make sure that you're not violating another producer's means of making money when you're trying to make some yourself.

Figure 9.2 You don't need the mark or any sort of label, but it does make sure others know your work is copyrighted.

"But I'm not trying to make any money with their art, so it's okay, right?" Well, that's a tough question with a few interesting rules attached.

Playing fair with copyrighted material

Video 9.7 *Fair Use and Copyright*

Can you use copyrighted material when you're practicing with Adobe Premiere Pro? Can you make a montage of clips from your favorite movie that you downloaded from YouTube as you're trying out new techniques Premiere Pro? Could you include those clips in a video in which you reviewed the movie? Could you re-imagine a scene from that movie or imitate its visual style in a parody or homage?

These uses of copyrighted material are completely legit. The people who came up with our copyright laws were careful to make sure that the laws don't limit—but instead promote—creativity. They did this with a set of ideas called fair use.

Fair use policy is a set of rules that make sure copyright protection doesn't come at the cost of creativity and freedom. Copyright can't be used to limit someone's personal growth or learning, freedom of speech, or artistic expression and creative exploration. Those ideas are more important than copyright, so copyright doesn't apply when it gets in the way of these higher ideals. You're free to use copyrighted materials in the pursuit of these higher goals. Some people (mistakenly) believe that fair use doesn't apply to copyrighted materials, but in fact, it applies only to copyrighted materials. Here is a list of issues that a court would consider when making a decision about fair use:

- **Purpose: If you use the work to teach, learn, voice your own opinion, inspire you to create a new piece of art, or report news, you're probably safe.** Protected reasons include educational purposes (teaching, research), freedom of speech (commentary or criticism), news reporting, and transformative work (parody or using the work in a new way). It isn't considered fair use if you're making money from the use, using it just for entertainment, or trying to pass it off as your own work.

- **Nature:** If the nature of the original work is factual, published information, or the work was critical to favoring education, you're probably safe. Was the content already published, fact based, and important for society to know? Then you're pretty safe to use the work. But if it was unpublished, creative (such as art, music, film, novels), and fictional, you're probably not cleared to use it.

- **Amount: If you use a small amount of a copyrighted work, it's more likely that your use of the work is fair use.** If you use only a small quantity—not the main idea or focus of the work, but just enough to teach or learn from— you're probably safe. If you use a large portion of the work or basically rip off the central idea or the "heart of the work," it isn't fair use.

- **Effect: If nobody is harmed because of the action you've taken, then your action is probably fair use.** If you use a legitimate copy of the original work, it doesn't affect the sale of another copy, and you have no other way to get a copy, you're in pretty good shape. But if your copy makes it less likely that someone would buy a copy or you made a large number of copies, you're probably hurting the original creator, and that's not fair use.

As mentioned earlier, copyright law addresses a simple question: "How can we promote more freedom and creativity in the world?" This is the question that copyright laws seek to answer. Fair use makes sure that beginning artists can experiment using anything they want. Just be sure not to share anything that might be another artist's copyrighted work.

But as a beginning video producer/editor, how can you get good-quality assets to use in real-world projects? Happily, you have access to more free resources than ever before in history via the Internet and free stock photo and footage sites. We'll look at some in the next section.

Uncopyrighting

▶ **Video 9.8**
*Licensing Strict
and Free*

You have a couple of ways in which to undo copyright. One is voluntary. An author can choose to release the copyright to her material. Believe it or not, this can be more difficult to do than you'd expect. Copyright law protects creators of their works, and it can be difficult to *not* be protected by copyright law.

The second way is to let the copyright expire. Copyrights normally expire between 50 and 100 years after the death of the original author, but exceptions to this rule and extensions can be requested. It's beyond the scope of this book to discuss copyright at length, but it's important to realize that some materials have expired copyrights. When copyright is expired or released, the work is said to be in the public domain. This means that copyright no longer applies to the content, and you can use the material without worrying about copyright infringement.

Licensing

Licensing is another way that you can legally use copyrighted material. For designers and artists, licensing is fairly common because it allows us to use copyrighted material for a certain time and in a certain way by paying a fee established by the copyright holder according to the use of the material.

Stock photos are popular items licensed by all sorts of designers, and you can find them from many sources at various prices. In fact, Adobe Stock is integrated into Premiere Pro itself. Stock photos are images for which the author retains copyright but you can purchase a license to use these images in your designs. For almost everyone, this is a much less expensive solution than hiring a photographer to go to a location and shoot, process, and sell you the rights to an image.

CREATIVE COMMONS

In the last decade or so, a lot of exploration has been done in finding alternative ways to license creative works. Creative Commons licensing (**Figure 9.3**) is built on copyright law but offers ways that artists can release their works for limited use and still choose the way the works are used and shared.

Creative Commons licenses include many different combinations of the following attributes, so you'll need to do some research when using Creative Commons–licensed materials and when releasing assets with Creative Commons licensing.

- Public Domain (CC0) licenses allow artists to release their works to the public domain. It's a bit difficult to give your materials away to the public domain, but CC0 is generally recognized as a way to do so and is respected in most parts of the world.

- Attribution (BY) requires that you credit the original author when using her work. You can do whatever you want with the work as long as you give that credit.

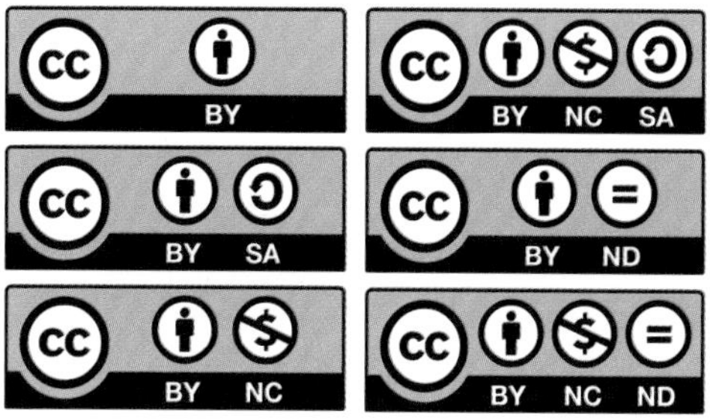

Figure 9.3 Creative Commons licenses allow for a variety of easy-to-understand licensing options.

- ShareAlike (SA) allows you to use the item in anything you want as long as your creation is shared under the same license as the original work.

- NoDerivs (ND) requires that you not change the material when you incorporate it into your own work. You can use NoDerivs material freely, but you must pass it along without changing it.

- NonCommercial (NC) means that people can use your work in their own creative works as long as they don't charge for it. You're getting it for free, so if you want to use it, then you have to be generous and also give away your work for free.

Creative Commons licenses are widely accepted and used, and you can find a ton of amazing resources that use this licensing. If you have any questions about Creative Commons licenses, you can find out everything from a general overview to detailed legal descriptions at *www.creativecommons.org*.

PEOPLE PERMISSIONS

Because many assets we use in interactive media projects include photographs and video, we need to talk about extra permissions such as model releases. This type of release is required when a person's face is identifiable in the footage and the video will be used to promote something, whether it's a product or an idea. Any work you do for a client is by definition a commercial use and will require a model release for every identifiable face.

Think Like a Boss

Some might say that the only thing you need to know to succeed in life is how to solve a problem. That's not how to solve a specific problem; that would be only an exercise in memory. A well-trained monkey can mimic a person's actions and get a similar result. But a monkey can't think with the depth of a human. My preferred way to solve problems is to work to understand things deeply and explore all the nuances of a potential solution. But for others, this process is a little outside their comfort zones and they find it faster and easier to copy someone else's solution.

In Premiere Pro, copying another solution or technique means following tutorials. In entry-level jobs, it's being a dutiful employee, efficient worker, and good follower who shows up on time.

But what do you do when you're the leader? What happens when you need to do something new and fresh for your job? What if the boss doesn't know how to do it and that's why she hired you? At times, your client's main request will be something as vague and daunting as "Do something that hasn't been done before."

That's where the problem-solving process comes in—the only skill you need to be successful. If you can do that, you can figure out anything.

 ★ *ACA Objective 1.3*

▶ *Video 9.9* Project Management Intro

Project management

Project management is really just the problem-solving process in action—geared toward supervising resources, people, and team-based projects. The DNA of project management is problem solving and organizing the process so that you tackle the right issues at the right time using the right tools. Project-management systems take on a million forms (as do problem-solving systems), but if you truly grasp the ideas behind the labels, you can translate them into whatever management strategy your client, team, or boss is using.

The problem-solving process is creative in itself. A good solution to a problem can be artistic in its elegance and efficient grace. If you can grasp problem solving, you can learn whatever you need to learn now and in the future.

The following procedure will help when you need to solve a technical problem on hardware or equipment, handle an editing issue within your Premiere Pro project, or figure out how to get your hand out of that jar you got it stuck in. It will help you translate a tutorial written for Premiere Pro CS6 into your current version (things change fast these days!). And it boils down to three simple steps: learn, think, and do.

Learn

The first step of a problem-solving process is to learn. It includes two important steps: learning what the problem is and learning how others have solved similar problems (research and investigate). It seems simple, but the process can be confusing. Most projects with major problems get stuck at this initial step because they didn't learn well—or at all. Let's talk about them.

▶ **Video 9.10** *Project Management— Understand the Problem*

UNDERSTAND THE PROBLEM

As we discussed earlier in this chapter, the first step of every project is to understand the problem. For most design projects, you must figure out how to most effectively help your client share their goals with the target audience. If the client is yourself, then it's about getting to the essence of what you want to communicate and communicating it so that your target audience can act on it.

Understanding the problem is the most difficult part of the problem-solving process. Mess it up here, and by definition, you're not solving the problem. You haven't properly identified the problem, so how can you solve it? Sometimes you can make the problem worse by implementing a plan that creates a new problem without solving the real one.

You can avoid trouble down the road by clearly understanding and defining the problem at the start. "I want to sell a million widgets" is not a problem you can solve; it's a desire the client has. So what's the problem you can help with? He hasn't sold as many as he wants? That's not it either. How do you get to the bottom of the problem?

Start with good questions: Do people need a widget? If so, do people know widgets are a thing? If so, do they choose a competing widget? If so, why do they choose this other widget? Why do you think they should use your widget instead? Who would be most likely to buy your widget? What is your budget for widget advertising? What do you want to spend on this particular project? What are your expectations?

Many clients become frustrated with this set of questions. They just want action to be taken so that they can feel like they're doing something. But let me repeat that old saying: "Aim at nothing, and you'll hit it every time." This is when you sharpen your axe so you don't have to chop at the tree all day.

This part of the project can be fairly informal on smaller projects but can be huge on large projects. Here's a list of critical questions to answer:

- **Purpose:** Why are you doing this editing project? What result would you consider a success?
- **Target:** Who needs this message or product? Describe your typical customer.
- **Limits:** What are the limits for the project? Budget and time are most necessary to nail down.
- **Preferences:** Aside from the results we've already discussed, are there any other results you'd like or expect from this project?
- **Platform:** Is the project targeting the web? A mobile device? A kiosk? DVD? Broadcast TV? What are the specifications of the particular device?

These examples are intended to show how quickly you can determine a client's expectations. The answers to these questions define the size of the job and how you'll best be able to work with the client.

Sketches and written notes from this initial step will help. Gather as much information as you can to make the rest of the project go smoothly. The more you find out now, the less you'll have to redesign later, because the client hates the color, the layout, or the general direction you took the project. Invest the time now, or pay it back with interest later. With a clear idea of what the problem is, you'll get the information you need to solve it in the next step.

RESEARCH AND INVESTIGATE

After you understand exactly what your client is expecting, you can start doing the research to arrive at the answers you need. Let's take a quick look at that word: *re-search*. It literally means "search again." Lots of people fail to research; they just search. They look at the most obvious places and approaches, and if things don't immediately click, they settle for a poor but quick and easy solution.

Depending on the job, researching can be a relatively quick process. Find out about the competitive products, learn about the problem you're trying to solve, and understand the demographic you're going to target. The more research you do, the better information you'll have about the problem you're trying to solve, which will help you with the next step.

Think

The next couple of steps represent the "thinking" phase. You can do this quickly using a pen and napkin, or you can do it in depth and generate tons of documentation along the way, particularly on large projects (**Figure 9.4**). But thinking is the part that most of us often mistake as the beginning. Remember that if the learning step isn't done well, your thinking step might be headed in the wrong direction.

▶ *Video 9.11* *Project Management— Think it Through*

Figure 9.4 As a producer and editor, you'll often do much of your thinking on paper, even if you're not producing traditional or formal storyboards. Sketch out your sequence first and have that reference to show the customer and to come back to for clarity.

BRAINSTORM

The next step is to brainstorm. As with research, you need to really grasp the meaning. It's a brain**storm**. Not a brain *drizzle*. A full-on typhoon of ideas. At this point, it's important to stop thinking analytically and start thinking creatively. If you start thinking critically instead of creatively, you'll change direction and you'll lose ground on your brainstorming task. If you start moving in the critical direction, that's the opposite of creative. Stop that! Don't try to work hard on brainstorming. Work relaxed instead.

At times, analysis will need to happen. You start analyzing how to complete your ideas when you should be creating them. Here are some things *not* to do when brainstorming and directions that trigger the critical mode of thinking:

- Judging your ideas
- Trying to finish an idea when you should still be brainstorming

- Getting stuck on a particular idea
- Planning out the project
- Thinking about how much time you have
- Thinking about the budget
- Thinking about numbers
- Grouping or sorting your ideas
- Developing the idea that you think is best.

Here are things you should be doing to get into creative mode:

- Listen to music.
- Look at cool clips on YouTube or Vimeo.
- Call a friend.
- Doodle on something.
- Read a poem.
- Take a break.
- Go for a walk.
- Watch a movie.
- Write a haiku. Meditate for five minutes.
- Exercise.
- Sleep on it.

When you're in brainstorming mode, don't edit your ideas. Let them flow. If a crummy idea pops into your head, put it on paper. If you don't, it will keep popping up until it's been given a little respect. Give the weak ideas respect; they open doors for the great ones. Brainstorming is a matter of creating ideas.

PICK AND PLAN

▶ *Video 9.12* Project Management— Get it in Writing

After brainstorming, you need to pick a solution that you generated in your brainstorming session and plan things out. You'll find that the plan you go with is rarely your first idea. Through the process of brainstorming, the idea will go through several iterations. A common mistake for beginners is to fall in love with an early idea—beware of this pitfall! Your best idea is lurking in the background of your mind, and you have to get rid of all the simple ideas that pop up first. For a small project or a one-person team, you might quickly hammer out a contract and get to work, but in larger projects, the planning needs to be detailed and focused.

The larger the project, the more formal this process will be. Small projects with just one person working on it will have little planning necessary for moving forward. However, larger projects will need a project plan to set the project requirements for the team.

SETTING PROJECT REQUIREMENTS

★ ACA Objective 2.2

This is where the action happens. Look through the ideas you've generated and pick the one that seems best and plan how to make it happen. This is where you determine exactly what has to be done, establish some direction, and identify a clear target. This planning stage (which most creative types naturally tend to resist, myself included) is where you clarify what needs to be done; it establishes your direction and identifies a clear target. We resist it because it seems to limit us. It ropes in our creative freedom, and it gives us a checklist—all things that many creatives hate. These things are creative kryptonite—or at least we *think* they are. But let's consider this for a moment.

If you don't perform this admittedly tedious step, what won't you have? You won't have a definition of what needs to be done, a direction to head in, or a target to hit. Everyone will be in the dark. Although this step doesn't seem creative in itself, creativity isn't the priority at this particular juncture. You're at a journey-versus-destination moment. Creativity without limits is a journey, which is great for your own work, but a disaster for a client-driven job. A client-driven project requires clearly defined goals—a destination. You need to arrive somewhere specific.

Two critical points that must be a part of every project plan are the project scope and project deadline. Every contract needs to have these critical components defined to focus the project:

- Project scope is the amount of work to be done. On the editor's side, this is the most important thing to establish. If the scope isn't clear, you're subject to the Achilles heel of editing and production work: project creep. This is a pervasive problem in our industry (you'll learn more later in this chapter), but simply writing down a defined scope can prevent the problem. Get in writing *exactly* what you need to do and make sure specific numbers are attached.

- Project deadlines dictate when the work needs to be done. This is the client's most important element. The deadline often affects the price. If the client needs ten animated banner ads in six months, you can probably offer a discount. If they need a draft by tomorrow morning, then they'll have to pay an additional "rush" fee. Deadlines on large projects also can be broken down into phases, each with its own fee. This division of tasks helps you pay the bills by generating cash flow during a large and lengthy project. It also limits the impact—for you—of payment delay.

I strongly encourage you to include the following additional items in your interactive media project plans. These items, when shared and discussed with your client, will save time, money, and disagreements. These additional deliverables are the raw materials of project planning and help convey the exact target of the project. The following two deliverables are critical for every production project:

- Storyboards are helpful to show the client how your project and edit will flow. It's even better when the client has an idea of what they're looking for and can give you their own storyboard, however crude. Does this limit your creative freedom? Yes, and it also saves you a ton of time. The goal of a client job is to get a project done to their satisfaction. If they're very particular and know what they want, you're not going to convince them otherwise. Sketches save time because they limit your direction to one that the client will accept, and they help you get to that acceptance faster. That means you get finished and paid sooner. The better the storyboards are before you get into actual editing, the fewer changes and revisions you'll need. You don't have to be a master sketch artist; just convey the idea. Sometimes sketches may just be wireframes—very rough representative sketches of how to lay out the project—especially in regard to interactive media projects.

- Specifications, or specs, are detailed, clear written goals and limits for a project. Many times, the specifications themselves will be referred to as the "project plan" and become part of the contract. This will involve the target platform and feature set of the interactive project. All project plans should include two critical pieces of information: the scope of the project and the deadlines that need to be met. Be sure to always include both of these items in your project specifications.

AVOIDING PROJECT CREEP

▶ **Video 9.13** *Project Management— Avoiding Creep*

Project creep occurs when a project starts to lose its focus and spin out of control, eating up more and more time and effort. It is important to be aware of this phenomenon. It happens all the time, and the main culprit in every case is a poorly designed project plan that lacks clear specifications and deadlines.

Here's how it happens: Joe Client creates a product and wants to sell it. He comes to you for marketing materials. You determine that he wants a series of promo clips for his website. You've settled on a price of $4,500 and you've got a month to get it done. You go to work.

Then Joe realizes that he also wants some images for social media. Could you just make a few? He also realizes that he needs a 10-second pre-roll to run before a company webinar. Oh, and he can't figure out how to post the videos to his favorite online marketplace. Could you just help him set that up? What about if we created some media for a mobile app as well? That would be pretty simple, right? Then he changes his launch date—he doesn't need it next month—he needs it next week because he just reserved a booth at a large convention. By the way, do you know anything about HDMI transmitters and setting up video loops? Would you be available to troubleshoot the setup if the client needs you during the convention?

This is why it's critical to create a detailed project plan with task definitions and deadlines attached. Sometimes the client asks for something and it takes you 30 seconds. It's a good idea to always happily deliver on these little items. A favor is any job that takes you five minutes or less. After that, the favor turns into work. And your only defense is your contract defining a clearly stated scope.

Just make sure that the project's scope is clearly stated. If the contract says that you'll provide *any* images for the company's web presence, you're in trouble. If it says that you'll specifically provide three 30-second clips for the client's website, you're in great shape. Taking the hour it requires to specify your project and its deadlines in detail will save you from many hours of work and contract revisions.

If the client has approved your project parameters and then asks for something different, you need to charge them for the change if it's going to take more than 5 to 10 minutes. Sticking to this policy helps the client think about changes before sending them to you. If you fail to charge when addressing impromptu changes, the client has no reason to think about the requests in advance. Charging your customer for additional changes focuses them on what they really want.

Of course, if the client asks for something that makes the job easier and faster, then make the change and do it for free. The bottom line is this: Establish goodwill whenever it's good for both you and your client. But when an 11th-hour alteration serves only one side of the relationship, the requesting side has to pay for the service. This arrangement ensures that everyone ends up winning.

Do

▶ **Video 9.14** *Project Management— Make It So*

The last phase of the project plan is to knock it out! This is the "two snaps and a twist" phase because it generally happens quickly when you have a good plan—unless there's a hitch. But at this point, on most design projects you're pretty much wrapping things up.

BUILD IT

This step is obvious: Make it happen. This phase is where most people think all the action is…but honestly, if you've done the prior steps well, this can be the fastest part of the process. You already know what to do—now just do it. The design decisions and feature specifications have been made and you can get to work. Of course, when doing this step, it's best to regularly refer to the specifications and keep the client informed. The best way to do so is to have a feedback loop in place.

FEEDBACK LOOP

★ *ACA Objective 1.4*

A feedback loop is a system set up to constantly encourage and require input and approvals on the project direction. Keeping your client informed is the best way to speed through the process. For an interactive media project, iterative work establishes effective guideposts to send to the client for review and input. Iterative work is work you're sharing as it's done. Doing so performs a couple of critical functions. First, it lets the client see that work's being done and helps reassure them that the process has momentum. Second, it lets the client chime in on anything that they don't like while it's still easy to make a change.

Establishing this open communication channel encourages and enforces a healthy exchange of opinions and can enable you to most efficiently adjust and fine-tune your project to suit your client.

TEST AND EVALUATE

This very last step can also be fast if you've had a good feedback loop in place. For Premiere Pro projects, it's essentially checking the work against your project plan and making sure that you met all the specifications to satisfy you and your client. If not, you should essentially start the problem-solving process again to understand the current problem. Find out exactly what the client believes doesn't meet the requirements.

Assuming a good project plan with storyboards and a good feedback loop, the test-and-evaluation phase should require only minor tweaks—no different from any other iterative work resolution. If you don't have a good feedback loop and the first time the client sees your work is upon delivery, that client could become unhappy and demand innumerable changes. Avoid this migraine headache with an effective and well-defined feedback loop as part of your plan. Those two tools are your weapons against project creep and unreasonable clients.

WORKING FOR "THE MAN"

Many video editors begin their careers working at larger firms, which can be a much easier way to get started than freelancing with your own business. If you're exclusively an artist, this type of job may require you only to do the tasks you're best at doing. In a large firm, someone else does the sales, manages client relationships and projects, and creates technical specifications.

As an artist at a larger firm, you're responsible only for working with footage and editing it. Everything else is handled by someone else, which is a good trade-off for artists who don't like the detail-oriented checklist work of project management and bookkeeping.

Working within an experienced company can also be an amazing education. You can develop your strengths, learn about the industry, and slowly increase your involvement in the other aspects of this career beyond Premiere Pro proficiency.

Video 9.15 The advantages of working at a firm

Conclusion

Much of this chapter digressed from the hands-on Premiere Pro work that similar books cover. But starting their careers without the information presented in this chapter can pose a problem for many beginning artists. You need to master a lot of industry information, creative knowledge, and business skills to be successful. We're stoked that you read this far. Many of us creative people have a hard time with the business side of the career, but it's best to understand these ideas and concepts now before a lack of understanding becomes a problem. The tips and techniques that you've read in this chapter will eliminate a lot of the inherent frustration in the complexity of working with and for other people.

Premiere Pro is an intensely creative and varied application that tends to attract adventurous individuals. The qualities that make us great at thinking outside the box and editing exciting videos are the same qualities that may make us less skilled at the organized detail work of business and client management.

Video 9.16 Wrapping Up Project Planning

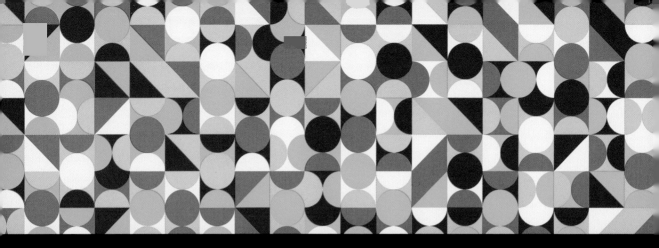

CHAPTER OBJECTIVES

Chapter Learning Objectives

- Extend Premiere Pro with Adobe Creative Cloud desktop apps.
- Extend Premiere Pro with Adobe Creative Cloud mobile apps.
- Identify useful web resources for Premiere Pro.

CHAPTER 10

Wrapping It Up!

You've almost made it to the end of this book—and by now you should be pretty good at using Adobe Premiere Pro CC to create video sequences targeting a variety of specifications and formats. As you've seen through the projects we've worked on, you can use Premiere Pro to create a diverse array of project types.

Premiere Pro is part of a larger family of applications and services that support it, so before we close, let's tie things up with a look at that big picture, including some resources that you can use to continue exploring Premiere Pro on your own.

Extending Premiere Pro CC with Adobe Creative Cloud

One of the first things you learned in this book is that video production is often a team effort. Although some small productions can be achieved by a single person, when quality is a priority, it quickly becomes necessary to work with specialists who have a deeper knowledge of specific disciplines such as audio recording and editing, still graphics, titles, and color grading.

That kind of deep specialization also extends to the software you use. Even if you can work on a project by yourself, you may find that some phases of production can benefit from more specialized software. Adobe has a strong lineup of desktop applications that can handle many aspects of video production, and Adobe mobile applications are becoming increasingly useful as well. If you have a full subscription to Adobe Creative Cloud (not a Premiere Pro–only subscription), it's a good idea to be aware of these resources because all of them are already included with your subscription. You can install most of the applications in this chapter directly from the Adobe Creative Cloud desktop application, and you can find out more about them at the Adobe Creative Cloud applications page (www.adobe.com/creativecloud/catalog/desktop.html).

Video production applications

Many Adobe Creative Cloud desktop applications support various aspects of video production. You may not need them all the time, but when you do, it's good to know that they're immediately accessible.

WRITING AND PLANNING WITH ADOBE STORY PLUS

Adobe Story Plus is a great tool for writing the script for your production, and it automatically helps your script conform to standard scriptwriting formats. It's also a planning tool that you or your production team can use to collaborate on developing scenes, characters, actors, props, and other preproduction details. From that production data, Story Plus can generate production reports and schedules.

You can import Story scripts into Premiere Pro, where the scripts become part of clip metadata and can be searched. You can use the script metadata to guide the assembly of those clips into your rough cut.

STREAMLINING CLIP LOGGING AND ROUGH CUTS WITH ADOBE PRELUDE

Adobe Prelude can simplify metadata entry, logging, and rough cut creation. It can be a useful tool for producers or directors who want to perform preproduction tasks before handing off clips for editing in Premiere Pro.

Do you remember how the Export Media dialog box lets you enter metadata such as keywords and rights information for the video you're exporting? Metadata can be even more useful when you enter it as you log video clips in preproduction. Many productions like to enter clip metadata such as scene numbers, actors, and notes, and Prelude is a simple way to do this. If you used Adobe Story Plus to organize your production, the metadata you entered there can flow through to Prelude and then into Premiere Pro. You can also use Prelude to associate parts of an Adobe Story script to clips you captured.

You can even do your rough cut in Prelude. When you're ready to refine your rough cut, you can send it directly to Premiere Pro, where you can continue editing it using the full range of editing tools in Premiere Pro.

EDITING AND MIXING AUDIO WITH ADOBE AUDITION

In Chapter 4 you briefly used Adobe Audition to edit an audio clip in a Premiere Pro sequence. You can turn to Audition to fix audio problems that are too challenging for Premiere Pro. For example, you can use Audition to clean up audio by removing noise and unwanted sounds such as pops. Doing so is easy because of the integration between Audition and Premiere Pro. You can jump to Audition from an audio clip selected in a Premiere Pro sequence, edit it, and return to Premiere Pro with the edited clip in place—without having to manually export or import files.

You can also use Audition for mixing video soundtracks using audio tools that are more powerful and versatile than those available in Premiere Pro.

COLOR-GRADING CLIPS WITH ADOBE SPEEDGRADE

Premiere Pro has a capable set of tools for color correction and grading. Colorists and other color grading specialists are accustomed to color analysis and correction tools that are even more powerful, and that level is available in Adobe SpeedGrade. In SpeedGrade you have a great deal of control over color across specific color ranges and tonal ranges. You can apply color settings that emulate film stocks. You can create color palettes, or *Looks*, that can be used in other applications such as Premiere Pro. You can also use SpeedGrade to more easily match the color and contrast of two clips.

Like Audition, SpeedGrade is directly linked to Premiere Pro, so it's easy to take clips in Premiere Pro to SpeedGrade and back.

CREATING HOLLYWOOD-STYLE SPECIAL EFFECTS WITH ADOBE AFTER EFFECTS

You learned how to make clips move, rotate, and scale adjust by using keyframes to animate settings such as Position, Rotation, and Scale in the Effect Controls panel in Premiere Pro. And you learned how to composite clips on different tracks using masks. But some productions require special effects at a level of detail and quality that's beyond what Premiere Pro can achieve, and when you need that, you can call on Adobe After Effects.

With After Effects you can produce cinematic visual effects. You have more precise, powerful, and flexible control over features such as masking and keyframes than in Premiere Pro, and you can also create animations and special effects in 2D and 3D. After Effects has features such as motion tracking (tying the animation of one layer to the motion of another) and rotoscoping (automatically tracking changes in a mask from frame to frame). These features make it easy to place actors in virtual sets or create animated fly-through logos. If you want to create the next great science fiction epic, After Effects will probably be a big part of your workflow.

Of course, the sophisticated effects shots you put together in After Effects can be imported into Premiere Pro and edited with other clips. Like SpeedGrade and Audition, After Effects and Premiere Pro can exchange data directly so you don't have to export and import files.

CREATING OUTPUT EFFICIENTLY WITH ADOBE MEDIA ENCODER

In this book you've seen how Adobe Media Encoder can increase your productivity. By sending final video from Premiere Pro to Media Encoder for rendering in the background, you free up Premiere Pro so you can continue working on another sequence. You don't have to stand by Premiere Pro watching for a job to finish just so you can manually start another one, because you can simply add multiple items to the Media Encoder queue and have it render each job in turn, unattended, until all of them are done. And if you need to create versions of the same sequence for different output formats, just duplicate it in Media Encoder and apply different export presets. After you start the queue, you can get some sleep or go out while it renders all the export jobs for you.

FINDING, ORGANIZING, AND INSPECTING MEDIA WITH ADOBE BRIDGE

While you can browse and inspect information about media using the Project panel and Media Browser panel in Premiere Pro, Adobe Bridge is also a great standalone tool for media browsing and organization, especially for files not yet imported into Premiere Pro and in file formats used by Adobe Creative Cloud applications. You can use Bridge to preview video files and view their specifications and metadata without having to open them.

In Bridge you can use powerful searching and filtering to find files quickly. For example, you can have Bridge show you all the files within a folder and its subfolders, and then you can use a filter to show you only the video files. Then you can drag those video files directly to the Project panel in Premiere Pro, because drag-and-drop importing works just as well from Bridge as from the folders on your desktop.

Bridge is also a convenient way to view add metadata for many file types. For example, you can select hundreds of still images and apply ownership information and keywords to all of the selected images at once. In short, you can think of Bridge as a more powerful version of your desktop, optimized for Creative Cloud applications.

OPTIMIZING STUDIO WORKFLOWS WITH ADOBE ANYWHERE

If you work with a group of people at a busy video production studio, whether independent or part of a larger organization such as a corporation or a television station, you might face challenges coordinating the flow of video, video metadata, and other files among members of your team in the office and remotely.

Adobe Anywhere is made for those kinds of enterprises. It isn't something a home user or one-person studio would use; a professional system integrator installs Adobe Anywhere on a server, where the video is also stored. Adobe Anywhere then lets members of a workgroup edit that video from their desks over the network instead of having to carry storage drives from person to person. It also has features such as version control that help the team know where specific files are in the production workflow and who is currently using them. In this way, Adobe Anywhere helps team members work more efficiently by reducing the amount of file transfer and file management they have to do.

Graphics applications

In this book you've imported photographic still images and other graphics into video sequences. Those types of media are typically prepared in two other important Adobe Creative Cloud applications.

EDITING PHOTOGRAPHS WITH ADOBE PHOTOSHOP

If there's any application in this chapter that you might have heard of, it's probably Adobe Photoshop, the standard for digital photographic editing and image processing for many years. When you have photographs that need to be adjusted, cleaned up, or composited before being imported into Premiere Pro, Photoshop is the tool to use. Premiere Pro understands the layered Photoshop file format directly, as well as other image file formats such as JPEG that Photoshop can also save and export.

Although many photographers shoot in a camera's raw file format, Premiere Pro doesn't read camera raw files directly. Photoshop includes the Adobe Camera Raw plug-in, which you can use along with Photoshop to adjust camera raw format files and save them in an image format that Premiere Pro can import.

CREATING SMOOTH LINE ART WITH ADOBE ILLUSTRATOR

A video production can also use non-photographic art and graphics, such as logos, charts, diagrams, and maps. These types of graphics are often created in a drawing program such as Adobe Illustrator. Whereas Photoshop creates *bitmap graphics*, or pictures made of a grid of pixels, with Illustrator you can create *vector graphics*, or pictures defined by points and paths. Remember when you drew a mask in Chapter 5? When you laid down points to define path segments, you were creating vector paths as you would in Illustrator.

For Premiere Pro users, the big advantage of Illustrator vector graphics is that they scale smoothly to any size. When you enlarge a bitmap graphic such as a photograph, scaling above a certain percentage results in blocky images and jagged-edged shapes because the pixels are too large. Vector graphics enlarge smoothly because the points and paths that define the shapes are recalculated at the current resolution. Because of that, the shapes always use all of the available frame pixels, so they always have a smooth edge.

Mobile apps

Smartphones and tablets continue to become more powerful as their cameras continue to get better, with some capable of recording 4K video. That combination makes video editing easier to achieve on a mobile device. Adobe has mobile apps that help you do that, and they can link up to Premiere Pro. Even if you're not interested in actually editing video on a mobile device, Adobe also has mobile apps that can support a production in other ways.

- **Adobe Premiere Clip** lets you edit video on a mobile device. You can create a video from media on your device, sync it to music, add titles, and apply slow motion and other effects. You can send a Clip project directly to Premiere Pro for further editing.

- **Adobe Capture** can sample multiple types of media and send them directly to Adobe applications. For video editing, Capture can sample colors from a mobile device's camera and create a Look (like the ones that can be created with SpeedGrade) that can be applied to clips in Premiere Pro to create a mood or visual style. You can also use Capture to convert a photo into a vector graphic that you can use in Premiere Pro.

- **Adobe Story** is the mobile version of the Adobe Story application you read about earlier in this chapter. The mobile apps lets you read and review Story scripts; you can add comments to a script and send it back.

- **Creative Cloud Libraries** are cloud-based storage of graphics and other assets that automatically sync among Creative Cloud desktop and mobile applications. For example, if you capture a Look with Capture, it's stored in your Creative Cloud Library.

  In Premiere Pro you'll find a Creative Cloud Libraries panel. Media assets you've added to Creative Cloud Libraries, such as a Look you created with the Adobe Capture app, appear in that panel so that you can instantly use them in a Premiere Pro project. If you need stock images or other media for your Premiere Pro projects, the Creative Cloud Libraries panel also has a Search Adobe Stock button that takes you directly to that service.

- **Prelude Live Logger** is an app that lets you use an iPad to log clips as they're being recorded with a tapeless camera. The metadata you log can be transferred to the Adobe Prelude desktop application, which can combine the metadata with their clips and then send them on to Premiere Pro for editing.

You can find out more about these apps at the Adobe Creative Cloud mobile apps page (www.adobe.com/creativecloud/catalog/mobile.html).

Most Adobe mobile apps are currently available on iOS, and some are available on Android. Check the system requirements for each app.

Where to Go Next

Adobe has several web-based resources that are designed to serve the Premiere Pro community, including the following:

- **Premiere Pro CC product page** (*www.adobe.com/products/premiere.html*): This is the main page for Premiere Pro, with links to product information, tutorials, and help resources.

- **Learn Premiere Pro CC** (*helpx.adobe.com/premiere-pro/tutorials.html*): Learn more about Premiere Pro by watching video demonstrations of features and techniques. This is also a great way to catch up when new features are added.

- **Main Premiere Pro CC support page** (*helpx.adobe.com/premiere-pro.html*): This page gathers links to a range of support resources on one page, including tutorials, articles, videos, common questions and top issues, community forums, and customer support contact information.

- **Premiere Pro CC help** (*helpx.adobe.com/premiere-pro/topics.html*): Browse or search the online user guide for Premiere Pro for descriptions of tools, commands, effects, and other features.

- **Premiere Pro CC community** (*forums.adobe.com/community/premiere*): Ask questions about Premiere Pro at Adobe Communities, where questions are answered by other community members.

- **Premiere Pro CC blog** (*blogs.adobe.com/premierepro*): As a Creative Cloud application, Premiere Pro may be updated with new features at any time. Posts on the Premiere Pro blog can keep you informed about changes and new features when you see a Premiere Pro update in the Creative Cloud desktop application. You may also see posts about previews of upcoming technologies and other developments you may want to be aware of.

Goodbye!

Congratulations! You've completed all the chapters in this book, and in this chapter you have explored some of the other creative capabilities and resources available to you in Adobe Creative Cloud. Keep practicing with your own projects so that the basics of editing become second nature. Use the resources in this chapter to continue exploring Premiere Pro CC, as you discover your working style and creative voice in video.

ACA Objectives Covered

DOMAIN OBJECTIVES	CHAPTER	VIDEO
DOMAIN 1.0 Setting Project Requirements		
1.1 Identify the purpose, audience, and audience needs for editing video.	**Ch 2** Identifying Job Requirements, 33 **Ch 3** Preproduction, 69 **Ch 4** Preproduction, 93 **Ch 5** Preproduction, 111 **Ch 6** Preproduction, 131 **Ch 9** Who You're Talking For and Who You're Talking To, 206	**2.1** Project Planning **3.1** New project Snowboarding highlight video **4.1** Introducing the activity bus video project **5.1** Introducing the weather report project **6.1** Introducing the memorial slideshow project **9.1** Discovering Client Goals
1.2 Summarize how digital video professionals make decisions about the type of content to include in a project, including considerations such as copyright, audience needs, permissions, and licensing.	**Ch 2** Identifying Job Requirements, 33 **Ch 3** Preproduction, 69 **Ch 4** Preproduction, 93 **Ch 5** Preproduction, 111 **Ch 9** Identifying your client's ideal customer, 208 **Ch 9** Copyrights and Wrongs, 210	**2.1** Project Planning **3.1** New project Snowboarding highlight video **4.1** Introducing the activity bus video project **5.1** Introducing the weather report project **9.3** Finding the Target Audience **9.5** About copyright
1.3 Demonstrate knowledge of project management tasks and responsibilities.	**Ch 2** Identifying Job Requirements, 33 **Ch 9** Project management, 216	**2.1** Project Planning **9.9** Project Management Intro **9.10** Project Management—Understand the Problem
1.4 Communicate with others (such as peers and clients) about editing plans.	**Ch 2** Identifying Job Requirements, 33 **Ch 6** Preproduction, 131 **Ch 9** Feedback Loop, 224	**2.1** Project Planning **6.1** Introducing the memorial slideshow project **9.14** Project Management—Make It So
DOMAIN 2.0 Understanding Digital Video		
2.1 Understand key terminology related to digital video.	**Ch 2** Editing in the Timeline panel, 47	**2.9** Fine tune the edit
2.2 Demonstrate knowledge of basic principles and best practices employed in the digital video industry.	**Ch 8** The Elements of Art, 167 **Ch 9** Setting Project Requirements, 221	**8.4** Design School: The Elements of Art

continues on next page

continued from previous page

DOMAIN OBJECTIVES	CHAPTER	VIDEO
2.3 Demonstrate knowledge of how to use transitions and effects to enhance video content.	**Ch 5** Compositing a Green Screen Clip with a New Background, 115 **Ch 6** Creating a Sequence from Multiple Files Quickly, 133 **Ch 8** The element of type, 187	**5.4** Key weatherman over weathermap **8.12** Design School: The Element of Type
2.4 Demonstrate knowledge of how to use audio to enhance video content.	**Ch 3** Designing Sound, 86 **Ch 4** Fixing Audio in Adobe Audition, 98 **Ch 8** The element of color, 181	**3.11** Sound Design **4.4** Sweeten the audio **8.9** Design School: The Element of Color
2.5 Demonstrate knowledge of how to use still images and titles to enhance video content	**Ch 3** Nesting a Sequence and Freezing a Frame, 81 **Ch 3** Creating a Lower-Third Title, 83 **Ch 3** Creating Rolling Credits, 87 **Ch 4** Add a Still Image to the Sequence, 103 **Ch 6** Creating a Sequence from Multiple Files Quickly, 133	**3.9** Creating a nested sequence **3.10** Add a lower-third **3.12** Add rolling credits **4.7** Add a photo and title

DOMAIN 3.0 Understanding Adobe Premiere Pro CC

DOMAIN OBJECTIVES	CHAPTER	VIDEO
3.1 Identify elements of the Premiere Pro user interface, and demonstrate knowledge of their functions.	**Ch 1** Starting Premiere Pro, 11 **Ch 1** Setting Premiere Pro Preferences, 17 **Ch 1** Exploring the User Interface, 18 **Ch 2** Using the Project panel, 36 **Ch 2** Working with the Timeline panel, 46 **Ch 4** Add a Still Image to the Sequence, 103 **Ch 7** Working in the Timeline Panel, 148 **Ch 7** Navigating in the Timeline panel, 150 **Ch 7** Selecting and Moving Clips in the Timeline Panel, 152 **Ch 7** Trimming Clips, 153 **Ch 7** Editing Keyframes with the Pen Tool, 156 **Ch 7** Finding Shortcuts That Make You More Efficient, 157	**1.4** Start Premiere Pro **2.3** Explore the Project panel **2.3** Work in the Timeline **4.7** Add a photo and title **7.2** Manage sequences in the timeline **7.3** Navigate the timeline **7.4** Select, arrange, and trim your clips **7.4** Select, arrange, and trim your clips **7.5** Use the Slip and Slide tools **7.8** Use the Pen tool
3.2 Define the functions of commonly used tools, including the Selection, Track Selection, Ripple Edit, Rolling Edit, Rate Stretch, Pen, Razor, Slide, Slip, Hand, and Zoom tools.	**Ch 2** Editing in the Timeline panel, 47	**2.9** Fine tune the edit

DOMAIN OBJECTIVES	CHAPTER	VIDEO
3.3 Navigate, organize, and customize the workspace.	**Ch 1** Using Workspaces, 27	

DOMAIN 4.0 Editing Digital Video Using Adobe Premiere Pro		
4.1 Editing Digital Video Using Adobe Premiere Pro.	**Ch 1** Setting Up the New Project Dialog Box, 13 **Ch 4** Setting Up a Project, 94 **Ch 5** Setting Up a Project, 112 **Ch 6** Setting Up a Slide Show Project, 132 **Ch 7** Setting Up a Project, 147	**1.5** Set up preferences **5.2** Organize your project **6.2** Organize your project **7.1** Introducing final review
4.2 Import media and assets into a project.	**Ch 2** Importing media into a project, 35 **Ch 2** Setting Up a Project, 70 **Ch 4** Setting Up a Project, 94 **Ch 5** Setting Up a Project, 112 **Ch 5** Importing layered Photoshop documents, 112 **Ch 6** Setting Up a Slide Show Project, 132 **Ch 6** Creating a Sequence from Multiple Files Quickly, 133 **Ch 7** Setting Up a Project, 147	**2.2** Import your video files **3.2** Set up the project **4.2** Access and import your media **5.2** Organize your project **6.2** Organize your project **7.1** Introducing final review
4.3 Demonstrate knowledge of how to set up and navigate a sequence in Premiere Pro.	**Ch 2** Using the Project panel, 36 **Ch 2** Creating a sequence, 39 **Ch 2** Creating a rough cut, 41 **Ch 2** Working with the Timeline panel, 46 **Ch 4** Setting Up a Project, 94 **Ch 5** Setting Up a Project, 112 **Ch 6** Setting Up a Slide Show Project, 132 **Ch 7** Setting Up a Project, 147 **Ch 7** Navigating in the Timeline panel, 150	**2.4** Create a sequence **2.7** Create a rough cut **2.8** Work in the timeline **5.2** Organize your project **6.2** Organize your project **7.1** Introducing final review **7.3** Navigate the timeline
4.4 Organize and manage video clips in a sequence.	**Ch 2** Creating a rough cut, 41 **Ch 3** Adding B-Roll Clips, 76 **Ch 3** Creating a Lower-Third Title, 83 **Ch 4** Creating a Rough Cut, 95 **Ch 7** Working in the Timeline Panel, 148 **Ch 7** Selecting and Moving Clips in the Timeline Panel, 152	**2.7** Create a rough cut **3.6** Add B-roll **3.10** Add a lower-third **4.3** Edit in the timeline **7.2** Manage sequences in the timeline **7.4** Select, arrange, and trim your clips

continues on next page

continued from previous page

DOMAIN OBJECTIVES	CHAPTER	VIDEO
4.5 Trim clips.	**Ch 2** Editing in the Timeline panel, 47 **Ch 3** Editing the Rough Cut, 71 **Ch 4** Creating a Rough Cut, 95 **Ch 7** Trimming Clips, 153 **Ch 7** Splitting a Clip, 155	**2.9** Fine tune the edit **3.4** Trim your video in the timeline **4.3** Edit in the timeline **7.4** Select, arrange, and trim your clips **7.4** Use the Slip and Slide tools **7.7** Use the Razor tool
4.6 Manage sound in a video sequence.	**Ch 2** Recording a voiceover, 49 **Ch 2** Editing audio, 51 **Ch 3** Filling a Stereo Clip with a Mono Recording, 70 **Ch 3** Applying Audio Transitions, 75 **Ch 3** Designing Sound, 86 **Ch 4** Fixing Audio in Adobe Audition, 98	**2.10** Record a voiceover **2.11** Sweeten the audio **3.3** Work with audio **3.5** Add transitions between audio clips **3.11** Sound design **4.4** Sweeten the audio
4.7 Manage superimposed text and shapes in a video sequence.	**Ch 2** Creating and adding a title, 56 **Ch 2** Adding a title to a sequence, 59 **Ch 3** Creating Rolling Credits, 87	**2.13** Add titles **2.14** Create an overlay **3.12** Add rolling credits
4.8 Add and manage effects and transitions in a video sequence.	**Ch 2** Using video transitions and effects, 53 **Ch 3** Applying Audio Transitions, 75 **Ch 3** Changing the Playback Speed of a Clip, 78 **Ch 3** Varying Clip Playback Speed Over Time, 79 **Ch 3** Nesting a Sequence and Freezing a Frame, 81 **Ch 3** Stabilizing Shaky Clips, 88 **Ch 5** Compositing a Green Screen Clip with a New Background, 115 **Ch 6** Adding a Ken Burns motion effect, 138 **Ch 7** Changing Clip Speed and Duration, 155 **Ch 7** Editing Keyframes with the Pen Tool, 156	**2.12** Add transitions **3.5** Add transitions between audio clips **3.7** Adjust clip playback speed **3.8** Time remapping **3.9** Create a nested sequence **3.13** Stabilize your video **5.4** Key weatherman over weathermap **6.6** Add motion to your images **7.6** Use the Rate Stretch tool **7.8** Use the Pen tool
DOMAIN 5.0 Exporting Video with Adobe Premiere Pro		
5.1 Demonstrate knowledge of export options for video.	**Ch 2** Exporting a Sequence to a Video File, 61 **Ch 3** Exporting Final Video, 89 **Ch 4** Reviewing with Your Clients and Exporting the Final Video, 107 **Ch 6** Exporting Multiple Versions with Adobe Media Encoder, 140	**2.15** Clean up the timeline and export your project **3.14** Fine-tune and export your video **4.8** Preview and review **6.6** Export your slideshow

Index

SYMBOL

\ (backslash), using in Timeline
panel, 46

NUMBERS

3D lighting, elements of, 177–178

A

Add Edit command, 156
Add Marker control, 46
additive color, 182
adjustment layers, applying,
101–103
Adobe
Capture app, 186
Communities forum, 19, 234
mobile apps, 232–233
website, 14
Adobe Cloud desktop applications
After Effects, 229–230
Anywhere, 231
Audition, 98–99, 229
Bridge, 230–231
Media Encoder, 63–64, 140–143,
230
Prelude, 228, 233
Speedgrade, 229
Story Plus, 228
.ai extension, 85
alignment, principle of, 195
Alpha Channel setting, 118
Alt key. See keyboard shortcuts
analogous colors, 185
animated logo, adding, 120–122
Anytown High School client, 93
application window, resizing, 26
art elements
color, 181–187
diagram, 168
form, 177–178
framework, 166–167
line, 172–174
shape, 175–176
space, 169–171
texture and pattern, 179–180
type, 187–194
value, 180–181
Assembly workspace, 28
asymmetrical balance, 199–200

B

audio. See also MP3 audio file
adding to Timeline panel, 48
designing, 86
editing, 51–53
editing to repair silence, 97
editing separately from
video, 48
fixing in Adobe Audition, 98–99
preventing on main video
track, 77
audio levels, varying over time,
52–53
audio meters, 23, 71
audio track controls, 46, 49–50
audio transitions, applying, 75–76
audio waveform, looking at, 74
Audition Adobe Cloud desktop
application, 98–99, 229

background, blurring, 106–107
backletter fonts, 190
backslash (\), using in Timeline
panel, 46
Backspace/Delete, 74
balance, principle of, 195, 199–200
balance and proximity,
creating, 166
bins, displaying as hierarchy, 37
black bars, appearance in Export
Settings, 63
blog, accessing, 20, 234
Brain Buffet Media Productions,
18–21, 111, 121
brainstorming, 219
Bridge Adobe Cloud desktop
application, 230–231
B-roll clips, adding, 76–77.
See also clips
Burns, Ken, 138–139
bus image, applying Fast Blur
to, 106
bus time title, preparing, 104
buttons. See panel buttons

C

Capture mobile app, 232–233
Capture window, importing
with, 38
cast shadow in 3D lighting,
177–178

CC (Creative Cloud) Libraries, 16
Cinema mode, using to review
projects, 108
client's needs, understanding,
206–209
clip instances, renaming, 75
clip logging, streamlining, 228
Clip mobile app, 232–233
clip speed and duration,
changing, 155
clip volume, adjusting, 52–53
clips. See also B-roll clips
adding for rough cuts, 41
changing playback speeds,
78–81
creating video sequences
from, 44
deleting parts of, 72–74
dragging, 52
extracting still frames from, 44
going to beginning of, 151
logging and naming, 9
moving in time, 48, 152–153
In and Out points, 155
removing from timeline, 48
selecting in Timeline panel,
152–153
slicing, 156
splitting, 155–156
stabilizing, 88–90
trimming in Timeline panel,
47–48
white balancing using gray
target, 113–114
closing panels, 24
CMYK (cyan, magenta, yellow,
black) color, 182
collaboration
coordinating, 8–9
on teams, 3
color, element of, 168, 181–187
Color workspace, 28
color-grading clips with
Speedgrade, 229
column order, changing, 37
commands. See also keyboard
shortcuts
accessing, 136
Add Edit, 156
Frame Hold, 155
complementary colors, 185

compositing with green screen effects
  animating graphics, 120–126
  clip with background, 115–119
  exporting final video, 126–127
  preproduction, 111–112
  project setup, 112–114
Constant Gain transition, 75
Constant Power transition, 75
content, importing, 6
context menu, opening for clips, 158
contrast
  including in images, 166
  principle of, 195, 197
cool colors, 183
copyrights, 210–214
Creative Cloud Libraries mobile app, 233
Creative Commons licenses, 214–215
creativity, skill of, 162–163
Ctrl key. See keyboard shortcuts
curved segments, creating, 117

D

decorative fonts, 190
default transition, selecting, 135, 137–138
Delete key, 74
deleting parts of clips, 72–74
demographic, targeting for projects, 208–209
design hierarchy, applying, 164–167
design principles, 196–202
desktop, revealing, 26
dialogue scene
  exporting final video, 107–108
  fixing audio, 98–99
  media files, 94
  preproduction, 93–94
  project setup, 94–95
  reviewing with clients, 107–108
  rough cut, 95–98
  still images in sequences, 103–107
  video adjustments, 99–103
dingbat fonts, 191
divider, dragging, 23–24
dragging
  clips, 52
  dividers, 23–24
  magnification scroll bar, 151
  media files, 36
  transitions, 53–55

drives, working with, 7–8.
  See also Scratch Disks tab
Drop Shadow video effect, applying, 125–126
Duplicate button, 126–127

E

Ease In command, applying, 122
editing
  audio, 51–53
  audio and video separately, 48
  audio to repair silence, 97
  keyboard shortcuts, 158
  keyframes, 122, 156–157
  rough cuts for interviews, 71–75
  in Timeline panel, 47–48
  titles, 87
  values, 58
editing interviews
  audio transitions, 75–76
  B-roll clips, 76–77
  exporting video, 89–90
  freezing frames, 83
  lower-third titles, 83–85
  nesting sequences, 81–83
  playback speed of clip, 78–81
  preproduction, 69
  project setup, 70
  rolling credits, 87
  rough cut, 71–75
  sound design, 86
  stabilizing clips, 88–89
  stereo clip with mono recording, 70–71
  video sequences, 39, 45
Editing workspace, 28–29
Effect Controls panel, 54
effects, finding, 76. See also After Effects; video effects
Effects panel, 22
emphasis, principle of, 196–197
End key, navigating sequences with, 72
evaluating projects, 224–225
Export Frame button, 44
Export Settings dialog box, 61–65
exporting
  final video, 89–90, 107–108, 126–127
  sequences to video files, 61–65
  versions with Media Encoder, 140–143

F

fair use policy, 212–213
Fast Blur, applying to bus image, 106
Fast Color Corrector fx button, 102, 114
feedback loop, using, 224
files. See also media files
  linking to, 6–7
  organizing into folders, 11
  storing, 7–9
final video, exporting, 89–90, 107–108, 126–127.
  See also videos
focal point, creating in design hierarchy, 165, 196–197
folders, organizing files into, 11
fonts
  accessing list of, 188
  types of, 190
form, element of, 168, 177–178
forward delete key, 74
Frame Hold commands, 155
frames
  freezing, 81–83
  identifying in time notation, 43
  moving back and forward, 90, 151
  searching timeline for, 151
Free Draw Bezier tool, 116
freezing frames, 81–83
fx button, clicking, 100

G

garbage matte, drawing, 115–119
General tab, configuring, 13–14
.gif extension, 85
GPU Acceleration option, 14
graphics. See also images
  adding and animating, 120–126
  file formats, 85
  importing with transparent backgrounds, 85
  resizing in titles, 85
graphics applications, 231–232
graphics cards, 14
gray target, using to white balance clips, 113–114
green background, keying out, 117–119
green screen clips, preparing to shoot, 114–115
green spill, addressing, 119

H

Hand tool, 47
handwritten fonts, 190
help, getting, 19–20
highlight in 3D lighting, 177–178
highlight videos, 69
Hollywood-style special effects, 229–230
Home key, navigating sequences with, 72
hover-scrubbing, 37
hues in color wheel, 183
human creativity, graph of, 162

I

Illustrator, graphics applications, 232
images. *See also* graphics
    adding to titles, 58–59
    including contrast in, 166
Import command, 147
Import Sequence option, 148
importing
    with Capture window, 38
    content, 6
    graphics with transparent backgrounds, 85
    layered Photoshop documents, 112–113
    media files into projects, 35–36
In and Out points
    adding for rough cuts, 43
    for clips, 155
    explained, 38
    settings, 41
information details, inspecting, 37
integration, explained, 3
interviews. *See* editing interviews

J

JKL keyboard shortcuts, 44, 46
job requirements, identifying, 33–34
Joe's Construction Cruisers video, 33
JPEG (Joint Photographic Experts Group), 85

K

Ken Burns motion effect, adding, 138–139
kerning in typography, 192
Key Color eyedropper, 117–118

keyboard shortcuts.
    See also commands
    adding points, 53
    Apply Video Transition, 137
    building rough cuts, 44
    editing, 158
    Import command, 147
    JKL, 44, 46
    Macs versus PCs, 74
    sequence navigation, 72
    Time Remapping, 81
    using, 157–158
keyboards, Mac and PC, 74
keyframes, editing, 122, 156–157

L

layered Photoshop documents, importing, 112–113.
    See also Photoshop
layers, applying, 101–103
leading in typography, 192
legal issues, addressing, 34
Levels effect, adjusting, 100
licensing, 214–215
ligatures in typography, 194
light source in 3D lighting, 177–178
line, element of, 168, 172–174
line art, creating with Illustrator, 232
List view, scrolling, 37
listing media files, 34
lists, sorting, 37
Lock icon, enabling, 48
Lock track control, 46
logging clips, 9
logo, animating, 120–122
lowercase letters, 193
lower-third titles, creating, 83–85.
    See also titles
Lumetri Scopes panel, 28

M

Mac keyboards, 74
magnification, 43, 151
map, adding weather graphics to, 123–126
margin guides, 60
markers
    adding, 43, 46
    adding items at, 136–138
    adding notes to, 138
masks
    previewing against black background, 119
    using, 169
Matte Cleanup options, accessing, 119

maximizing panels, 29
Media Browser panel, 36
Media Encoder CC
    exporting files with, 63–64, 140–143
    features, 230
media files. *See also* files
    finding, organizing and inspecting, 230–231
    importing into projects, 35–36
memorial slide show, 131
Mercury Playback Engine, 14
metadata
    adding to videos, 62
    customizing columns, 37
    repeating for exported sequences, 62
Metadata panel, reopening, 25
microphone, selecting in Audio Track Mixer panel, 49–50
mobile apps, 232–233
mono recording, filling stereo clip with, 70–71
monochromatic colors, 185
monospaced fonts, 190
motion, adding to images, 138–139
movement
    and alignment, 166
    principle of, 195, 202
moving clips in Timeline panel, 152–153
MP3 audio file, setting up, 126–127.
    See also audio
Mute audio track control, 46

N

naming clips, 9
negative space, 171
nesting sequences, 81–83
New Project dialog box.
    See also projects
    General tab, 13–14
    Scratch Disks tab, 15–16
notes, adding to markers, 138

O

object shadow in 3D lighting, 177–178
opacity mask, drawing, 115–119
opening titles, creating with video, 82. *See also* titles
OS X, starting Premiere Pro in, 11–12
Out points. *See* In and Out points
output, creating with Media Encoder, 230

P

panel buttons, customizing, 51
panels
    arrangement of, 20–21
    arranging, 23–27
    closing, 24
    displaying, 19
    dragging dividers, 23–24
    maximizing, 29
    types of, 22–23
    undocking, 26
pattern
    principle of, 195, 201
    and texture, 179–180
PC keyboards, 74
Pen tool
    editing keyframes with, 156–157
    identifying, 47
    using with audio level, 52
performance, accelerating, 14
permissions, obtaining, 34, 215
perseverance, importance to
    creativity, 162
photos. *See also* graphics; images
    adding to timeline
        automatically, 135–136
    organizing in Project panel, 134
Photoshop, 231. *See also* layered
    Photoshop documents
playback
    controlling in timeline, 151
    improving during editing, 45
    resolution, 43, 45, 125
playback speed
    changing for clips, 78–81
    increasing, 46
playhead
    control, 46
    moving in time, 46, 151
    Position time display, 43, 46
    transport controls, 43
.png extension, 85
points, adding, 53
Position keyframe, adding, 121
preferences, setting, 16–17
Prelude
    Adobe Cloud desktop
        application, 228
    Live Logger mobile app, 233
Premiere Pro
    blog, 20, 234
    product page, 233
    starting, 11–12
    support and updates, 19

presets
    basing sequences on, 133–134
    dropping onto sequences, 127
primary colors, 183–184
problems, understanding, 217–218.
    See also solutions
Program Monitor panel,
    controls, 43
Program panel, 20–21
project creep, avoiding, 222–223
project folders, managing, 9
project management, 216–217
Project panel
    contents of, 20–22
    organizing photos in, 134
    using, 36–37
project requirements, setting,
    221–222
projects. *See also* New Project
    dialog box
    editing settings, 16–17
    locating, 16–17
    reopening, 19
    reviewing with Cinema
        mode, 108
    setting up, 147–148
    setup for dialogue scene, 94–95
    setup for edited interviews, 70
    setup for weather report,
        112–115
    testing and evaluating, 224–225
promo video, elements of, 33
proportion, principle of, 195, 201
.psd extension, 85

Q

quiet passages
    removing, 74
    repairing, 97

R

radial balance, 200
Rate Stretch tool, 47–48, 78,
    120, 155
Razor tool, 47–48, 155–156
recording voiceovers, 49–50, 103
reflected highlight in 3D lighting,
    177–178
releases, obtaining, 215
renaming clip instances, 75
render bars, colors of, 45
repetition
    principle of, 201
    and rhythm, 167
research, conducting, 218

resizing
    application window, 26
    graphics in titles, 85
    still images, 105
resources, 233–234. *See also*
    websites
reviewing projects with clients,
    107–108
RGB (red, green, blue) color, 182
rhythm, principle of, 202
ripple deletes, 73–74
ripple edits, performing, , 47–48,
    72, 96, 153
Roll/Crawl Options dialog box, 106
rolling credits, creating, 87
Rolling Edit tool, 47, 96, 153
rotation angles, specifying, 122–123
Rotation keyframe, adding, 121
rough cuts
    creating, 41–45
    dialogue scene, 95–98
    editing for interviews, 71–75
    getting enough coverage, 98
    streamlining, 228
rubber band, displaying for clips,
    156–157
rule of thirds, 170

S

safe margins, 60
sans serif fonts, 189
scale
    principle of, 201
    and proportion, 166–167
Scratch Disks tab, configuring,
    15–16. *See also* drives
script fonts, 190
scriptwriting with Story Plus, 228
scrubbing
    explained, 151
    using Shift with, 125
Selection tool, 47, 52, 117, 152
sequences
    adding items at markers,
        136–138
    adding items at regular
        intervals, 135–136
    adding titles to, 59–60
    basing in presets, 133–134
    creating, 39–41
    creating from clips, 44
    creating from multiple files,
        133–139
    editing, 39
    editing in Timeline panel, 47–48
    exporting to files, 61–65

extracting still frames from, 44
going to beginning of, 151
importing, 148
navigating, 72
nesting, 81–83
preparing items for, 134
rough cuts, 41–45
transitions, 53–55
serif fonts, 189–190
settings
    editing for projects, 16–17
    icon, 43
shades in color wheel, 183
shadow in 3D lighting, 177–178
shape
    adding to title, 57
    element of, 168, 175–176
Shift key. *See* keyboard shortcuts
Show/hide track in Program
    Monitor, 46
shortcuts. *See* keyboard shortcuts
slicing clips, 156
slide show. *See* video slide show
Slide tool, 47–48
Slip and Slide tools, using, 47–48,
    153–155
Snap button, identifying in
    Timeline panel, 149
snapping to time, 83
snowboarding highlight videos, 69
Solo audio track control, 46
solutions, picking and planning,
    220. *See also* problems
sorting lists, 37
sound. *See* audio
Source Monitor
    controls, 43
    setting In and Out points, 41
Source panel, 20–21
space, element of, 168–171
specifications, using, 222
Speedgrade Adobe Cloud desktop
    application, 229
splitting clips, 155–156
SSD (solid-state drive) storage, 8
stereo clip, filling with mono
    recording, 70–71
still frame, extracting, 44
still images
    adding to sequences, 104–105
    placing at markers, 137
    resizing, 105
Story mobile app, 232–233
Story Plus Adobe Cloud desktop
    application, 228
storyboards, using, 222
studio workflows, optimizing, 231

T

target audience, defining, 208–209
targeting tracks, 149–150
temperature, adding to sun, 123
testing projects, 224–225
text, adding to titles, 57
texture
    element of, 168,
    and pattern, 179–180
themes and feeling, creating, 167
Thumbnail view, 36–37
.tif extension, 85
time, snapping to, 83
Time magnification control, 46
time notation, 43
Time Remapping, 79–81
time values, altering, 83
Timeline panel
    \ (backslash) in, 46
    controls, 46
    editing in, 47–48
    locating, 20–21
    navigating in, 150–152
    selecting and moving clips in,
      152–153
    settings, 46
    Snap button, 149
    using, 46
    working in, 148–150
tints in color wheel, 183
title sequence, nesting in main
    sequence, 82–83
titles. *See also* lower-third titles;
    opening titles
    adding images to, 58–59
    adding text to, 57
    adding to sequences, 59–60
    crawling left and holding,
      105–106
    creating, 56
    dropping into timeline, 59
    editing, 87
    editing duration of, 60
    resizing graphics in, 85
    superimposing over images, 104
tonal range adjustments, 99–103
tones in color wheel, 183
Tools panel, 23, 47
Track labels controls, 46
Track Select tools, 47–48

tracking in typography, 192
tracks
    adding, 120
    adding to sequences, 122
    controlling, 46
    expanding, 149
    preventing locking, 48
    targeting, 149–150
transcoding, 64
transitions
    previewing, 76
    setting defaults for, 135–136
    using, 53–55
trimmed clips, adding, 41–42
trimming
    clips, 152–155
    locking at, 47
    with tools, 48
type, element of, 168, 187–194

U

unity
    principle of, 195
    ranging to variety, 166
uppercase letters, 193
user interface, guidelines, 19

V

value
    editing, 58
    element of, 168, 180–181
variety, principle of, 198
versions, exporting with Media
    Encoder, 140–143
video adjustments, applying,
    99–103
video and audio, editing
    separately, 48
video clips. *See* clips
video effects, using, 53–55.
    See also effects
video sequences
    adding items at markers,
      136–138
    adding items at regular
      intervals, 135–136
    adding titles to, 59–60
    basing in presets, 133–134
    creating, 39–41
    creating from clips, 44
    creating from multiple files,
      133–139
    editing, 39
    editing in Timeline panel, 47–48
    exporting to files, 61–65
    extracting still frames from, 44

subtractive color, 182
support, getting, 19, 233–234
swashes in typography, 194
sweetening audio, 98–99
symmetrical balance, 199

DISCARD

going to beginning of, 151
importing, 148
navigating, 72
nesting, 81–83
preparing items for, 134
rough cuts, 41–45
transitions, 53–55
video slide show
creating sequences, 133–139
exporting, 140–143
preproduction, 131
project setup, 132
versions with Media Encoder, 140–143
video transitions
previewing, 76
setting defaults for, 135–136
using, 53–55
Video/audio track separator, 46
videos. *See also* final video
adding metadata to, 62
lighting, 114–115
markers for placing photos, 136–138
sweetening audio, 98–99
trimming, 71–75, 153–155

Vocal Enhancer audio effect, applying and editing, 51–52
voiceovers, recording, 49–50, 103
volume of clips, adjusting, 52–53

W

warm colors, 183
Warp Stabilizer, 88–89
weather graphics, adding to map, 123–126
web-based resources, 233–234
websites. *See also* resources
Adobe, 14
Adobe Communities forum, 19
Adobe Creative Cloud mobile apps, 233
color combinations, 185–186
fonts, 188
keyboard shortcuts, 44
Welcome screen, 12
white balancing clips, 113–114
white space, 170
Windows, starting Premiere Pro in, 11–12
workflows, optimizing, 231
workspaces, using, 26–29

Y

YouTube, exporting sequences for, 62–63

Z

ZIP files, unpacking, 10
zooming, 46–47